ARMY RECORDS

A Guide for Family Historians

urned to any branch of the

the

ARMY RECORDS

A Guide for Family Historians

William Spencer

the national archives

8108017611

First published in 2008 by
The National Archives
Kew, Richmond
Surrey TW9 4DU
United Kingdom

www.nationalarchives.gov.uk

The National Archives brings together the Public
Record Office, Historical Manuscripts Commission,
Office of Public Sector Information and Her Majesty's
Stationery Office.

A catalogue card for this book is available from
the British Library.

ISBN 978 1 905615 10 0

Jacket, typographic design and typesetting by
Ken Wilson | point 918

Printed in Great Britain by
The Cromwell Press Ltd., Trowbridge, Wiltshire

Some of the material in this book previously appeared in
Army Records for Family Historians published in a revised
edition by the Public Record Office in 2000 (first edition
1998).

ACKNOWLEDGMENTS

I owe thanks to so many people who over the
years have asked me a question which has lead me
to ferret amongst the records to satisfy my own
curiosity, and in so doing learn more. Just a
question, medal or a photograph has given me the
stimulus to keep getting my hands dirty.

I must, as is becoming perhaps a pleasurable
habit, thank Catherine Bradley for giving me the
chance to revise this guide. I'll keep taking the
rope! My favourite editor Janet Sacks once again
has reined me in when I go off at tangents. Mrs
Brass saved my neck and sanity. Thanks Amanda.

Additional thanks must go to Major Martin
Everett, archivist of the South Wales Borderers
Regimental Museum for providing further details
about John Harding, to Tony and Liz Light for
information about William Freke Williams and
Dennis Woodman for his work on WO 22.

Thanks to my colleagues in DSD for producing
the documents, many at very short notice and
from afar. My thanks must also go to Brian
Carter for producing the images.

Marstons' Pedigree is still keeping me happy
but the brewery has yet to notice!

My final thanks must go to Kate, Lucy and
Alice.

WILLIAM SPENCER

CONTENTS

USING THE NATIONAL ARCHIVES

Most of the records described in this guide can be consulted at The National Archives, Ruskin Avenue, Kew, Richmond, Surrey, TW9 4DU. The Office is open from 09:00–17:00 Mondays and Fridays, 09:00–19:00 on Tuesday and Thursday, 10:00–17:00 on Wednesday and 09.30–17:00 on Saturday. The National Archives is closed on Sundays, public holidays and for annual stocktaking. The National Archives website address is:

http://www.nationalarchives.gov.uk

The archives are about ten minutes' walk from Kew Gardens Underground Station, which is on London Transport's District Line, as well as the London Overground Service. For motorists it is just off the South Circular Road (A205). There is adequate parking.

Getting access to the records is simple. You will need to obtain a reader's ticket, which is free, when you first arrive. Please bring two forms of identity, such as a driving licence, credit card, bank card, something with your address and signature on it. If you are not a British citizen you should bring your passport. For further information see:

www.nationalarchives.gov.uk/visit/whattobring.htm

It is possible to get photocopies and/or digital copies of most documents you find: please ask the staff for details. It is possible for you to use your own digital camera to copy documents. There is a public restaurant and a well-stocked bookshop on site. Self-service lockers are available to store your belongings.

In order to protect the documents, each one of which is unique, security in the reading rooms is tight. You are only permitted to take a notebook and any notes into the reading rooms. You must also only use a pencil. Eating and drinking are not permitted in the reading rooms.

The archives can be a confusing place to use. If you are new it is a good idea to allow plenty of time to find your feet. The staff are both knowledgeable and friendly, and are happy to help if you get lost.

The records held by the National Archives are described and ordered using a three-part reference. The first element is known as the 'department' and takes the form of letters. The 'department' denotes which government department created the records. The second element is known as the 'series' and collects together records of a similar type and is denoted by numbers. The third and final element of a document reference is known as the 'piece' and this usually is just numbers but occasionally may include letters.

Over time, terminology used to describe the document references at the National Archives has changed and you may hear terms such as 'letter codes' and 'class' still being used. Letter codes refers to the department and class refers to the Series. Whilst the terminology is interchangeable, many of the department identities are obvious, for example WO is the War Office, ADM is the Admiralty and AIR is the Air Ministry. Other department identities are not so obvious; the records of MI5 for example, are identified by the letters KV (it is an anagram of significance for you to work out) and the Welsh Office uses BD.

Thus most War Diaries for the First World War are in the series WO 95. It is these department and series references that are referred to throughout this guide.

Brief descriptions of every document ('piece' is the term used by the National Archives) are in the class lists. Several sets of lists are available in the Open Reading Room and other locations. The class list gives you the exact reference of the document you want. This is what you order on the computer terminal. Occasionally in this Guide we use the full reference, written thus: WO 95/5467.

An increasing number of documents are available on microfilm, microfiche or in digitized format. Where this is the case, the fact is noted in the text. You do not need to order microfilms on the computer as you can help yourself to them in the Open Reading Room.

Some lists have been published by the Public Record Office/The National Archives. Probably the most useful of these publications is the *Alphabetical Guide to War Office and certain other Military Records preserved in the Public Record Office* (PRO Lists and Indexes LXIII, 1931, reprinted 1963).

In addition, there are various other finding aids for genealogists. The best general overview is provided by Amanda Bevan's revised *Tracing Your Ancestors in the Public Record Office* (7th edition, TNA, 2006).

The structure and development of the War Office is fully described in Michael Roper's handbook *The Records of the War Office and related departments, 1660–1964* (PRO Handbook No 29, 1998).

INTRODUCTION

I have been using the National Archives as a reader and member of staff for over 25 years. During this time there have been many changes, the most significant being the opening of new records and new ways of making them available.

The records discussed in this book reflect the lives, and in many cases the deaths, of millions of men and women over the past 400 years and more. Record keeping over that time has improved and become more egalitarian in dealing with both the officers and ranks as the years from 1660 to the end of the 20th century have passed by.

The National Archives (TNA) holds many sources of great importance to family historians who had ancestors serving in the British Army. This book is a major revision of *Army Records for Family Historians*, last published by the PRO in 2000. A number of new sections and appendices have been added, in particular to take account of the growth of interest in records of the two world wars and the release of army service records from the First World War.

There is now more information about some of the records relating to the First World War (only partially released in 1998), and records held by the British Library concerning the Indian Army and its predecessors. Many of the records discussed in this guide are now available on computer and of course the TNA Catalogue can now be searched more effectively by key word.

This book describes the main series of records of the War Office and other government departments which provide information about officers and soldiers who have served in the British Army and to a lesser extent in the armies of the East India Company and the Indian Army. Almost all War Office records give some information about individuals, but this guide concentrates on those series containing material of greatest potential interest to the family historian.

The records discussed in this book are produced in a variety of different ways. The majority of the records are produced in their original form—that is, on paper—but others are produced on microfilm or microfiche, and many are only available in a digitized form. Digitized records are becoming more common and in future many military-related records will only be available this way. There are records mentioned in this guide that are currently available in one medium but that may soon be made available in digitized format. Although advice may say the records are available in one format, when you attempt to order any of the records at the National Archives the computer should tell you in what format the records are produced. So any changes that occur between me writing the guide and you, the user, actually trying to look at a particular record should quickly become apparent when you go to order an item.

Many of the records at the National Archives are now being digitized, either by the institution or in partnership with other bodies. Records digitized by the archives are usually placed onto the DocumentsOnline section of the National Archives' website. Whilst it is possible to search these digitized records by name of person or organization or military unit, downloading such records from outside of the archives will require the payment of a fee. Searching DocumentsOnline while at Kew is free; only the printing incurs a charge.

Interest in Army records is as strong as ever, unsurprising given current military activity. It is worth noting parallels between the British Army and its experience in previous Afghan Wars and in the present war in Afghanistan. Perhaps the only thing that has changed is the technology. Future historians may well find it interesting to study the men involved in Afghanistan in 1839, 1880, 1919 and 2007. The media have already asked if I can find families who had an ancestor who took part in the Second Afghan War and who have a current family member similarly employed in the same region.

Researchers are now able to use many electronic resources at the National Archives, enabling them to use the data captured electronically in their quest for original (paper) records. As archives select, preserve and make available records electronically, so research techniques may change, yet the lives and experiences of the soldiers will still remain similar to those who have served before them.

WILLIAM SPENCER

1 ORGANIZATION OF THE ARMY

The status, structure and organization of the army has changed frequently over the last 600 years and it is necessary to explain this a little in order that the records can be approached with greater understanding.

Until the Civil War in 1642 there had been no standing army in England, although there had been a militia (part-time/voluntary/short-term service) in various forms since the tenth century. Bodies of men were raised for campaigns as required, and they were often known by the names of the officers who both raised and commanded them. There was no central organization of these units and therefore no systematic records were created for them.

Upon the restoration of Charles II in 1660, a standing army became a permanent feature of government. Its administration was the responsibility of the secretary at war, with the help of an established bureaucracy that slowly developed into the War Office. As a result, records are somewhat fuller than for the period before 1660, although sparse compared with later periods. There was also a Board of Ordnance, which was responsible for the supply of armaments and the erection and maintenance of fortresses. It also controlled the gunners and engineers who, until the early eighteenth century, were normally civilians.

Due to parliamentary suspicion of a standing army, organization of the Army remained minimal until the 1750s. The numerical strength of the Army was fixed annually by Parliament (until 1878 in the preamble to the Mutiny Act and thereafter in the Army Act); its peacetime strength rarely exceeded 20,000 in the eighteenth century, rising to 100,000 in the first half of the nineteenth century and to 200,000 after 1855. Regiments were created and abolished as necessary. In general, regiments owed allegiance as much to their commanding officers as to the monarch and, until 1751, were usually known by the names of their colonels. Records relating to regiments that might be run more like private businesses are more likely to have survived with private collections than with the public records.

1.1 The Army from 1751 to 1870

By the 1750s, the regiment was established as the basic unit in the Army. In 1751 each regiment of foot—the infantry, in other words—was given a regimental number, in order of precedence within an elaborate hierarchy of regiments. This numbering system was used until the 1880s and informally for many years thereafter. A number of books give lists of regiments and their numbers, including *A Companion to the British Army, 1660–1983* by David Ascoli, *Guide to regiments and corps of the British Army and the regular establishment* by J.M. Brereton, *Regiments and corps of the British Army* by I. Hallows, and *The family historian's enquire within* by F.C. Markwell and Pauline Saul.

The actual organization of the Army, however, remained a very loose affair. In the 1780s, after the American War of Independence, there were in effect four separate armies: the regular army; the Board of Ordnance (which included the Royal Artillery and the Royal Engineers); the Militia, which was under the control of the Home Office; and the Volunteers, which existed as a series of private clubs.

Damning reports of general mismanagement in the Crimean War led to a series of reforms in 1855, in which the Board of Ordnance was abolished and all its responsibilities passed to the War Office, which was given responsibility for all military matters. (For more detail on the pre-Crimean origins of reform, see *Wellington's Legacy: Reform of the British Army, 1830–1854* by Hew Strachan.) At about the same time, a number of specialist corps—medical services, supply, transport and so on—were set up to deal with functions that had hitherto been carried out on an *ad hoc* or regimental basis or by civilian contractors. (See chapter 14.)

Until the Union of Ireland with Great Britain in 1801, Ireland had its own military establishment and parallel administrative structure. Records of the Army in Ireland are largely in WO 35 and CO 904, with entry books of the Muster Master General of Ireland, 1709–1823, in WO 8. The Scottish Army was also a separate establishment until 1707.

1.2 The Army from 1870 to 1945

The Cardwell army reforms of the early 1870s radically reorganized the administration of the War Office by localizing forces. The localization of forces led to regiments being linked together in units of two, with a common depot. The two regiments were, in effect, brigaded together. This brigading system led to a new system of regimental numbering for individual soldiers. It was possible for a man to be given a specific regimental number when he joined the army, but after 1870 he was more likely to be given a brigade number first. Further information about brigading and which regiments were in which brigade can be found in any Army List for *c.*1871–1881 and also at *www.regiments.org/regiments/uk/depot/1873.htm*.

In 1881 under the Childers reforms, the whole structure of regiments was greatly changed. Many regiments were merged (the 48th and 58th Foot, for example, were combined to form the Northamptonshire Regiment), and many were linked to a county, although the linking of regiments to county titles was not new and had first been formalized in 1782. A typical regiment would have two battalions, one serving at home, which would provide fresh drafts of men for the other, which was stationed abroad. Local militia forces, which had been autonomous, became the third battalion of the regiment. The use of numbers to identify foot regiments was discontinued. For a description of the organization of a regiment, see 1.3.

These reforms, however, did nothing to improve the machinery by which the Army was serviced and supplied, at home or in the field, although it is from this period that serious attention was first paid to the commissariat and to medical services. In addition, no reform was made of the Royal Artillery or cavalry regiments.

The Haldane reforms of 1907 to 1912 altered the central organization of the Army, creating a General Staff, under a chief of imperial general staff, to direct military operations. In addition, an expeditionary force of six infantry battalions and six cavalry regiments was formed. This force could be mobilized within twelve days and was the nucleus of the 'Old Contemptibles' of 1914.

The slimming down of the British Army after 1945 has led to further amalgamations and changes. These are covered in David Ascoli's book. An up-to-date structure of the British Army can be found at *http://www.army.mod.uk/unitsandorgs/index.htm*.

1.3   The Regiment

The regiment is the basic unit within the British Army. The regiments were, and are, of various types: guards or household troops (both horse and foot), cavalry (originally divided into horse and dragoons) and infantry (foot or line). Artillery and engineers are discussed in chapters 5 and 6. The Artillery and Engineers grew out of irregular units raised privately by noblemen and others to fight particular campaigns or battles.

An infantry regiment consisted of one or more battalions, each of which had a paper strength of 600–1,000 men. Each battalion might have between eight and twelve companies, with a paper strength of 60, 100 or 120 men per company. By the time of the First World War infantry regiments were based around four companies, when the whole regiment numbered approximately 1,000 officers and men. From 1803, each battalion had two lieutenant colonels. Each company came to be commanded by a captain and two subalterns, who were lieutenants or second lieutenants.

In terms of administration, a regiment came to be divided into two arms —a depot and a service arm. The depot acted as the regimental headquarters and recruited and trained men for service. Before 1881, the depot moved quite frequently within the British Isles but rarely went overseas. Quelling civil disturbances at home was another responsibility of the depot companies. The locations of depots are given in the *Army Lists* (see 3.1).

During the two world wars the numbers of recruits in the British Army increased many times and numerous extra Territorial Army and 'service' battalions were formed for each regiment. Battalions of a given regiment were identified by a number. These numbers could take several forms—for example:

1st Dorsets (1st Battalion Dorsetshire Regiment)
4th Grenadiers (4th Battalion Grenadier Guards)
1/4 East Lancs (1st Line of the 4th Territorial Battalion East Lancashire Regiment)

The composition of cavalry regiments was slightly different. A regiment of horse consisted of between six and eight squadrons of fifty men each. Each squadron was commanded by a captain, who was assisted by a number of subalterns. Squadrons could be broken down into troops and yet the term 'troop' was sometimes used in the early nineteenth century instead of squadron. Many cavalry regiments were originally called light dragoons, but most of these eventually became lancer regiments.

In 1922, cavalry regiments were reorganized in a similar manner to their infantry counterparts. The artillery were usually divided into batteries, brigades or regiments (see chapter 5).

A brief history of each regiment, together with a list of the principal campaigns and battles it fought, is given in *Register of the Regiments and Corps of the British Army*, edited by Arthur Swinson. Individual regimental histories may be identified from A. S. White's *A Bibliography of the Regiments and Corps of the British Army*.

1.4 Location and Records of Units

There are several ways to locate the whereabouts of a regiment or battalion. With the exception of the period between 1914 and 1918, the location of each battalion is given in the monthly *Army Lists*. From 1829 the stations of army units are also listed in the monthly *United Service Journal Naval and Military Magazine* (later renamed *Colburn's United Service Magazine*).

The monthly returns in the series WO 17 and WO 73 also record the location of units. The returns in WO 17 cover the period between 1759 and 1865, while those in WO 73 are for 1859 to 1914. Both classes consist of returns to the adjutant general showing the distribution of each regiment at home and abroad, and its effective strength for all ranks.

Since 1866, the information contained in the monthly returns has been abstracted and printed in the *Annual Returns of the Army* which are published as parliamentary papers and are available at Kew. Returns for 1750 and 1751 are in WO 27/1–2.

By far the most effective way of finding a location of a unit of the British Army is to use the records in WO 379, Disposition and Movement of Regiment, Returns and Papers (Regimental Records) 1737–1967. The earlier records relating to the infantry regiments continue to use the numbers by

The Duke of Cambridge's Own (Middlesex Regiment).

1st Batt., Buttevant.
2nd Patt., Kamptee, Madras.] *Formerly the 57th (West Middlesex) and* [*Regimental District No. 57.—Hounslow.*
the 77th (East Middlesex—Duke of Cambridge's Own) Regiments.

(The 3rd and 4th Battalions are formed of the Elthorne and East Middlesex Militia respectively.)

The Plume of the Prince of Wales. The Duke of Cambridge's Coronet and Cypher. "MYSORE" "SERINGAPATAM" "ALBUHERA" "CIUDAD RODRIGO" "BADAJOZ" "VITTORIA" "PYRENEES" "NIVELLE" "NIVE" "PENINSULA" "ALMA" "INKERMAN" "SEVASTOPOL" "NEW ZEALAND" "SOUTH AFRICA, 1879."

Years' Ser. Full Pay.	Half Pay.	
26	...	Colonel.—Sir Edward Alan Holdich,[1] *KCB. Ensign,* 2 July 41; *Lt.* 26 July 44; *Capt.* [2]22 Feb. 50; *Brevet Major,* 2 Aug. 50; *Brevet Lt.Colonel,* 28 May 53; *Colonel,* 28 Nov. 54; *Major,* 26 May 58; *Major General,* 3 Sept. 67; *Lt.General,* 28 Apr. 75; *General,* 1 Oct. 77; *Colonel* 57th Foot, 11 Dec. 75.
24	...	Lieutenant Colonels.—1 Arthur Lang Tickell, *Commanding the Battalion,* 4 July 88; *Commandant Wellington Depot; Ensign,* 5 Aug. 64; *Lt.* [31]31 July 67; *Capt.* [27]27 Sept. 71; *Major,* 1 July 81; *Lt.Colonel,* 17 Dec. 85; *Colonel,* 17 Dec. 89.
		2 Hamlet Dalton Wade-Dalton, *Ensign,* [14]14 Sept. 66; *Lt.* [15]15 Dec. 69; *Capt.* 24 Sept. 73; *Major,* 1 July 81; *Lt.Colonel,* 18 Sept. 89.

Years Full	Half	MAJORS.	ENSIGN OR 2ND LIEUT.		LIEUT.		CAPTAIN.		BREV. MAJ.		MAJOR.	
21	...	*p.s.c.* Henry Thomas Hughes Hallett[7]	13 Jan.	69	27 Oct.	70	28 April	75	......		4 Jan.	8
28	... 2	Cockburn Forte	[11]11 Mar.	62	[30]30 Dec.	64	12 Feb.	75	......		29 Apr.	8
19	... 1	Alfred Allan Garstin[8]	23 Sept.	7	28 Oct.	71	12 Aug.	80	......		14 April	8
27	...	Thomas Harris,[9] *District Staff Officer, Secunderabad*	[18]18 Dec.	63	7 Jan.	68	10 Oct.	74			8 Jan.	8
26	... 2	Herbert Michael Williams[10]	5 July	64	28 Oct.	68	23 Jan.	70	......		30 Sept.	8
23	... 1	Richard Chicheley Thornton	[23]23 Oct.	67	[22]22 Mar.	71	1 Feb.	75	......		28 June	8
17	... 2	Augustus West Hill[12]	......		1 Jan.	73	27 Sept.	80			8 May	8
22	...	George Fenton, *D.A.A. General for Musketry, Ireland*	2 Sept.	68	[14]14 Oct.	71	6 Aug.	79	......		21 Dec.	8
22	... 1	Frederick Graham	8 Jan.	68	28 Oct.	71	15 Nov.	79	......		21 Dec.	8
17	... 1	*p.s.c.* James Grove White[13]	......		12 Nov.	73	2 Jan.	81	......		18 Sept.	8

		CAPTAINS.										
17	... 1	Napoleon Joseph Rodolph Blake[14]	......		12 Nov.	73	14 Mar.	81				
21	...	Ruscombe Field Westmacott,[15] *Adj.* 2 Vol.Bn.Argyll & Sutherld.Highldrs.	[9]9 Oct.	69	28 Oct.	71	23 Mar.	81				
17	... 1	Cecil Bowcher Duff Michel[16]	......		12 Nov.	73	1 April	81				
17	...	Adoniah Graham Schuyler, *Adjutant Burmah State Railway Volunteers*	......		12 Nov.	73	1 June	81				
16	... 2	Richard Woodroofe Graham[13]	......		21 Jan.	74	1 July	81				
16	...	Sydney Edwin Bellingham,[17] *Adjutant Hyderabad Rifle Volunteers*	......		24 Jan.	74	1 Oct.	82				
16	...	Ernest Edward Foley	......		28 Feb.	74	23 Nov.	82				
16	... 1	Charles Wallace Warden[18]	......		13 June	74	29 Dec.	83				
16	... 1	Ernest Vernon Bellers,[13] *Adj.* 1 July 86	......		21 Sept.	74	23 May	84				
15	...	Francis Douglas Lumley, *Adjutant* 4 *Battalion* (6 *Middlesex Militia*)	......		10 Mar.	75	28 June	84				
15	... 1	Alexander Towers-Clark[19]	......		22 May	75	1 Jan.	85				
14	...	Robert Theophilous Hewitt Law,[20] *Ordnance Store Department*	......		24 Mar.	76	8 May	85				
14	... 1	Robert Douglas Longe[13]	......		11 Sept.	76	8 May	85				
14	...	*p.s.c.* Edward John Sharpe,[21] *District Staff Officer, Madras*	......		31 May	76	23 Sept.	85				
14	...	Godfrey Charles George Norton, *Adjutant* 3 *Bn. Middlesex Regt.*	......		19 Aug.	76	17 Dec.	85				
12	... 2	William Scott-Moncrieff,[13] *Station Staff Officer, Nusseerabad*	1 May	78	10 Mar.	80	21 Dec.	85				
12	...	*p.s.c.* Nathaniel Walter Barnardiston, *A. D. C. to Lt. Gen. E. N. Newdegate*	14 Sept.	78	11 Mar.	80	21 Dec.	85				
11	... 2	George Beresford Lempriere	21 June	79	13 Mar.	80	14 June	87				
11	... 2	George Walter Wrey Savile, *Adjutant* 7 Oct. 86.	6 Aug.	79	15 Mar.	80	14 June	87				
11	...	Lionel Grant Oliver, *Adjutant Coorg and Mysore Volunteers*	13 Aug.	79	21 July	80	18 Sept.	87				
12	... 2	*p.s.c.* Louis William Bodé[13]	11 May	78	12 Aug.	80	8 Sept.	87				
10	... 2	Charles Robert Dyer	11 Aug.	80	1 July	81	21 Nov.	88				
10	... 2	Reginald de Hardewicke Burton, *Station Staff Officer, Kamptee*	11 Aug.	80	1 July	81	17 Jan.	89				
10	...	Ernest Albert Bennett[23]	23 Oct.	80	1 July	81	11 May	89				

		LIEUTENANTS.										
9	... 2	Henry Herriott Woollright	......		22 Oct.	81						
8	... 2	Francis Sapte	......		10 May	82						
8	... 1	Bertram Edmund Ward	......		10 May	82						
8	... 2	Edmund Douglass Harvest[24]	......		10 May	82						
7	... 2	Evelyn William Medows Norie, *on special service, Burmah*	......		25 Aug.	83						
6	... 1	James Eyre Drummond Ward	......		30 Jan.	84						
6	... 1	Ernest William Rokeby Stephenson	......		23 Aug.	84						
6	... 1	Algernon Forbes Randolph	......		23 Aug.	84						
6	... 2	Wallace Nelson[25]	......		23 Aug.	84						
5	... 2	Robert Mandy Osborne Glynn	......		6 May	85						
5	... 1	Henry Montague Eustace	......		29 Aug.	85						
5	... 1	Robert Hall Hayes	......		29 Aug.	85						
5	... 1	Jenkin Stephen Jones	......		25 Nov.	85						
5	... 1	Frank George Mathias Rowley	......		30 Jan.	86						
4	... 2	William Edward Scarth Burch	......		7 July	86						
4	... 2	Robert James Ross	......		25 Aug.	86						
4	...	Philip Byron Bohun Forster	......		10 Nov.	86						
4	... 1	Andrew Ducrôt	......		10 Nov.	86						
3	... 2	Charles Leslie Muriel	5 Feb.	87	11 May	89						

		SECOND LIEUTENANTS.										
3	... 2	William Charles Stuart Prince	16 Nov.	87								
3	... 1	Charles Hallyburton Campbell Grace	16 Nov.	87								
3	... 2	William Francis Leader	19 Nov.	87								

[19] Captain Towers-Clark served with the 57th Regiment in the Zulu campaign of 1879, including the action of Gingindhlovu and relief of Ekowe. Served afterwards to the end of the war as Orderly Officer to Lt. Colonel Clarke while commanding successively the 2nd Brigade 1st Division and "Clarke's Column." Made several road surveys, including the road in Zululand from St. Paul's to the Middle Drift of the Tugela River (Medal with Clasp).
[20] Captain Law served in the Zulu war in 1879 (Medal with Clasp).
[21] Captain E. J. Sharpe served with the 57th Regiment in the Zulu war of 1879, and was present at the action of Gingindhlovu and relief of Ekowe and throughout the operations of "Clarke's Column" (Medal with Clasp). Served in the Egyptian war of 1882 (Medal, and Khedive's Star).
[23] Captain Bennett served with the Zhob Valley Expedition in 1884.

Fig. 1 Hart's Army List *1891: List of Officers of the Middlesex Regiment.*

which regiments of foot were known before they were given county and other names in 1881. The bulk of the cards in pieces 18–129 are arranged in the order of the infantry as it existed in the late 1960s. The arrangement of the rest of the cards, which include many miscellaneous units and formations, follows no particular formal order or precedence.

The series WO 380, Establishments and Stations of Regiments, Returns and Papers (Regimental Records Series I–IV) 1803–1991, is also very useful. For the period 1803 to *c.* 1922, the records are arranged in three series; series 4 continues up to *c.* 1953. Most records relating to the infantry regiments continue to use the numbers by which regiments of foot were known before they were given county and other names in 1881.

In both of the above series, find the piece that covers the unit and date and it will tell you where the unit was. If you don't know the unit but know the place and date, you may find WO 17 or WO 73 quicker to use.

A summary of returns is published in *In Search of the 'Forlorn Hope': a Comprehensive Guide to Locating British Regiments and their Records, 1640 to World War One* by John M. Kitzmiller II, but while this book is still useful it has been surpassed by the release of WO 379 and WO 380.

Orders of battle also contain lists of units, and give their location and their place in the command structure. Those for the First World War are in WO 95/5467–5494, and those for the Second World War are in WO 212. Other orders of battle from 1939 are in WO 33.

Regimental records may be held locally by regimental museums or local record offices—see chapter 20—although much of what they have is duplicated at the National Archives. Chance survivals from individual units in the National Archives are listed in Michael Roper's *The Records of the War Office and related departments 1660–1964* (PRO, 1998).

1.5 Higher Command

During wartime, regiments and other units were grouped together for operational purposes. Although they remained part of their parent regiments, battalions (usually three or four in number) came to be grouped together to form a brigade. Three brigades together formed a division. The division was a self-contained fighting force that, during both world wars, had its own artillery and support services. During the First World War, for example, its strength was about 20,000 men of all ranks. However, the demands of that conflict required larger formations and two, or sometimes more, divisions were grouped together as a corps. A group of two or more corps was designated as an army. These groupings are referred to in different ways: armies in capital letters (THIRD ARMY), corps in Roman numerals (XVI Corps) and divisions in Arabic numerals (30th Division). The term corps can mean both a grouping of divisions and a regiment of specialized troops, such as the Royal Artillery, (Royal) Army Service Corps or Royal Engineers. An even larger formation, the Army Group, was established in the Second World War. 21 Army Group was made up of the 1st Canadian Army and the 2nd British Army. 21 army group was commanded by general Bernard Law Montgomery. Other unit formations outside of those expected include the Commonwealth Division and Commonwealth Brigade from the Korean War period and units such as Dunster Force, the Elope Force and Grigg's Force from the First World War period.

It is possible to search the TNA Catalogue using key words and this will enable you to look for the operational and other records for units with unusual names or designations.

A simple organization chart for infantry regiments is in appendix 1.

1.6 Ranks

The Army comprised commissioned officers (usually from the wealthier classes), warrant officers, non-commissioned officers, and other ranks. The other ranks were often drawn from the very poorest sections of society, including agricultural labourers, paupers and even criminals. Before the First World War, it was very unusual for an ordinary soldier to become an officer. Over the years, very different sets of records grew up for officers and other ranks. These records are therefore treated separately in this guide.

There was no uniform set of titles for the various ranks, and the titles used might reflect either the type of work performed or regimental custom. A list of ranks is given in appendix 2.

2 RECORDS OF THE ARMY BEFORE 1660

Before the creation of the standing army in 1685, armies required to fight the king's enemies were only gathered together when that need arose. One key reason why a standing army was not created prior to 1685 was the fear that it may be used to overthrow the crown. A standing army is a professional army that is permanent rather than a creation of necessity.

2.1 Medieval Sources

The earliest way an army was raised was under the terms of what was known as 'knight service'. A knight holding land on behalf of the crown was obliged to provide his king with 40 days' service per year and to bring with him whatever arms and, more importantly, men that the king needed. This was the feudal system. This use of 'knight service' to raise armies died out in the early fourteenth century.

The feudal system was gradually replaced by one based on contracts or 'indentures' between the king, or others, with those who were to serve directly and raise troops to serve with them. Commissions of array and commissions to musters, authorizing lords to raise forces in the king's

Fig. 2 *Indenture for military service 1415.* E101/69/6

name or inspect troops mustered, were also issued. Useful sources in print relating to knight service include the *Books of Fees 1198–1293* and *Feudal Aids* (6 volumes for 1284–1431). *Parliamentary Writs and Writs of Military Summons* is also a useful source for names of those engaged on military service. However, original records relating to soldiers are likely to be formal, with little personal detail, and are normally written in Latin or Norman French.

Exchequer accounts in E 101 include wages for knights and soldiers as well as some indentures for war (see Fig. 1) and E 404 includes warrants for indentures for war and knights' fees and wages in war. Accounts may also be found in E 36, E 364 and E 358, which includes the 'Agincourt Roll' (E 358/6) recording payments to those who fought at the Battle of Agincourt in 1415. Other sources relating to knights' fees include DL 40, DL 42, E 179, E 164, E 198 and the main series of Chancery enrolments, many of which have been published in detailed summaries known as calendars. These include the Scutage Rolls in C 72 (1214–1328), which record relief from 'shield tax' (payment made for soldiers), the Close Rolls (C 54–C 55), the Patent Rolls (C 66), Norman Rolls (C 64), Scotch Rolls (C 71) and Welsh Rolls (C 77). Chancery Miscellanea (C 47) includes some returns of commissions of array (C 47/2 and 5) and indentures of war for service in Ireland (C 47/10).

With the advent of the online catalogue, finding many of these early musters in E 101 is much easier. The most effective way to find a muster in E 101 is to restrict your search to 'muster' and E 101 only. If you seek a muster for Henry V's campaign, which included the Battle of Agincourt, use 'muster AND harfleur' and E 101. Further accounts including names of participants at Agincourt can be found in E 358/6. It is possible to search the E 358 catalogue by name of knight.

Research by Anne Curry of Southampton University is currently looking at the Exchequer (E) records for participants in the campaigns in France. Much of the research involves improving the E 101 and E 358 catalogues.

The Research Guide *Medieval and Early Modern Soldiers Military Records Information 1* can provide further advice.

2.2   Tudor and Stuart Muster Rolls and Accounts

From Anglo-Saxon times, men were liable to military service as a local home-defence force. In 1285, the Statute of Winchester required all those aged between 15 and 60 to be assessed to equip themselves with weapons and armour, according to their means; those holding less than 40 shillings' worth of land were expected to equip themselves with scythes and knives, while the wealthiest individuals would have to provide horse and armour. In the sixteenth century, the responsibility for making and inspecting such assessments lay with local commissioners of array, or the lord lieutenant of

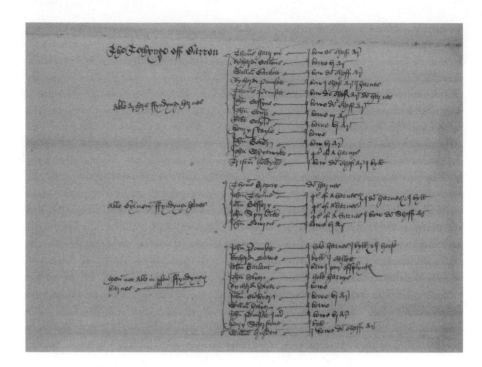

Fig. 3 *Tudor Militia Muster Roll for Somerset 1539.* E 101/59/21

the county, assisted by local officials such as the parish constable.

Muster rolls list the names of local inhabitants who were liable to military service and the equipment that they were required to have. The earliest known muster roll dates from 1522, but obviously musters had been held for centuries before. The rolls, or sometimes certificates of musters giving only total numbers of men, were forwarded to the Exchequer or the Privy Council, and have therefore became part of the public records.

Some muster rolls have only survived with the private papers of those local gentry families who served as commissioners of array or deputy lieutenant; these may be deposited in local record offices. The private papers of a John Daniel of Daresbury, in Cheshire, which are held at Kew under the reference SP 46/52, give an idea of the sort of material that can be found: they contain correspondence and papers relating to musters and commissions, and several muster rolls of the trained band of which he was captain.

For the present location of muster rolls, consult *Tudor and Stuart Muster Rolls—A Directory of Holdings in the British Isles* by J. Gibson and A. Dell. This is arranged by county, and then by hundred (a division of the county containing a number of parishes). For each county, you will find a list of what is held by the National Archives, with full document references; what is held by local record offices; and what has been transcribed and published. Many publications by local record societies are held by the National Archives library.

Muster rolls do not represent a complete census of the male population: we can see this by comparing the names with those listed in surviving taxation returns in E 179. It has been estimated that, on average, either a muster or tax return is likely to omit one-third of the names it was supposed to contain. The unfit and those too poor to provide the necessary equipment (and who might not be trusted to use their weapons in defence of property) may be omitted altogether.

Muster rolls for 1522–1547 are found in the record classes E 101/bundles 58–62 and 549; E 36/16–55a; E 315/464 and 466 and SP 1–SP 2; see Fig. 3 for an example. Many are listed in *Letters and Papers of the Reign of Henry VIII*. A few from 1548 are in SP 10/3–4.

For the reign of Elizabeth I (1558–1603), and especially for the years 1569, 1573, 1577 and 1580, muster rolls and certificates are in SP 12 and E 101/bundles 64–66. From 1570, most are not lists of men but certificates, listing the numbers of men only, grouped by hundred and according to the equipment they provided; names in such musters may only be of the 'trained bands'—that is, those men who were selected for special training.

Musters for the reign of James I (1603–1625) are in SP 14 and for Charles I (1625–1640) in SP 16–SP 17. Most of these State Paper classes are seen on microfilm and are well listed and indexed by printed calendars. These records are more fully described in Military Records Information 2 *Tudor and Stuart local soldiery: militia muster rolls*.

Other sources for this period in which references to individual officers and men, including applications by widows for pensions, may sometimes be found include the published *Calendars of State Papers Domestic*, *State Papers Foreign*, *State Papers Ireland*, and *Privy Council Registers*; all these are indexed by personal name. Exchequer and Audit Office accounts in E 101, E 351 and AO 1–AO 3 may occasionally list the names of individuals serving in particular campaigns. The 'licences to pass beyond the seas' in E 157 record oaths of allegiance by soldiers serving abroad, notably in the Low Countries.

2.3 The English Civil War

Although there are no individual military service records as such for this period, it can be possible to identify individual soldiers in the State Papers and in numerous accounts, but no comprehensive indexes of names exist for these records. There is a useful overview of the sources in M. Bennet's 'All embarqued in one button: an introduction to sources for soldiers administrations and civilians in civil war Britain and Ireland', *Genealogists' Magazine* (December 1996), vol. 25, no. 8.

Edward Peacock's *Army Lists of the Roundheads and Cavaliers* (London, 1863), a reprint of a contemporary pamphlet, is arranged by regiment and lists officers only in the royalist and parliamentary forces in 1642. Royalist officers can also be found through the personal name indexes to the printed *Calendars of State Papers Domestic*; *Calendar of the Committee for Compounding with Delinquents* (delinquents being royalists who were fined) and the *Calendar of the Committee for the Advance of Money*.

An article by P. R. Newman, 'The Royalist Officer Corps 1642–1660', *Historical Journal*, XXVI (1983), describes other sources, including *Docquets of Letters Patent 1642–6*, edited by W. H. Black (1837), which lists commissions granted by King Charles I to raise regiments and appoint senior officers. Such senior officers usually made their own personal appointments of junior officers in their regiments, reference to which may sometimes be found in private papers. A few isolated examples of commissions issued by Prince Rupert are in c 115/126/6515–6517.

After the Restoration of Charles II in 1660, many royalists petitioned the King for rewards for loyalty to his father and such petitions appear in the printed *Calendars of State Papers Domestic* for his reign. A special fund was set up to reward officers who had seen military service and a list of over 5,000 names was printed and indexed in the 1663 *List of Officers Claiming to the Sixty Thousand Pounds* (SP 29/68, ff 42–107). An article by P. R. Newman, 'The 1663 List of Indigent Royalist Officers', *Historical Journal*, 30 (1987) discusses the value of this source. Another list of soldiers of the rank of major and above of the same date is SP 29/159, no 45.

An initial search for Parliamentary officers is also best made in printed sources such as R. R. Temple's 'The Original Officer List of the New Model Army', *Bulletin of the Institute of Historical Research*, LIX (1986) for 1645; Anne Lawrence's *Parliamentary Army Chaplains 1642–1651* (Royal Historical Society, 1990); C. H. Firth and G. Davies' *The Regimental History of Cromwell's Army* and *The New Model Army* by Ian Gentles. The *Calendars of State Papers Domestic* draw on the State Papers (SP 16–SP 17) and records of the Council of State (SP 18 and SP 25), and the Committee of Both Kingdoms (SP 21), amongst other sources, and may also prove a fruitful source of names.

For ordinary Parliamentary soldiers, speculative searches in accounts and other records of payments are time-consuming but may be rewarding. The Commonwealth Exchequer Papers in SP 28, which are not included in the printed calendars, contain warrants, accounts, certificates, testimonials and muster rolls, with numerous references to individuals, but there are no indexes and most are arranged topographically. (SP 28/265, for example, contains a muster of the 55 officers and men of Captain Hicke's cavalry troop and list of 'distressed widowers whose husbands were slaine in the service'.)

SP 28/142 has a number of regimental lists c.1649–1650 purporting to bear the signatures of officers and men in certain regiments and appointing representatives to negotiate for pay arrears. Other accounts, mainly relating to payments to officers, are in E 101, E 315, E 351, WO 47, WO 49, WO 54 and WO 55. Arrears of pay owing to soldiers that were to be secured on the sale of crown lands (in England and Wales only) are recorded in E 121. These contain thousands of names and identify the company and troop and regiment in which a man served, but they are not indexed and are arranged by the county in which the property was situated. An example is illustrated in Fig. 4.

As well as the basic accounts, there are a few examples of certificates of entitlement issued to individual soldiers. Similar debentures were issued to soldiers who had served in Ireland and were granted confiscated Irish lands but these records, which were kept in Dublin, have not survived. There is a calendar of some of the grants of land that were confirmed after 1660, with an index of names, in the *Fifteenth Report* of the Irish Record Commission (1825). Further references to men, mainly officers, who served in Ireland, may be found in the *Calendars of State Papers Ireland*.

Muster rolls for the Scots Army in England in 1646, arranged by regiment, are in SP 41/2.

A little used source, that may give a brief service history, is the records of the Committee for Indemnity in SP 24, set up to protect soldiers from legal actions arising out of their military service during the fighting. SP 24/31, for example, has the case of Issac Appleton, an apprentice tailor who was sued by his master for breaching his apprenticeship contract by leaving to serve with the parliamentary forces in 1643. Cases are arranged in alphabetical sequence and there are indexed order books. These records are further described in Research Guide Military Records Information Sheet 3 *Civil War Soldiers 1642–1660*.

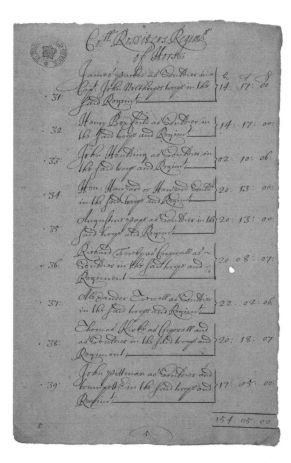

Fig. 4 *Civil War payments concerning Colonel Rossiter's Regiment of Horse.* E 121/3/3

3 COMMISSIONED OFFICERS

A commissioned officer is an individual whose authority to command and to discharge his duties as an officer is derived directly from the sovereign. All officers received a commission document signed by the sovereign. To trace the service record of an officer in the Army you need to know his regiment, because the War Office kept no continuous central record of officers until the late nineteenth century.

The most important source for the career of an officer in the Army is the printed *Army Lists*. If your ancestor does not appear in these lists, it is very unlikely that he was an officer. The *Army Lists* have been produced since 1740. They are arranged by regiment, and are more effectively name-indexed after 1867.

There are two main types of service record—those created by the War Office, which are in WO 25, and those produced by the regiments themselves, which are in WO 76. There are incomplete card indexes to these records in the Open Reading Room at Kew. Further information about them is in section 3.5.

Records giving personal information about an army officer were created routinely upon the granting of a commission, promotion, resignation or his being placed upon the half-pay list, and occasionally at other stages in his career.

There were four distinct categories of commissioned officer:

1 GENERAL OFFICERS, who co-ordinated the efforts of the whole army. They had the rank of field marshal, general, lieutenant general and major general.
2 FIELD OFFICERS, who commanded a regiment; that is, colonel, lieutenant colonel and major.
3 COMPANY OFFICERS, who were in charge of units within a regiment; that is, captain (in command of a company) and his subalterns, lieutenant, cornet (in the cavalry), ensign (infantry). In 1871 cornets and ensigns became second lieutenants, although the term cornet is still used by the Household Cavalry.
4 OTHERS: paymasters, riding masters, quartermasters, surgeons and chaplains.

There were also some other ranks, such as brigadier general, colonel commandant, and brigade major. Officers were graded by seniority, which ruled promotion within the regiment. Brevet officers were officers who were raised to the next rank in name only, but with first refusal on the next substantive rank. Some officers held two ranks at the same time—the regimental rank, which was higher and was usually a special appointment, and the Army rank, which was the actual rank of his commission. This often occurred during the two world wars when vacancies at a higher rank had to be filled because of casualties.

A list of Army ranks is given in appendix 2.

There are numerous printed sources listing officers by name and identifying their regiments as found below.

3.1 Army Lists

The broad outline of an officer's career should be fairly easy to discover from the official *Army Lists*.

Brief details of army officers have been gathered together since 1702 and published in regular series from 1754. Sets may be available in large reference libraries, although the earliest volumes are very rare. Incomplete printed sets are available at Kew but there are also complete record sets, with manuscript amendments, of the annual lists between 1754 and 1879, and of the quarterly lists from 1879 to 1900, in WO 65 and WO 66 respectively. The manuscript lists up to 1765 are indexed by name. WO 65/164–168 includes special lists of forces in North America, 1778; British–American half-pay officers, 1782; and Foreign Corps, 1794–1802.

There are five distinct types of *Army Lists* depending on date with, in many cases, more than one type covering a similar period.

Annual Army Lists
These date from 1754 to 1879 and are arranged by regiment. Volumes from 1766 are indexed. Engineer and artillery officers are included in the index from 1803 only. The series was replaced by a quarterly *Army List* from June 1879.

Monthly Army Lists
These date from 1798 to June 1940 and are arranged by regiment. In addition, they include some idea of the location of each unit. Officers of colo-

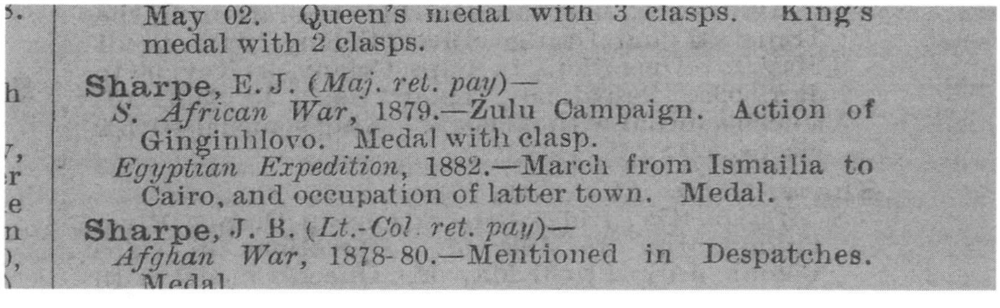

Fig. 5 *A 'war services' entry from the 1904 Army List.*

> May 02. Queen's medal with 3 clasps. King's
> medal with 2 clasps.
>
> **Sharpe,** E. J. (*Maj. ret. pay*)—
> *S. African War*, 1879.—Zulu Campaign. Action of
> Ginginhlovo. Medal with clasp.
> *Egyptian Expedition*, 1882.—March from Ismailia to
> Cairo, and occupation of latter town. Medal.
> **Sharpe,** J. B. (*Lt.-Col. ret. pay*)—
> *Afghan War*, 1878-80.—Mentioned in Despatches.
> Medal.

nial, militia and territorial units are included. The lists are indexed from 1867. After July 1939 the lists were given a security classification and not published. In 1940, they were replaced by the quarterly *Army List*.

Quarterly Army Lists

There are two separate series of quarterly *Army Lists*:

1879–1922 These lists have two distinctive features. Firstly, in addition to the regimental list (which was discontinued in 1908) they include a gradation list; that is, lists of officers in seniority order, with dates of birth and promotions. In addition, from April 1881 details of officers' war service are included. Between 1909 and 1922 these details appear in the January issue only. This series of the quarterly *Army List* was replaced by half yearly *Army Lists* in 1923.

JULY 1940–DECEMBER 1950 Quarterly *Army Lists* were produced in place of the monthly *Army List* from July 1940. They were classified documents and not published. Despite the new name, the lists continued to be produced monthly or bi-monthly until December 1943. From then on, they were issued quarterly until January 1947. They are not regimental lists and do not include the gradation list or details of officers' war services. From April 1947, although still styled the quarterly *Army Lists*, they were published in April, August and December each year.

Half yearly Army Lists

These lists exist for the period between 1923 and February 1950. They replaced and took a similar form to the quarterly *Army Lists*. They were issued in January and July each year and included a gradation list of serving officers. The January issue also includes a list of retired officers. From 1939 they became a restricted publication. From 1947 they were issued annually in February.

Army Lists *and* Army Gradation Lists

The *Army List* was revised in 1951, and now consists of three parts: part 1, a list of serving officers; part 2, a list of retired officers; part 3, a brief biography of officers, called the Gradation List. Part 1 is published yearly. Part 2 is now published only every four years. Part 3 is a restricted publication, and is not available to the general public, although old copies do sometimes appear for sale second hand.

3.2 Other Lists

Details of officers granted commissions before 1727, compiled from State Papers and other TNA sources, can most easily be traced in Charles Dalton, *English Army Lists and Commission Registers, 1661–1714* and *George I's Army, 1714–1727*, both by Charles Dalton. Copies of Dalton's books are available at Kew.

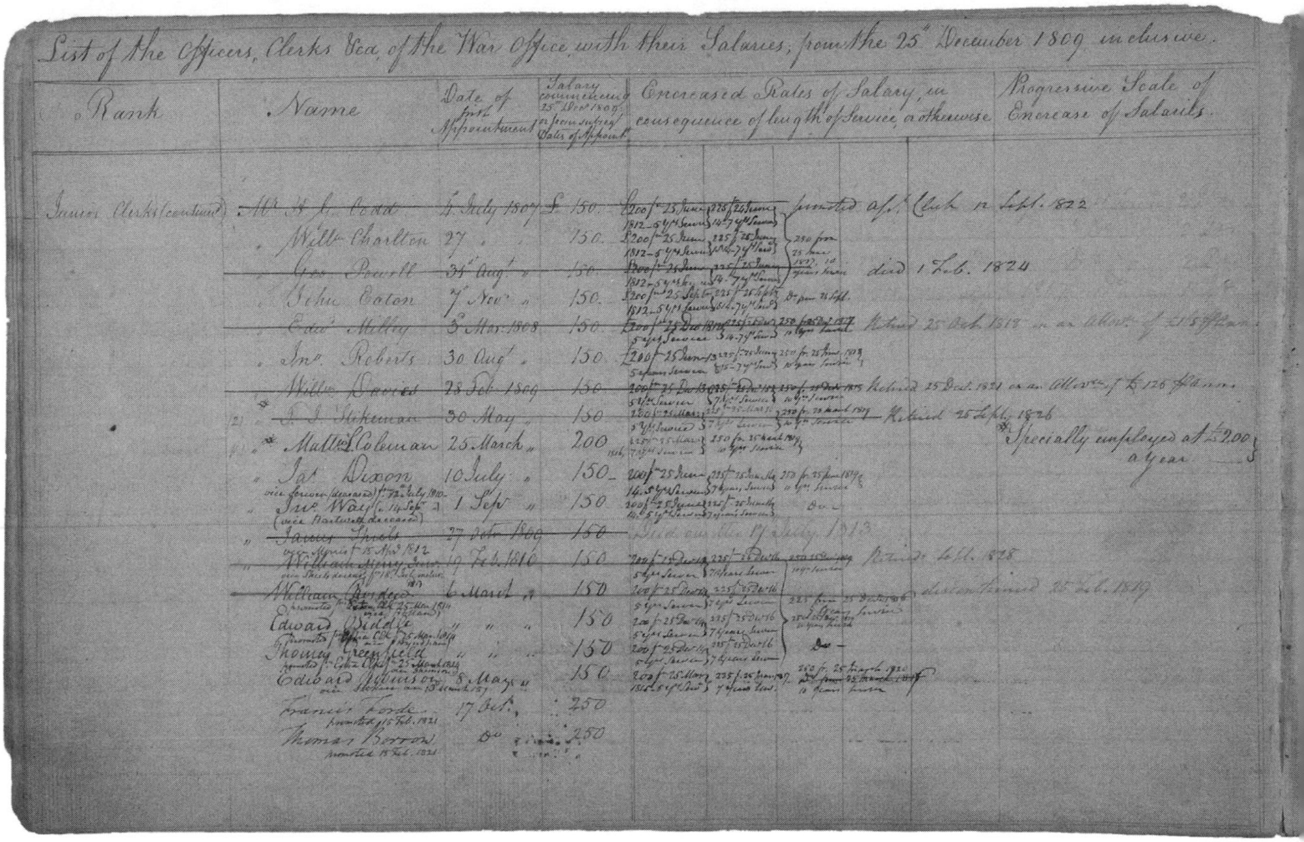

List of the Officers, Clerks &c. of the War Office, with their Salaries, from the 25th December 1809 inclusive.

Rank	Name	Date of first Appointment	Salary commencing 25th Dec 1809 or from subseq. Dates of Appoint.	Encreased Rates of Salary, in consequence of length of Service, or otherwise	Progressive Scale of Encrease of Salaries

Fig. 6 *List of War Office clerks* c. *1809–1819*. WO 381/4

You may also find the following useful:

The Military Register, published from 1768 to 1772 and in 1779, which includes Army and marine officers.

The Royal Military Calendar, published in 1820, which contains service records for officers from field marshal down to major, who held the rank at the date of publication. The Calendar, however, contains no personal information or details of officers' families. These books are available at Kew.

Lieutenant General Henry Hart started an unofficial army list in February 1839, in part to fulfil the need for a record of officers' war services, which he felt were inadequately covered in the official Army List. He noted them meticulously in extensive footnotes. *Hart's Army Lists* cover the period between 1839 and 1915 and were issued quarterly. An annual volume, which contained additional information, was also published. Hart's own copies of his *Army Lists*, 1839–1864, with material used to compile them, are in WO 211. An incomplete set of Hart's lists between 1840 and 1915 is available on open shelf in the Open Reading Room. Certain volumes have been reprinted by the Naval and Military Press. An example is reproduced as Fig. 1.

Lists of artillery officers were published in *List of Officers of the Royal Regiment of Artillery, 1716–June 1914*. A similar list was compiled for the Royal Engineers: *Roll of Officers of the Corps of Royal Engineers from 1660 to 1898*. In addition, there is a published *List of Commissioned Medical Officers of the Army, 1660–1960*. These books are available at Kew.

General staff officers and War Office staff (including civilian employees) are listed in the *War Office List,* published by the War Office itself between 1861 and 1964.

A few manuscript lists of army officers between 1702 and 1823 may be found in WO 64 and there is a manuscript index to entries in the *Army Lists* between 1704 and 1765 in the Open Reading Room.

3.3 Commissions, Appointments, Transfers and Promotions

Officers held their rank by virtue of a royal commission, and the issue of a commission—or warrant of appointment—is likely to be recorded in several places. A small collection of original commissions between 1780 and 1874 is in WO 43/1059. Appointments and promotions of officers were also announced in the *London Gazette* (hence the term 'gazetting') and, from 1829, in the *United Service Journal and Naval and Military Magazine*.

The military entry books in the State Papers (SP 44/164–203) contain warrants for the issue of commissions between 1679 and 1782. For the period from 1782 to 1855, warrants are in HO 51.

Commission books between 1660 and 1803 are in WO 25/1–121. Similar information can be found in the notification books (a one-line entry recording a commission or promotion) 1704–1858 (WO 4/513–520, WO 25/122–203).

Appointments and subsequent transfers and promotions are also recorded in the succession books (recording movement of manpower) of the secretary at war. They were compiled retrospectively from the notification and commission books. They are in two series:

BY REGIMENTS	1754–1808	(WO 25/209–220)
BY DATE	1773–1807	(WO 25/221–229).

WO 103 contains original submissions and entry books of submissions to the sovereign of recommendations for staff and senior appointments, rewards for meritorious service, and for commissions and appointments, 1809, 1871–1914.

For artillery and engineer officers, see chapters 5 and 6.

3.4 Purchase of Commissions

Before 1871 many commissions up to the rank of colonel were purchased, although in time of war there were opportunities for promotion by ability.

There were set prices for commissions, but they were widely exceeded, especially in fashionable regiments such as the foot guards. Once a commission had been purchased, officers were then able to buy up to the next rank as the opportunity presented. The whole system was widely condemned during the mid-Victorian period, and was finally abolished in 1871 by the Army Purchase Commission. The system is fully described in Anthony Bruce's *The Purchase System in the British Army, 1660–1871*. However, pay for officers remained relatively poor and in many regiments, even in the twentieth century, many officers had private means as well as army pay. Officers continued to be drawn largely from the upper strata of society.

Applications to purchase and sell commissions between 1793 and 1870 are in the Commander in Chief's memoranda in WO 31. Accompanying correspondence may also be included; examples can be seen in *In Search of Army Ancestry* by G. Hamilton-Edwards. These records are arranged chronologically by the date of appointment or promotion, usually in monthly bundles. The date upon which an officer was commissioned or promoted can be ascertained from the *Army List*, as it is here that the date upon which an individual was commissioned or promoted and announced in the *London Gazette* will be recorded. These applications may shed considerable extra light on the individual concerned. The supporting documents often contain statements of service, certificates of baptisms, marriages, deaths and burials (some of which have been removed to WO 42), and letters of recommendation. For an example, see Fig. 8.

Correspondence about the purchase and sale of commissions between 1704 and 1858 is contained in a series of indexed letter books in WO 4/513–520.

Hart's Army Lists note whether an officer bought his commission or not, and give the date when the purchase was made. Using this information, it is thus possible to discover which bundle in WO 31 is likely to contain details of the purchase. Both the official *Army Lists* and *Hart's Army Lists* record when an officer sold his commission. Unfortunately an exact date is not given, but the month or quarter can be determined.

Registers of service of every officer holding a commission on 1 November 1871 are in the papers of the Army Purchase Commission in WO 74, together with a series of applications from officers on the British and Indian establishments, 1871–1891, to which certificates of service are attached. Papers and applications are indexed by regiment, but not by name of applicant.

3.5 Records of Service

Records of service of officers held by the National Archives fall into two main groups—those compiled by the War Office and those compiled in regimental record offices.

The records described below are only for officers who had retired before the end of 1913. Records of service of officers who served in the First World War and later wars and campaigns are described in chapters 16–18.

3.5.1 *War Office returns of service*

The War Office did not begin to keep systematic records of officers' service until the early nineteenth century, having relied until then on records retained by regimental record offices. During the nineteenth century, however, the War Office compiled five series of statements of service; these are based on returns made by officers themselves:

Reference	Dates of Compilation	Notes
WO 25/744–748	1809–1810	Arranged alphabetically, they contain details of military service only.
WO 25/749–779	1828	Made by officers who had retired on full or half pay and refers to service completed before 1828. Arranged alphabetically, they give the age at commission, date of marriage and children's births as well as military service. Related correspondence from officers whose surnames begin with the letters D to R only is in WO 25/806–807.
WO 25/780–805	1829	Made by serving officers, these are arranged by regiment and give similar information to the 1828 series. The Army List for 1829 serves as an index to it.
WO 25/808–823	1847	Completed by retired officers, these pieces refer to service completed before this date. Arranged alphabetically, they contain the same information as the 1828 series.
WO 25/824-870	1870–1872	Includes a few returns before 1870 and after 1872. It is arranged by year of return and then by regiment.

An incomplete name index to service records in WO 25 is available in the Open Reading Room.

3.5.2 *Regimental service records*

Until the early nineteenth century, when the War Office began to take an interest, service records were kept by the regiments only. There are two indexes to both the early Regimental and War Office series (WO 76 and WO 25), one being an index to regiments and the other to names. The records of service of officers for the late nineteenth century to 1920 are in WO 339 and WO 374.

Regimental records of officers' services start in 1755. Those for service prior to 1914 are generally in WO 76; the records of the Gloucester Regiment, 1792–1866, are in WO 67/24–27, and those of the Royal Garrison Regiment, 1901–1905, are in WO 19. There are also some oddments in WO

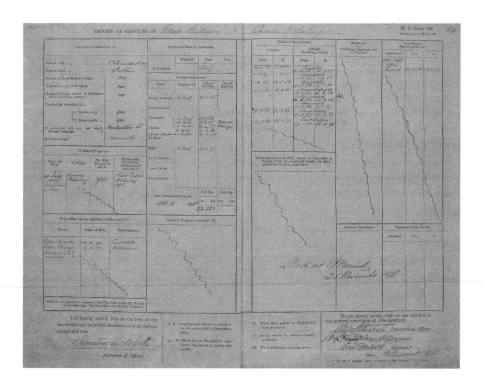

Fig. 7 *Regimental Officers record of service 1878.* WO 76/261

25. Artillery officers' services, 1727–1751, are in WO 54/684: for 1771–1870, they are in WO 76. Returns of engineer officers, 1786–1850, are in WO 54/248–259, with service records, 1796–1922, in WO 25/3913–3919. Not all regiments are represented, and the records of some were lost.

The information kept by the regiments varies a great deal, but it usually gives the ranks held, service details and some personal particulars. The WO 76 service record for Major W. C. Wolseley is described in the case study in section 3.8.2 and also reproduced as Fig. 7. There is an incomplete card index to regimental service records in the Open Reading Room, Kew. There are many regimental publications of officers' services.

Not all officers were regimental officers. For staff officers, there is a staff pay index, 1792–1830 (WO 25/695–699), lists of staff at various dates between 1802 and 1870, some with addresses (WO 25/700–702), and general returns of staff in British and foreign stations, 1782–1854 (WO 25/703–743). In WO 61/1–2 can be found general returns of the service of commissariat officers, who were not military officers, for 1798–1842; WO 61/5–6 contains a register of Commissariat and Transport staff, 1843–1889. Senior staff of the War Office are included in the *Army Lists*.

3.5.3 Records of service kept by the Military Secretary, 1870–1922

In 1871 it was decided to cease the system of obtaining commissions by purchase. In conjunction with these changes a new system of personal record keeping was begun by the Military Secretary's Department of the War Office. From 1870 individual units would keep details on individual officers on an Army Form B 194-1 and these would in turn be bound into Army Books 83. These records are in WO 76. A confidential report on each officer was completed yearly by the Commanding Officer of the unit and kept by the Military Secretary. Very few confidential reports have been preserved. Many files for officers who were commissioned before 1901 have not survived.

Together with these two forms was a correspondence file which, depending on length of service, could become very bulky. These correspondence files, covering the service of any officer between 1870 and 1922, are arranged in two separate record classes, WO 339 and WO 374, and contain military correspondence. They can contain details of an officer's estate, should he have died in service, reports made by repatriated prisoners of war, details relating to pensions, medical records, and so on.

WO 339 is arranged by War Office 'Long Number' and the alphabetical index providing these numbers can be found in WO 338 (available on microfilm). WO 374 is arranged in alphabetical order. In total some 217,000 individual files can be found in these two classes. Unfortunately, many files of officers who obtained their commissions prior to 1901 were destroyed in the 1930s. Files of those officers who saw service after 1922 are still maintained by the Ministry of Defence.

Further details about these records can be found in *First World War Army Service Records* by W. Spencer (4th ed., TNA, 2008).

3.5.4   *Further information and miscellaneous series*
A few papers and correspondence relating to individual officers are in WO 43. Particulars of service and some personal information for a small number of mainly senior officers, 1830–1961, can be found in a series of selected personal files in WO 138. A few confidential reports on officers, 1872–1905, are included in WO 27/489.

Inspection returns for the period 1750 to 1857, in WO 27, record the presence or absence of officers from their regiments at the time of inspection and may contain a brief record of service. The absence of officers is also recorded in the monthly returns, 1759–1865, in WO 17.

Additions to the list of general officers receiving unattached pay—that is, pay other than from their regiment—during the period 1835–1853 are recorded in WO 25/3230–3231. Staff paybooks and returns, 1782–1870, are in WO 25/689–743. Ledgers of the payment of unattached pay, 1814–1896, are in PMG 3. Alphabetical registers of those receiving unattached pay, 1872–1880, are in WO 23/66–67.

Wellington's despatch of 29 June 1815, printed as a supplement to the *London Gazette* of 1 July 1815, contains a list of officers killed and wounded at the Battle of Waterloo: copies can be found in ZJ 1/138 and MINT 16/111. A list of officers (and men) present during the siege of Fort Mary, Lydenburg, South Africa, in 1881 is in WO 32/7820. A list of officers present during the siege of Ladysmith, South Africa, in 1899–1900 is in WO 32/7114B.

3.6 Half Pay and Pensions

3.6.1 *Half pay*

It was not until 1871 that officers were entitled to a pension on retirement. Before then, officers who wished to retire either sold their commissions, thus recouping their capital investment, or went onto half pay. The system of half pay was set up in 1641 for officers of reduced or disbanded regiments. In time, it became in essence a retaining fee, which was paid to officers so long as a commission was held; thus they were, in theory if not in practice, available for future service. It might also be paid to officers who were unfit for service and this was officially sanctioned after 1812.

During the nineteenth century the system was more and more heavily abused. Officers who could afford to go onto half pay could avoid service abroad or any unwelcome posting. It was also possible to buy a commission and then go onto half pay the next day, which made officers eligible to purchase the next commission without serving any time with the regiment. Officers receiving half pay are listed in the Army List but do not always appear in the index.

Registers of half-pay officers are in WO 23. A series of alphabetical registers of those in receipt of half pay between 1858 and 1894, giving name, rank, regiment, date of commencement, rate and a record of payments, is in WO 23/68–78. These are often annotated with the date of the officer's death.

Ledgers recording the issue of half pay from 1737 to 1921 are in PMG 4. Until 1841 these are arranged by regiment and unindexed; thereafter, they are arranged alphabetically by name. Deaths, the assignment of pay, and sales of commissions are noted in the ledgers, and from 1837 addresses are also given. Later volumes also give dates of birth.

Lists of those who were entitled to receive half pay between 1713 and 1809, arranged by regiment, are in WO 24/660–747. WO 25/2979–3002 contain further nominal lists for the period from 1712 to 1763, and registers of warrants for half pay between 1763 and 1856. Replies to a circular of 1854, with details of the fitness for service of half-pay officers, may be found in WO 25/3009–3012. Further miscellaneous lists relating to half pay are in WO 25/3003–3008, 3013–3016.

Registers of half pay disbursed to officers living abroad are in WO 25/3017–3019; these cover the period from 1815 to 1833. WO 25/3232 is a register of permissions granted to officers on half pay to be abroad between 1815 and 1833.

Claims from wounded officers for half pay between 1812 and 1858 are contained in a series of letterbooks in WO 4/469–493.

3.6.2 *Retired full pay*

A few officers were entitled to retired full pay—mainly those with a letter of service for raising an invalid or a veteran corps. Registers of those receiving such pay from 1872 to 1894 are included in WO 23/66–74. Further registers covering the period from 1830 to 1870, are in WO 25/3000–3004.

Ledgers of payments from 1813 to 1896, are in PMG 3.

Registers of payments made to Army (and Royal Marines) officers in reduced circumstances between 1720 and 1738 are in WO 109/55–87.

3.6.3 *Pensions for wounds*

A system of pensions for wounded officers was set up in 1812 and was available to officers who were wounded before 1812. Registers of those who received such pensions between 1812 and 1897 are in WO 23/83–92. Correspondence on claims between 1812 and 1855 is in WO 4/469–493. Other correspondence, from 1809 to 1857, is in WO 43, for which there is a card index in the Open Reading Room. Ledgers for these payments from 1814 to 1920, are in PMG 9.

3.6.4 *Widows' pensions and powers of attorney*

Although officers had no entitlement to a pension, from 1708 provision was made for the payment of pensions to widows of officers killed on active service. From 1818, fifteen annuities were also paid to widows of officers whose annual income did not exceed £30 a year, out of a fund created by the will of Colonel John Drouly. Correspondence relating to widows' pensions, 1764–1816, is in WO 4/1023–1030. These volumes are internally indexed.

There are several series of registers of those receiving widows' pensions and the Drouly Annuities:

Reference	Dates	Notes
WO 24/804–883	1713–1829	
WO 25/3020–3050	1735–1769	Indexes, 1748–1811, are in WO 25/3120–3123.
PMG 11	1808–1920	Not April 1870–March 1882 (in PMG 10).
WO 23/105–113	1815–1892	
PMG 10	1870–1882	Continuation of PMG 11.

In addition, there are several series of application papers for widows' pensions and dependants' allowances:

Reference	Dates	Notes
WO 42	1755–1908	These papers may include proofs of birth, marriage, death and probate.
WO 25/3089–3197	1760–c.1818	Arranged alphabetically, with abstracts of the applications between 1808 and 1825 in WO 25/3073–3109. There is an index in the Open Reading Room.
WO 43	1818–1855	A few applications only.

Provision of an authentic baptismal certificate was mandatory for those in government service: membership of the established church implied loyalty to the crown. As a result there are many baptismal certificates for Army

34 · *Commissioned Officers*

officers in the War Office records. There are two main caches, for 1777–1868 in WO 32/8903–8920 (code 21A) and for 1755–1908 in WO 42. The latter also contains certificates of marriage, birth of children, death and burial (see below). Indexes to both are available in the Open Reading Room.

Reports by officers of their marriage, 1830–1882, are in WO 25/3239–3245; some of the marriages date from the early years of the century. The various military registers of births, marriages and deaths include references to officers' families, if they had followed the drum.

Other than this, more information is likely to be found in military records only if the officer died leaving his family in want. From 1708 there was provision for the payment of pensions to the widows of officers killed on active service; from 1720, pensions were also paid to the children and dependent relatives (usually indigent mothers over fifty) in similar cases, out of the Compassionate Fund and the Royal Bounty. These pensions were not an automatic right, and applicants had to prove their need. Application papers for widows' pensions and dependents' allowances, 1755–1908, which can include proofs of birth, marriage, death, and wills and so on, are in WO 42: other such papers, of uncertain date (1760–c.1818) are in WO 25/3089–3197, arranged alphabetically, with abstracts of applications, 1808–1825, in WO 25/3073–3089. There is an index in the Open Reading Room.

There are lists of widows receiving pensions, 1713–1829 (WO 24/804–883), and 1815–1892 (WO 23/88–92). Registers of payments, 1735–1811, are in WO 25/3020–3058, with indexes to pensions for 1748–1811 (WO 25/3120–3123). Similar registers for 1815–1895 are in WO 23/105–123. Ledgers of payments of widows' pensions, 1808–1920, are in PMG 11, but they give little information. Correspondence relating to widows' pensions, 1764–1816, is in WO 4/1023–1030: the volumes are internally indexed, and contain details on many widows. Selected correspondence on widows' pensions is also in WO 43: there is a card index in the Open Reading Room.

There are registers of compassionate allowances awarded to dependents, 1773–1812 (WO 25/3124–3125). Registers of those placed on the Compassionate List, 1858–1894, are in WO 23/114–119, with a summary for 1805–1895 in WO 23/120–123. There are also about 2,000 'compassionate papers' for 1812–1813 (WO 25/3110–3114), which are affidavits by the widows and children, in receipt of a compassionate pension, that they received no other government income. They are in rough alphabetical order, and give details of the officer, often the age of the children, and sometimes the name of the guardian, as well as some indication of county or country of residence. (These affidavits were sworn before local justices.) Correspondence relating to the Compassionate Fund, 1803–1860, is in WO 4/521–590. There are ledgers of payments, for 1779–1812 (WO 24/771–803), and for 1812–1915 (PMG 10), but they give little information. Ledgers of pension payments for the widows of foreign officers, 1822–1885, are in PMG 6 and PMG 7. For pensions and compassionate allowances to the widows and dependants of commissariat officers, 1814–1834, see WO 61/96–98.

Registers of pensions to the widows of Royal Artillery and Royal Engineer officers, 1833–1837, are in WO 54/195–196, with ledgers of payments, 1836–1875, in PMG 12. There is also a series of indexed registers of letters of attorney, 1699–1857, relating to Ordnance officers, civilian staff and creditors who expected to receive payments of any kind from the Ordnance Office (WO 54/494–510): many of these letters were made in favour of the wife or other close relative, or were letters granted by the probate courts to the widow as executrix.

Similar registers of powers of attorney for Army officers in general are in PMG 14 and PMG 51. There are entry books of powers of attorney apparently arranged by date, for 1759–1816 (PMG 14/104–125). For 1811–1814, there are alphabetical entry books (PMG 14/126–137). Registers of letters of attorney, 1756–1827, are in PMG 14/142–167: they include separate volumes of letters of attorney granted by widows, 1802–1821 (PMG 165–167). There is a single register of letters of attorney, 1755–1783, at WO 30/1. Later registers, 1836–1899, are in PMG 51.

3.6.5 *Children's and dependent relatives' allowances*

From 1720 pensions were also paid out of the Compassionate Fund and the Royal Bounty to children and dependent relatives of officers. There are registers of compassionate allowances awarded to dependants, 1773–1812 (WO 25/3124–3125). Registers giving the names of those placed on the Compassionate List, 1858–1894, are in WO 23/114–119, with a summary for 1805–1895 in WO 23/120–123. Applications for grants from the Fund, for 1812 and 1813 only, are in WO 25/3110–3114. Ledgers recording payments for 1779–1812 are in WO 24/771–803 and those for 1812–1815 are in PMG 10. Correspondence relating to the Compassionate Fund, 1803–1860, is in WO 4/521–590.

3.7 Recruitment and Training

Before the nineteenth century, little formal training was provided to new recruits, other than those recruited to those branches of the service requiring technical skills. In 1741 the Royal Military Academy was established to train artillery and engineer officers. This was merged in 1947 with the Royal Military College, founded in 1807 and based at Sandhurst since 1812. Sandhurst holds registers of cadets from *c*.1790 and applications for entry, which may include baptism certificates. These records may be consulted by arrangement with the commandant. See also 14.11.

3.8 Case Studies

These two case studies illustrate how a detailed picture of an individual's service history can be built up using a variety of different sources.

3.8.1 Major General William Freke Williams

This officer was brought to my attention by a friend of many years who had in her possession a privately printed family history, written and produced just after the turn of the twentieth century. As it had been written without access to many of the official records of the War Office, was the information in the family history correct?

William Freke Williams was born in 1792. On 30 August 1810, he obtained a commission without purchase as an ensign in the Royal African Corps (WO 25/60 f 303), signalling the beginning of what was to be a very successful military career.

On 10 June 1811 (WO 25/61, f 172), a lieutenancy in the Royal African Corps followed. During his time in the Royal African Corps, Williams saw service in Senegal, Goree and Sierra Leone, all on the west coast of Africa. On 26 March 1813, Williams purchased a commission as a lieutenant in the 85th Foot. Service with the 85th Foot was to take him to the Iberian Peninsula, fighting the French at the battles of San Sebastian, Nivelle and Nive. For his service at these battles, he was awarded the Military General Service Medal with three clasps (WO 100/1).

After service in the Peninsular War, the 85th Foot went to America where Lieutenant Williams was wounded at the battle of Bladenburg on 24 August 1814 (WO 1/141, f 33). He then purchased a captaincy in the 85th Foot on 31 October 1814 (WO 25/64, f 258).

Subsequent service in the West Indies and Canada brought him to the attention of the commander in chief. The next steps in his still rising career were his promotion to major in 1825 (WO 25/193, f 28) and being created a Knight of Hanover in 1834/5. After service in Canada in 1838, Williams was promoted to lieutenant colonel in June of that year. Further special service was to follow. An appointment as assistant adjutant general (AAG) in Belfast in 1844 lasted until 1855. During his time as AAG at Belfast, Lieutenant Colonel Williams became Colonel Williams (WO 25/77, f 254).

In 1855, to assist the British forces participating in the Crimean War, Williams was promoted to brigadier general and given command of a brigade of some 4,000 men on Malta. On 14 April 1857, he was promoted to major general and given command of a brigade at Gibraltar. When the garrison at Gibraltar was reduced, he returned to England to command a brigade at Shorncliffe.

Ill health in the early part of 1860 forced Major General W. F. Williams reluctantly to resign his command. He died at Bath on 12 December 1860 and is buried in the parish churchyard at Widcombe in Bath.

Much of this record of service was contained in the family history, although certain minor omissions had been made. Apart from missing the information about the Royal African Corps most of the basic facts were present and could be confirmed by the Official Army List, *Hart's Army List*, War Office Notification Books in WO 25 and Field Officers Records of Service in WO 25/3998–4001. A sample entry from the *Hart's Army List* of 1891 is reproduced as Fig. 1.

3.8.2 Major W. C. Wolseley

The wealth of detail about the career of an officer who died in service can be demonstrated by the case of William Charles Wolseley.

As with looking for any officer from 1757 onwards, the first place to look for an officer is in the *Army List* (see 3.1). This will not only provide you with the individual's rank and regiment, it will also tell you the dates on which the officer obtained a commission at a given rank. When using the *Army List*, it is important to find the first and last entry for an individual, as many officers saw service in more than one regiment.

For any officer who obtained a commission between 1793 and 1870, whether it be by purchase or on merit, the place to begin research, once you have checked the *Army List*, is WO 31 Commander in Chief (C in C), Memoranda Papers. Before an individual could be granted a commission, the Commander in Chief had to sanction it. The papers in WO 31 are arranged in date order: the class list, in the left-hand column of the document description, provides the date of the relevant memoranda, while the date on which the commission was announced in the *London Gazette*, which is the date in the *Army List*, in the right-hand column.

The kind of information contained in a commander in chief's memorandum can vary. If the commission was purchased, the memorandum will record the amount paid, the rank being purchased and the regiment. For commissions granted on merit, the reasons why such a commission should be granted are usually given. First commissions granted to individuals, usually as an ensign (infantry) or cornet (cavalry), are generally accompanied by a lengthy letter from a member of his family, or a suitable patron, describing his potential and character and explaining why such a commission is being sought.

The Commander in Chief's memoranda for the appointment of William Charles Wolseley as an ensign into the 16th Foot, dated April 1855, can be found in WO 31/1078. Within the memoranda is a letter dated 3 March 1855, from Reverend Cadwallada Wolseley, asking for a commission for his eldest son, William Charles Wolseley—see Fig. 8. The letter describes his attributes; his family (noting a connection with Captain Garnet Wolseley, who was later to become Field Marshal Viscount Garnet Wolseley), his physical description and his current place of residence. The letter also provides information about the writer of the letter, noting that he was chaplain to the Lord Lieutenant of Ireland and also to the Archbishop of Dublin.

Charles Wolseley's next two commissions were both by purchase. A Royal Commission in 1821 set the amount that should be paid, but these levels were exceeded on numerous occasions. The memoranda for Wolseley's commission as a captain in the 6th Foot, dated 19 December 1862, are in WO 31/1307. For his captaincy in the 6th Foot Wolseley paid the sum of £1100 which, interestingly, is the difference between the sum paid for a lieutenancy and a captaincy as set by the Royal Commission back in 1821.

Apart from the records in WO 31 and information contained in the *Army*

List, records of service of army officers can be found in the record class WO 76. A name index for this class is in the Open Reading Room. The records of service for the 6th Foot are in WO 76/261, with Wolseley appearing on folio 14 (see Fig. 7). This record of service notes the date of his birth, the dates of all of Wolseley's commissions, together with the regiments he served in, service overseas, details of his wife and children and, most importantly, his date of death at Meerut in India on 25 November 1878.

As a widow of a British Army officer, Annie Wolseley applied for a pension. Records of widow's pensions can be found in PMG 11, which is arranged in chronological order and alphabetically by name of the deceased. Details of the pension granted to Annie Wolseley can be found in PMG 11/74, which shows that a pension of £68 7s 2d per year was authorized on 2 May 1879.

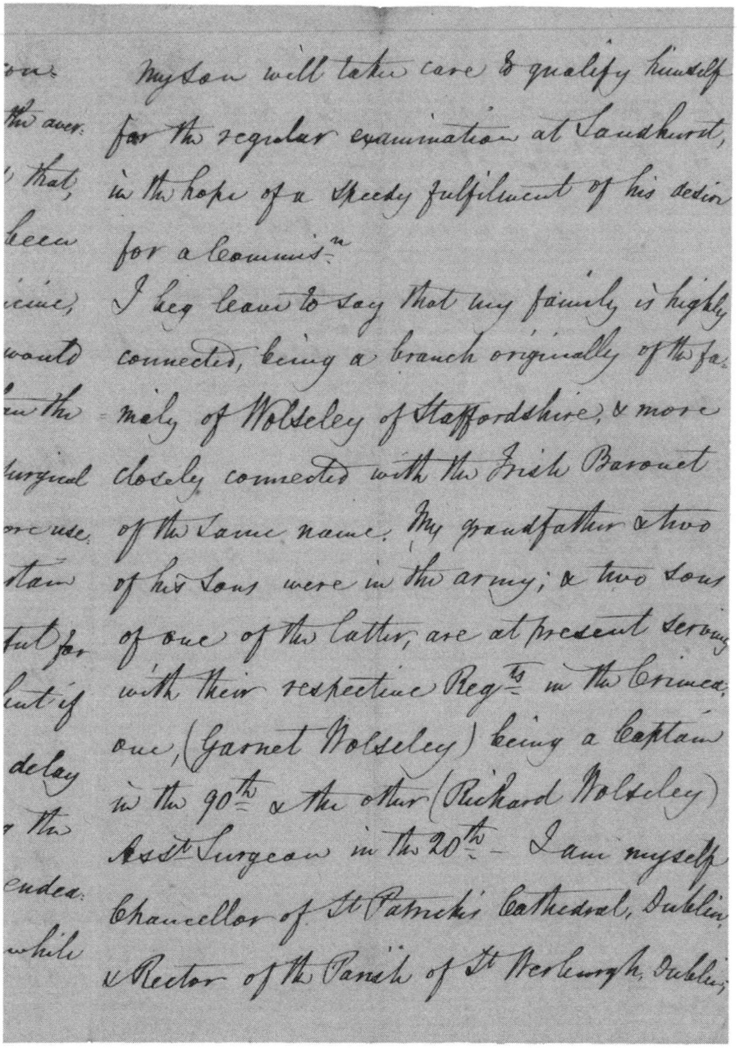

My son will take care & qualify himself
for the regular examination at Sandhurst,
in the hope of a speedy fulfilment of his desire
for a Commissn.
I beg leave to say that my family is highly
connected, being a branch originally of the family of Wolseley of Staffordshire, & more
closely connected with the Irish Baronet
of the same name. My grandfather & two
of his sons were in the army; & two sons
of one of the latter, are at present serving
with their respective Regts in the Crimea;
one, (Garnet Wolseley) being a Captain
in the 90th & the other (Richard Wolseley)
Asst Surgeon in the 20th – I am myself
Chancellor of St Patrick's Cathedral, Dublin
& Rector of the Parish of St Werburgh, Dublin;

Fig. 8 *Letter concerning W. C. Wolseley found in the Commander in Chief's Memoranda 1855.* WO 31/1078

3.8.3 *Lieutenant Colonel E. J. Sharpe*

The records of service of many officers commissioned before 1901 and who served in the First World War are quite rare. The key reason for this is the different forms of record keeping for officers commissioned pre and post 1901.

Edward John Sharpe was born in Esher, Surrey on 10 April 1858. After time as a cadet, Sharpe was commissioned on 31 May 1876 as a Sub Lieutenant on the unattached list (not into a specific regiment), but on the same day he was appointed to the 23rd Foot.

Transferring to the 57th Foot in February 1877, Edward Sharpe was to serve with the 57th , later the 1st Battalion Middlesex Regiment or the 2nd Battalion of the same regiment or on staff duties for the remaining part of his career up to 1903.

With the 57th Foot, Sharpe saw operational service during the Zulu War in 1879 for which he received the South Africa Medal with 1879 clasp.

In 1882, Lieutenant E. J. Sharpe managed to get himself attached to the 3rd Battalion King's Royal Rifle Corps and saw further operational service with them in Egypt. For this service Sharpe received the Egypt 1882 Medal and Khedive's Star.

According to Sharpe's record of service in WO 76/55 he was promoted to captain in 1885 and he served in various staff positions in India until 1892. A faint note on the record of service indicates that Sharpe was seconded for service in India in 1898.

Sharpe's record of service in WO 76/55 ends with the note mentioned above. However, the *Army List* records that Major E. J. Sharpe resigned in 1903.

Edward Sharpe, like many other retired officers, was drawn back to the army at the outbreak of the First World War. Interestingly for an officer commissioned pre 1901, Sharpe has a file in WO 339, which says it covers 1903–1924, but actually contains his letter of resignation from 1903, the reason for that resignation, a synopsis of his career between 1876 and 1903, together with information about his First World War career.

During the First World War, Major Edward Sharpe was promoted to temporary Lieutenant Colonel, initially seeing service as second-in-command of the 13th Battalion Middlesex Regiment. Seeing service in France between 30 August 1915 and 15 January 1916, Sharpe earned the 1914/15 Star, British War Medal and Victory Medal to add to his earlier awards. Sharpe was Mentioned in Despatches for his service in the war and this was announced in the *London Gazette* on 24 December 1917. After returning from France, Sharpe commanded the 8th (Reserve) Battalion, Middlesex Regiment.

Retiring again from the army before the end of the war, Edward John Sharpe died on 17 December 1923.

Sharpe's file can be seen in WO 339/12521.

4 OTHER RANKS, 1660–1913

In the Army, the 'other ranks' were the privates (infantry) and troopers (cavalry), gunners (Royal Artillery), sappers (Royal Engineers), trumpeters and drummers, supervised by corporals and sergeants who were non-commissioned officers (NCOs) promoted from the ranks. NCOs were in turn supervised by Warrant Officers (individuals whose position had been affirmed by a written warrant granted by their commanding authority). Specialist corps and regiments, however, used different names. A basic outline of ranks in the Army is in appendix 2.

Most men enlisted voluntarily and for 'life' (which, in practice, meant for twenty-one years), and served until they were disabled by wounds or old age, although in wartime enlistment for a limited period was sometimes permitted. Discharges could be bought, but few had the money to do so. The Army Enlistment Act 1870 introduced a scheme whereby men could join the Army on a short-service engagement of twelve years, of which six would be spent with the colours and six on reserve. However, men could still re-engage for a maximum service of twenty-one years. Pay was poor and further reduced by stoppages for food and clothing. Before the late eighteenth century, information about 'other ranks' is sparse and largely to be found in accounts or pension records.

To trace the service record of an individual, it is important to know the approximate dates of his service and the regiment or corps in which he served. Almost all service records were kept by the individual regiments, not by any central authority. As a result, if you are searching for an individual soldier, you really do need to know the regiment in which he served, unless you are prepared for a lengthy and speculative search. There are, however, two series of Army-wide returns of service of non-commissioned officers and men. One contains statements of periods of service and of liability to serve abroad, as on 24 June 1806 (WO 25/871–1120). The other contains returns of the service of non-commissioned officers and men not known to be dead or totally disqualified for service, who had been discharged between 1783 and 1810 (WO 25/1121–1131). Both series are arranged by regiment, and only then alphabetically.

The main everyday service records of men in active service kept by the Army were the regimental muster book and the regimental pay list. These provide a fairly complete guide to a soldier's Army career from enlistment, through movements with the regiment throughout the world, to discharge. However, because there are so many muster books and pay lists, and because they each cover such a short space of time, it can be a very lengthy task to search through them. It is worth investigating other records first, particularly the service records of soldiers retired to pension, where the personal information is consolidated and is far more easily found, even if you are not sure that your ancestor received a pension. If you find that he was discharged without a pension before 1883, you may have to use the muster books and pay lists. If your soldier died in service and you know the regiment, you may be able to find out quite a lot of information by using the casualty returns: if these prove no use, try the muster books.

4.1   Identifying a Regiment

There is a computerized index recording the names of soldiers who were discharged to pension between 1760 and 1854 whose records are in the record class WO 97 (see 4.2). It does not include regiments on the Irish establishment before 1822. A supplementary collection of discharge papers covering the period 1843–1899 in WO 97 is not covered by the database.

It may be possible to identify the unit from old photographs. A useful article is D. J. Barnes's 'Identification and dating: military uniforms' in *Family history in focus*, edited by D. J. Steel and L. Taylor. There is also a chapter on the subject in Norman Holding's *More Sources of World War I Army Ancestry*.

The registers of births of children of army personnel held by the General Register Office are indexed and it may be possible to determine a regiment from them, if you have some idea of when children were born or the area in which a soldier served. For further details about these registers see 19.1 and appendix 4.

If you know the county or country in which your ancestor was living between 1842 and 1862 for England or Scotland, or between 1842 and 1882 for Ireland and abroad, you may be able to pinpoint the regiment from the records of payment of pensions in WO 22 and PMG 8, which include the names of regiments in which individuals served. For further details of these records see 4.6. If the soldier died in service, another possibility would be to check the records of soldiers' effects, which survive between 1810–1822, 1830–1844 and 1862–1881. They are in WO 25, arranged by initial letter of surname, and they give the regiment. This source is unlikely to be of use if the soldier died owing money to the Army.

The National Army Museum holds a set of Soldiers' Effects Ledgers for April 1901–March 1960. These ledgers were created as a list of the monies owed to a soldier who died in service. They do not list any personal items that may have been returned to the next of kin. The information they typically contain is: full name, regimental number, date (and sometimes place) of death, next of kin and monies paid to the next of kin. The records from

1901–1914 also detail the date of enlistment and trade of enlistment.

As these records are not held in the main collections of the National Army Museum but in off-site storage, there is a fee, currently of £10, charged for the provision of a transcript of an individual's entry. Please contact The National Army Museum, Royal Hospital Road, Chelsea, London, SW3 4HT.

If you have an idea of the place of service, you may be able to identify the regiment from one of the sources listed in section 1.4.

There are other possibilities as well, although using the following suggestions may be a lengthy process. Depending on the known information, an area of records to be searched can be limited. If a rough date of discharge is known, it may be possible to trace the regiment in which a soldier served by using various registers of discharges. These are not complete but, especially before the records in WO 97 are arranged purely alphabetically, they are a useful potential source of information. A number of these pieces contain information on soldiers whose discharge document would not, in any case, be contained in WO 97. These discharges were:

Date	Reason	Reference
1817–1829	By purchase	WO 25/3845–3847
1830–1838	By own request	WO 25/3848–3849
1830–1856	With modified pension	WO 25/3850
1838–1855	Free or free deferred pension	WO 25/3851–3858
1856–1861	Free permanent pension	WO 25/3859–3861
1861–1870	Free permanent pension, modified/deferred pension, or purchase	WO 25/3863–3868
1852–1870	First period, incorrigible, ignominy, penal servitude, or 21 years with militia	WO 25/3869–3878
1856–1857	Regiment under reduction	WO 25/3879–3882
1866–1870	Limited Service Act	WO 25/3883–3893
1863–1878	On return from India	WO 12/13077–13105
1871–1884	General register	WO 121/223–238
1882–1883	Gosport discharge depot musters	WO 16/2284
1883–1888	Gosport discharge depot musters	WO 16/2888–2916
1884–1887	Without pension (gives address to which discharged)	WO 121/239–257

4.2   Service Records

You could describe a service record as everything about a soldier, collected together in one neat file. In many instances this is so and it can be a case of getting the maximum amount of information about the soldier—when he joined, where he served and when he left—for the minimum amount of effort.

Service records are in fact made up of different elements and to create one requires you to consult a large number of sources, each arranged differently. Attestation and discharge papers, description book, muster and pay lists and medal records may all need to be consulted in order to create a record of service. However, many researchers don't look at them all.

4.2.1 Soldiers' documents

The most important service records are attestation and discharge papers. These form the class known as soldiers' documents in WO 97, and cover the period between 1760 and 1913. Until around 1895, these service records are normally only for men who were discharged and received a pension, whether it be for length of service or disability. Documents for soldiers who died on service, or who did not receive a discharge certificate for any reason, have not survived. In the early years, the level of detail is limited; later documents, however, give information about the soldier's age, physical appearance, birthplace and trade or occupation on enlistment in the Army. They also include a record of service, including any decorations awarded, promotions and reductions in rank, crimes and punishments, and the reason for the discharge to pension. In some cases, the intended place of residence after discharge and the date of death are given. However, many soldiers moved from that address shortly after discharge.

These documents are arranged by discharge date. The order in many boxes has been considerably disturbed over the years, so you may need to look through a whole box to find a particular individual.

The documents fall into four series:

1760–1854　These documents are arranged alphabetically by name within regiments, which is why you must know the regiment in which a soldier served. There seem to be relatively few for men who enlisted before 1792. This series is available on microfilm at Kew and has been indexed recording the name, regiment, birthplace, age at discharge and years of enlistment and discharge. It is possible to search for records in this part of WO 97 by using the catalogue.

1855–1872　Again, these are arranged alphabetically by name within a regiment, and it is vital to know the regiment in which a man served.

1873–1882　These are arranged alphabetically by name of soldier within the categories—cavalry, artillery, engineers, foot guards, infantry and miscellaneous corps.

1883–1913　This series covers both soldiers discharged to pension and those discharged for other reasons, such as the termination of limited engagements or discharge by purchase. As widow's pensions as a matter of right were first granted during the 2nd Boer War (1899–1902), it is possible to find records for men who died in service. The documents are arranged in surname order. Details of next of kin, wife and children are also given.

SUPPLEMENTARY SERIES   There are two supplementary series towards the end of WO 97. One series covers 1843–1899 and the other 1900–1913. The collection for 1900–1913 is in WO 97/6323–6354 and the collection for 1843–1899 in WO 97/6355–6383. A significant percentage of the records in these two collections are for men who joined the army under a false name, with their true identity becoming known later. Some of these supplementary records have been digitized and placed on DocumentsOnline.

4.2.2   Additional series of service records

For men discharged between 1787 and 1813 and awarded Chelsea out-pensions (that is, those pensioners who were not living in Chelsea hospitals), certificates of service similar to those in WO 97 are in WO 121/1–136. They are arranged in chronological order based on the date at which a pension was awarded.

General registers of discharges from 1871 to 1884 are in WO 121/223–238. Registers of men discharged without pension between 1884 and 1887 are in WO 121/239–257. Many of the pieces in WO 121 are in very poor condition and access to them may be restricted.

Certificates of service of soldiers who were awarded deferred pensions between 1838 and 1896 are in WO 131. The date range of 1838–1896 reflects the date of issue of the certificate; in many of the earliest cases the date the man started serving was very early in the nineteenth century. A name index for WO 131 is available in the Open Reading Room.

Certificates of service for Irish soldiers awarded out-pensions by the Board of Kilmainham Hospital between 1783 and 1822 are in WO 119 (see also 4.6). They are arranged by discharge number, which can be traced in the admission books in WO 118.

4.2.3   Description books

Description books describe recruits of a given regiment on enlistment. There are two main series of description books. The regimental description and succession books (which record changes of manpower within a given unit) are in WO 25/266–688: they cover the period between 1778 and 1878, but not all the regiments' books start so early or go on so late, and only a small percentage of all soldiers are included. Some are arranged alphabetically, others by date of enlistment. The books give a description of each soldier, his age, place of birth and trade and successive service details. An example is reproduced as Fig. 9. The depot description books in WO 67, covering the period from 1768 to 1908, give the same information, gathered as recruits were assembled at the regimental depot.

The regimental description books in WO 25 do not contain details of every man in the regiment who served between the covering dates. They began to be compiled in approximately 1825, or slightly earlier, after an investigation into fraudulent claims of service. Regiments had to write down the services of every man in the regiment who was still serving at that time, and to list them in chronological order of enlistment (or alphabetically).

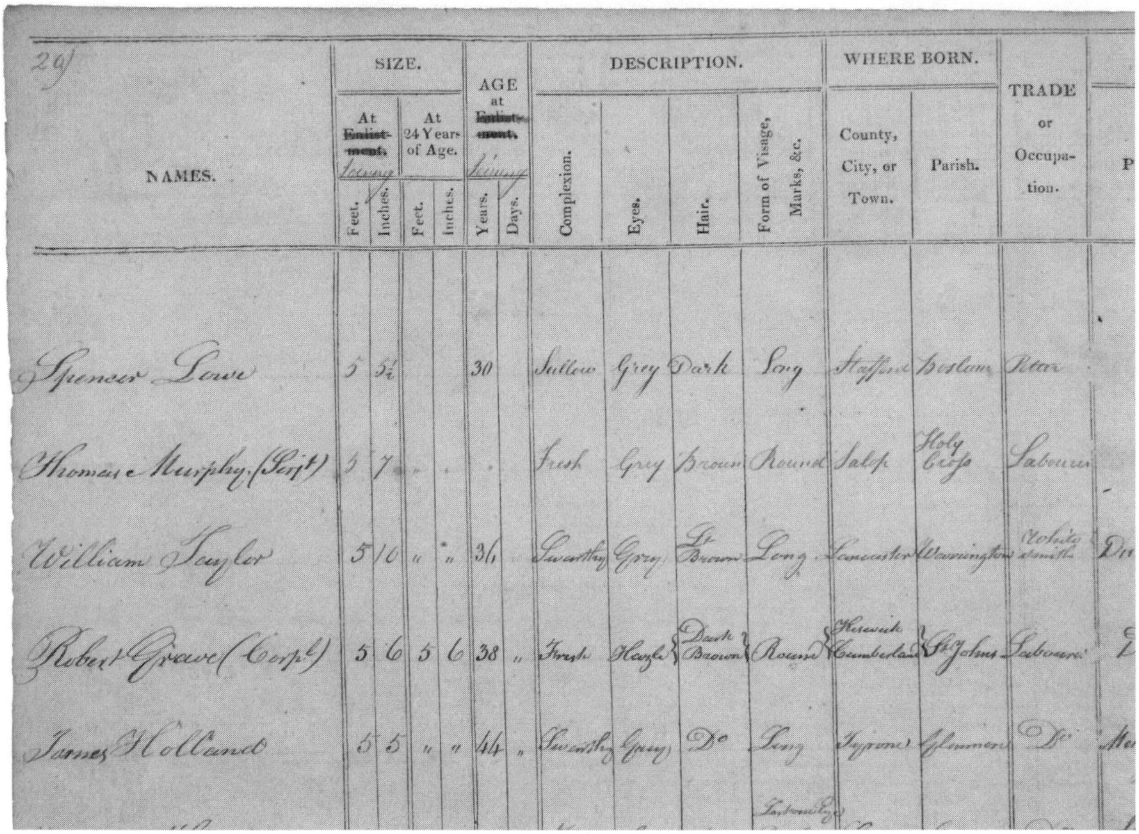

NAMES.	SIZE. At Enlistment Feet.	Inches.	At 24 Years of Age Feet.	Inches.	AGE at Enlistment Years.	Days.	Complexion.	Eyes.	Hair.	Form of Visage, Marks, &c.	WHERE BORN. County, City, or Town.	Parish.	TRADE or Occupation.	P.
Spencer Lowe	5	5½			30		Sallow	Grey	Dark	Long	Stafford	Beslem	Potter	
Thomas Murphy (Serjt)	5	7					Fresh	Grey	Brown	Round	Salop	Holy Cross	Labourer	
William Taylor	5	10	"	"	36		Swarthy	Grey	Brown	Long	Lancaster	Warrington	Whitesmith	Do
Robert Greave (Corpl)	5	6	5	6	38		"	Fresh	Hazel	Dark Brown	Round	Cumberland Keswick	St Johns	Labourer
James Holland	5	5	"	"	44		"	Swarthy	Grey	Do	Long	Tyrone	Clonmore	Do	Ma

Fig. 9 *A typical Description Book entry* c. *1813–1816.* WO 25/608

Most books would appear to have between 1,000 and 1,500 names (some have a lot more), but considering that regimental strength was 1,000 and the regiments had been through twenty-two years of war and wastage, this is a small percentage of the total number.

Depot rolls or description books (WO 67) are usually much fuller. Men were usually allotted a number, but this number does not appear on any forms until the 1830s. Depot rolls, however, do not list soldiers who enlisted where the regiment was stationed. Nor do they list soldiers who transferred from one regiment straight into another.

Regimental numbering began as a direct result of this commission of inquiry into fraudulent claims of service. When he joined, each man was allotted a consecutive number. This would not be carried throughout his career: if he transferred into another regiment, he would be allotted a new number. It is possible to estimate when a soldier enlisted in a particular regiment if a point of reference is known—for example, if a muster provides details of a man with a regimental number close to that of the ancestor. It is then possible to guess a year of discharge (add 21!).

In 1917 the system changed and the first series of Army numbers came in. This was very short-lived and the second series (superseding the first) was introduced in 1922. This allotted 'blocks' of numbers to particular regiments; when he first enlisted, a man would be given a number in the relevant block, which he would retain even if he transferred to another regiment. This numbering system ran out in c.1941 and another began.

4.2.4 *The Imperial Yeomanry*

The Imperial Yeomanry was created in 1899, when the need for mounted infantry was bought sharply into focus by events in the first few months of the Boer War (1899–1902). It enabled men to join for one year's service and for many, serve overseas in South Africa.

The Imperial Yeomanry records of service for other ranks can be found in the series WO 128, with the indexes in WO 129. The series WO 128 is arranged by service number and, while it would be possible to find the service number by using WO 129, details of which are given below.

There is an easier way to identify an Imperial Yeomanry (IY) service number by consulting *The Roll of The Imperial Yeomanry, Scottish Horse and Lovats Scouts, Second Boer War Africa 1899–1902*, by Kevin Asplin, which is an alphabetical list of nearly all the men of the Imperial Yeomanry, published in two volumes. This index will give you the all-important service number that you need to access the records in WO 128. Copies are held at the National Archives.

Reference	Number range		
WO 129/1	IY	Service numbers	1–7299
WO 129/2	IY	Service numbers	7300–19999
WO 129/3	IY	Service numbers	20000–23999
WO 129/4	IY	Service numbers	24000–29799
WO 129/5	IY	Service numbers	29800–35999
WO 129/6	IY	Service numbers	36000–42199
WO 129/7	IY	Service numbers	42200–45124

If an Imperial Yeomanry trooper completed his one year's service and then signed on for a further period of service, you may find that he was given a new number. The records of those members of the Imperial Yeomanry who were medically discharged during the period 1900–1913 can usually be found in WO 97.

The Queen's South Africa Medal and King's South Africa Medal rolls for the Imperial Yeomanry are arranged by battalion, and you need to know which company was in which battalion in order to use the rolls effectively. A breakdown of company to battalions can be found in appendix 4.

There are no consolidated records of service for Imperial Yeomanry officers. Some details can be found in WO 108 and others by using the *Army List*.

4.3.5 *The Household Cavalry*

The records of service of men discharged from the Household Cavalry can be found in the records series WO 400. This record series is arranged by regiment, date of discharge and in alphabetical order.

Regiment	Discharge dates	WO 400 piece range
1 Life Guards	1801–1856	1–4
1 Life Guards	1859–1920	5–55
2 Life Guards	1799–1856	56–86
2 Life Guards	1856–1919	87–166
Royal Horse Guards	1805–1856	167–199
Royal Horse Guards	1856–1886	200–229
Royal Horse Guards	1886–1919	230–285

4.3 Pay Lists and Muster Rolls

If you know the regiment in which a soldier served, or have ascertained it from other records, the muster rolls and pay lists provide a comprehensive means of establishing his date of enlistment, his movements throughout the world and his date of discharge or death. Most of these records cover the period from 1760 to 1898, although those for the artillery go back to 1708.

The quarterly muster rolls normally contain three monthly musters and note where the regiment or unit was located, the names of officers and men on the strength and their rank, pay, enlistment date (or death or discharge), punishments, time spent in hospital and other absences. The entry may show a man's age on enlistment, as well as the place in which he enlisted. Under 'men becoming non-effective', which is sometimes found at the end of each quarter's muster, you may find the birthplace, trade and date of enlistment of any soldier who had died or been discharged during that quarter.

From about 1868 to about 1883, at the end of each muster (or at the beginning for regiments stationed in India) may be found a marriage roll, which lists wives and children for whom married quarters were provided. The amount of information contained in the married establishment may vary according to date and who actually completed that section of the muster. It could be possible for date and place of marriage and the number, sex and ages of any children to be recorded.

The main series of muster books and pay lists are arranged by regiment and are bound in volumes covering a period of twelve months. They are in the following separate classes:

Unit	Dates	Class reference
Artillery	1708–1878	WO 10
Engineers	1816–1878	WO 11
General	1732–1878	WO 12
Foreign Legions	1854–1856	WO 15
Scutari Depot	1854–1856	WO 14
Militia and Volunteers	1780–1878	WO 13
All regiments and corps	1878–1898	WO 16

WO 12 includes household troops, cavalry, Guards, regular infantry, special regiments and corps, colonial troops, various foreign legions and regiments, and regimental, brigade and other depots. WO 14 and WO 15 relate to troops engaged in the Crimean War.

WO 16 continues the material in classes WO 10, WO 11 and WO 12, from 1888 as company muster rolls only, arranged chiefly by regimental districts. From 1881 the arrangement of the musters in this class reflects the reorganization of the Army on a territorial basis. The *Army Lists* contain indexes to regiments with their regimental district numbers.

4.4   Deserters

Army life was hard and discipline severe, hence desertion was common. Registers of deserters, 1811–1852, are in WO 25/2906–2934. Until 1827 these volumes consist of separate series for cavalry, infantry and militia (the latter up to 1820 only). After 1827 they are arranged in one series by regiment. They give physical descriptions of the individual concerned, dates and places of enlistment and desertion; they may also indicate what happened to deserters who were caught. An example from WO 25/2925 relates to a Private Thomas Brown of the 30th Regiment of Foot. It records that he deserted in London on 5 January 1844, having only joined up at the end of the previous December. He was then 17½ years old and is described as being 5 feet 6⅛ inches tall, with fresh complexion, brown hair and hazel eyes.

Registers of captured deserters, 1813–1848, with indexes to 1833, are in WO 25/2935–2954. They include registers of deserters who were caught or who surrendered, and give the name of the individual and his regiment, the date of his committal and place of confinement; what happened to him (that is, whether he returned to his regiment or was discharged from the Army), and the amount of the reward paid (if the man had not surrendered) and to whom it was paid.

Returns of deserters captured and held as prisoners on the Savoy Hulks in the Thames Estuary, 1799–1823, are in WO 25/2956–2961. These returns are not indexed. Deserters who surrendered under amnesty between 1803 and 1815 are in WO 25/2955.

Casualty returns in WO 25/1359–2410, 3251–3260, indexed in WO 25/2411–2755, 3261–3471, list deserters as well as casualties for 1809–c.1875 (the indexes contain some entries up to 1910). Miscellaneous correspondence relating to individual deserters, 1744–1813 and 1848–1858, is in WO 4/591–654.

In addition, the *Police Gazette* included in each issue a current list of men who had deserted from the Army (and Royal Marines), with a detailed description of each individual. Copies between 1828 and 1845 are in HO 75. Local newspapers may also carry descriptions of deserters.

Information about deserters, 1716–1830, can also be found in the deserter bounty certificates, which are included in numerous other types of accounts in E 182. These certificates record the payment of rewards to the captors of deserters and there is an incomplete card index by surname of deserter. E 182 is arranged by county and then in chronological order by date of correspondence.

A list of deserters at large in Australia has been published in Yvonne Fitzmaurice, *Army deserters from HM Service*, a copy of which is available at Kew.

4.5 Women in the Army

Until women nurses were first recruited during the Crimean War (see 14.7), no woman formally served in the British Army. One or two did enlist pretending to be men, although there are no separate records for them. Perhaps the most famous of these was Dr James Barry, whose record of service can be found in WO 138/1.

In each company, six wives of soldiers were carried on strength to act as unofficial cooks, laundresses and servants to officers. There were also a large number of camp followers who, unlike the army wives, were not entitled to an issue of 'the King's victuals'. Little is known about these women.

Wives of soldiers are recorded in the soldiers' discharge documents, in WO 97, from the 1850s onwards. Occasionally women retained on strength may appear in the muster rolls in WO 12 and WO 16 under the 'Married Establishment'. Generally, however, there are very few records available.

4.6 Pension Records

Men discharged from the army after a certain period of time, or on account of sickness or wounds which caused their services to be dispensed with, were usually awarded a pension. Service pensions for long service were awarded for service in excess of 12 years full-time service but, in most cases, men who received such pensions had served over 18 years and more.

Pensions given to men who had been discharged on account of sickness or wounds were not necessarily for life, yet their records can still be found in WO 97 or PIN 71.

Some men were given deferred pensions and they were quite often paid only after a man had reached a given age.

4.6.1 Administration of pensions

Before the late seventeenth century, there was little provision for disabled soldiers, although they might sometimes be licensed to beg. Petitions from disabled soldiers for relief or places in almshouses may be found with the State Papers and applications c.1784–1922 may be found in HO 56 and other warrant books for appointments 1750–1960 in HO 118. Formal provision was first made in the late seventeenth century and, from 1686, pensions were to be paid to 'all non-commission officers and soldiers that are or shall be disabled by wounds in fight or other accidents in the service of the Crown ... also ... to all such non-commission officers and soldiers as having served the Crown 20 years are or shall become unfit for service'. It was financed by a levy on the sale of commissions and an annual deduction of one day's pay from the wages of every soldier in the Army.

Pensions were provided in the form of accommodation for disabled soldiers in the Royal Hospital, Chelsea, which was opened in 1692. Most army pensioners (other than officers) eventually became known as Chelsea Pensioners, whether they lived in the Royal Hospital or not. Soldiers on the Irish establishment were accommodated at the Royal Hospital, Kilmainham, which was established in 1679 and opened in 1684. These pensions became known as in-pensions.

Within a few months, the accommodation became insufficient to meet the demand and a system of out-pensions for non-residents was devised to supplement the original in-pensions. Out-pensions could be claimed on the grounds of disability or unfitness arising from service. In the 1750s regulations were passed to make length of service and character the principal reasons for award of pensions, and not disability. Responsibility for the out-pensions of Irish pensioners passed to Chelsea in 1822, and for in-pensioners in 1929.

Except for a few officers admitted as in-pensioners, the two hospitals were not concerned with officers' pensions. The Board of Ordnance was responsible for paying pensions to its own troops until 1833.

The major series of records created as a result were the Soldiers' Documents (WO 97) described in 4.2. Additional information can be found in many further series.

For a brief account of both the Royal Hospitals see *The Guide to the Public Records* Part 1, section 704/6/3.

4.6.2 Out-pensions

Out-pensioners were formed into Invalid, Veteran and Garrison companies for garrison duties in wartime. In the nineteenth century, they were often sent out to colonies as settlers; see 4.7 and 14.5.

There are three main series of records containing information about out-pensioners: admission books, regimental registers and pension returns. These series cover the vast majority of pensioners at home and abroad.

4.6.3 Admission books

Admission books are arranged chronologically by date of examination for the award of an out-pension, and are not indexed. Therefore you need to know at least the approximate date of a man's discharge from the army and his application for a pension before a search becomes practicable. For 1806–1838, there is a name index in WO 120.

For pensions awarded between 1715 and 1913 by the Royal Hospital, Chelsea, to cover disability, there are two series of admission books in WO

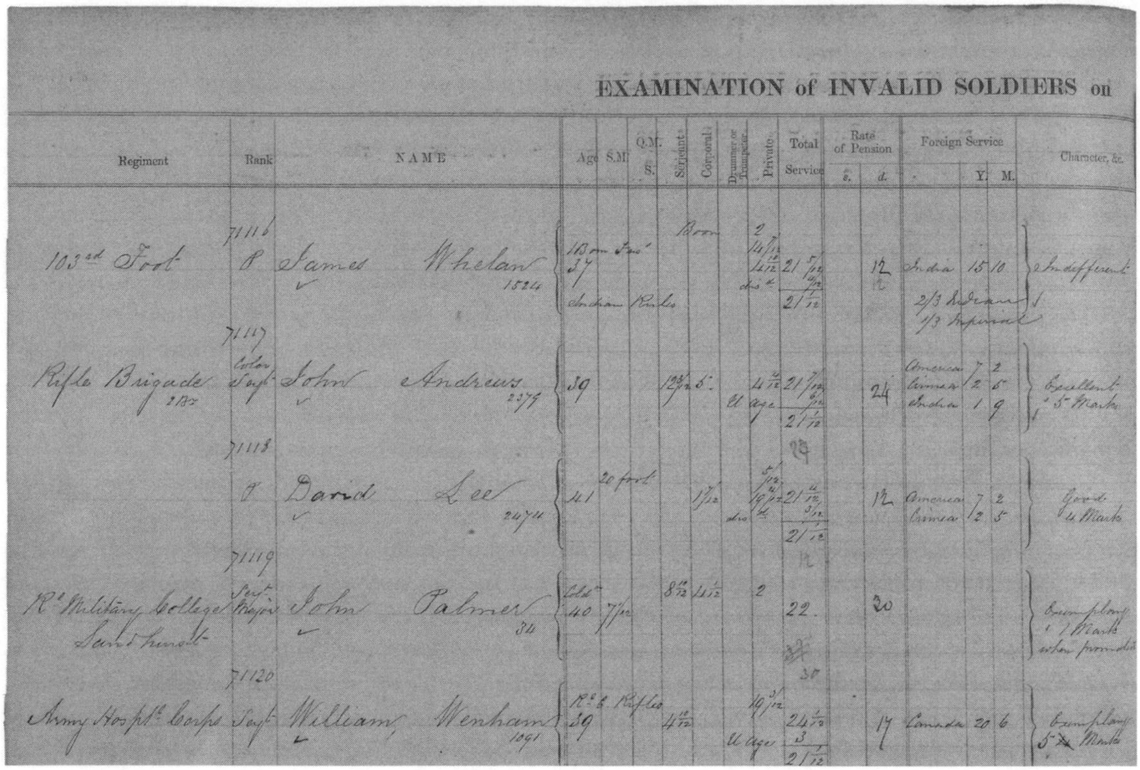

Regiment	Rank	NAME	Age S.M.	Q.M.S.	Sergeant	Corporal	Drummer or Trumpeter	Private	Total Service	Rate of Pension £. d.	Foreign Service Y. M.	Character, &c.
103rd Foot	P James Whelan										India 15 10	Indifferent
Rifle Brigade	Colour Sergt John Andrew									24	America 7 2 / America 2 5 / India 1 9	Excellent 5 Marks
	P David Lee										America 7 2 / Crimea 12 5	Good 4 Marks
Rl Military College Sandhurst	John Palmer									20		Exemplary
Army Hospl Corps Sergt William Wenham											Canada 20 6	Exemplary

Fig. 10 *Chelsea Hospital admission to pension register 1866.* WO 117/14

116/1–124 and 186–251. Details of pensions awarded for length of service, 1823–1913, are in WO 117. There is just one series for pensions awarded by the Royal Hospital, Kilmainham, between 1704 and 1922, in WO 118. An example of a page from a WO 117 admission book is reproduced as Fig. 10.

Each book gives the date of examination, a brief record of service, the reason why a pension was awarded, the place of birth and a physical description. Between 1830 and 1844, the Chelsea admission books are duplicated by registers in WO 23/1–16 where, in addition, the intended place of residence is given. The registers 1838–1844, in WO 23/10–16, are indexed.

4.6.4 Regimental registers

Each regiment kept registers of men who were discharged to pension and these are in two distinct series in WO 120. The first, 1715–1843, in WO 120/1–51 is arranged chronologically within regiments, and gives date of admission, age, a brief record of service, rate of pension, 'complaint', place of birth and a physical description. The volumes for 1839 to 1843 are indexed. In addition, a name index to some infantry regiments, 1806–1858, in WO 120/23–26, 29–30 is kept at Kew. WO 23/20–30 is indexed by J. D. Beckett, *An index to the regimental registers of the Royal Hospital Chelsea 1806–1838*.

The second series (WO 120/52–70) records pensions being paid between 1814 and 1857. Admissions before 1845 are arranged by rate of pension, while those between 1845 and 1857 are set out chronologically. The registers give the rate of pension, date of admission and residence, and are marked up with the place of payment of the pension and date of death. These registers are duplicated and extended to 1876 in wo 23/26–65. A similar series of registers of pensions being paid from 1806 to 1807 is in wo 23/136–140.

4.6.5   Pension returns

Before 1842, out-pensions were paid by convenient local officials, such as excise officials. In 1842 payment became the responsibility of staff officers of pensioners, in a number of districts. Each staff officer made a monthly return to the War Office in which he recorded pensioners who had moved into, or out of, his district, whose pension had ceased, or who had died. Pension returns in wo 22 record pensions paid or payable from district offices between 1842 and 1883. There were about one hundred districts in Great Britain and Ireland.

The records in wo 22 contain periodical returns of pensions paid or payable by the Royal Hospital, Chelsea. These are bound up in volumes and arranged under the various districts in the United Kingdom, the Channel Islands, and in India, the Colonies and certain foreign stations. They include returns of out-pensioners of Chelsea and Greenwich Hospitals, of those belonging to the East India Company, and of mercantile marine pensioners (found under 3rd East London District), as well as annual mortality returns showing the number of deaths at different ages. In addition to the statistical information that these returns supply, they are useful for tracing changes of residence and dates of death of individual pensioners.

These returns, which are arranged by district, give the pensioner's name, regiment, rate of pension, date of admission to pension, rank, and the district to which, or from which, he had moved. Also included with the returns are various items of statistical information. Returns for British payment districts cease in 1862, but returns relating to pensions paid overseas and in the colonies extend into the 1880s.

Many of the overseas volumes are arranged under subheadings. The following names are a list of places, subheadings and unusual regiments found in wo 22:

Australia: New South Wales, Queensland, South Australia, Tasmania and Victoria
Black Pensioners
Canada
Cape of Good Hope
Ceylon Rifles and Gun Lascars
China
Colonies Miscellaneous
Consuls
Hanoverian (King's German Legion)
India (East India Company and British Army): Bengal, Bombay, Madras
Malta
New Zealand

MONTHLY RETURN of Changes which have taken place among the Out-Pensioners of Chelsea and Greenwich Hospitals, and those belonging to the East India Company, in the _Bristol_ District, from the _1st July_ to the _31 July_ 1854, inclusive.

I. Pensioners transferred from the District.

Regt. or Number	Rate of Pension	Date of Admission to Out-Pension	Rank	Name of Pensioner	District to which transferred	Date to which Pensioner was paid previous to transference	Remarks stating whether the Pension is permanent or temporary, &c.
22 ft	7	9 Aug 1853	Pte	Daniel Sweeney	1st Cork	30 July 54	Temp 30 Aug 55
43 "	1/1	10 Oct 1848	"	John Webber	2 East London Tower Hill	30 June "	Permanent
47 "	1/4	13 July 1852	Corpl	William Taylor	Gloucester	30 July "	— do
61 "	9	6 July 1844	Pte	John Elliott	1st Portsmouth	30 Sept "	— do
67 "	1/1	9 Dec 1845	"	Absolom Cox	2 Manchester	30 July "	do
74 "	9	25 Sept 1829	"	John Clements	Bath	30 July "	do
81 "	1/3	23 Nov 1852	Corpl	Ephraim Carter	2 Dublin	30 June "	do
96 "	1/5	8 Nov 1837	Dm	Thomas Dodd	Halifax	30 Sept "	do

Mercantile Marine

126	9 2.0	May 1851	Sea	John Bailey	Chatham	30 Sept 54	Permanent
683	4.8.0	–	Widow	Thomasina Townsend	} Cardiff {	30 Sept 54	Widowhood
563	2.4.0	–	Children	John Townsend			Temp 30 Jan 1859

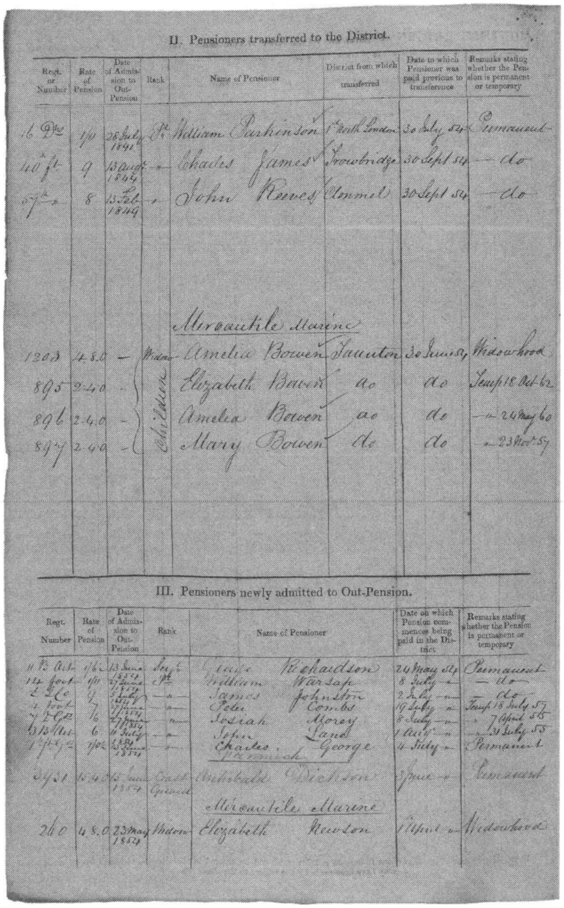

Figs 11–13 *Pension Return: Bristol District 1852–1862.* WO 22/10

For each area, place or district, there are usually two volumes—one covering c.1842–1852 and the other c.1852–1862. Some of the volumes for payments made overseas continue to c.1880.

In order to find out in which district a pensioner drew his pension, you need to use the registers in the series WO 23. Because of the way this series is arranged, it can be difficult to identify the most appropriate piece. However, there are a number of sequences of regimental or corps indexes that I would advise you to consult first—most notably WO 23/26–65 (covering 1845–1875), WO 23/136–140 (covering 1806–1807) and WO 23/147–152 (covering admission as out-pensioners between 1817 and 1875 where payments were made in the colonies 1817–1875).

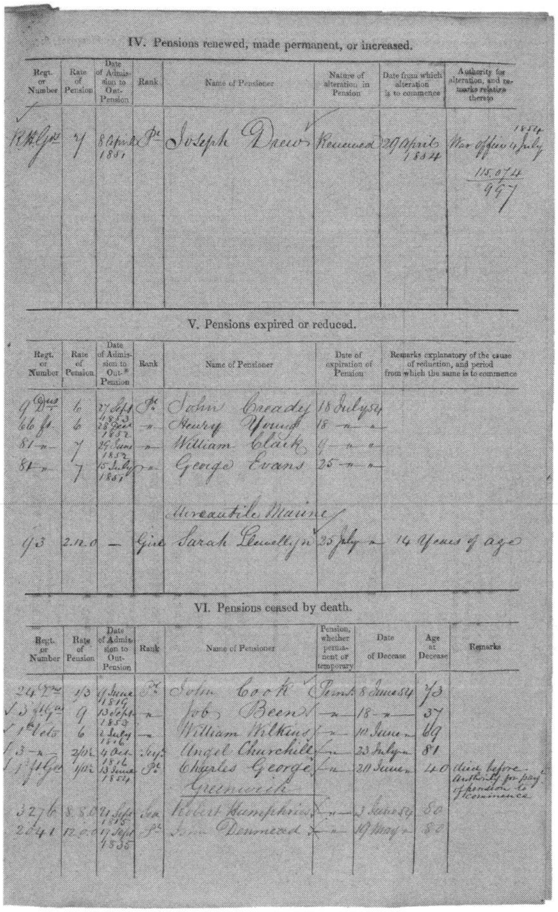

Many of the districts in the WO 22 catalogue are described by a place name in which the pay office was based and therefore the local area it covered. However, some districts covered large cities, metropolitan areas or large areas of sparsely populated Scotland and Ireland. To assist in locating the correct payment district, the following table may be of use.

WO 22 District	Local Pay Office	WO 22 District	Local Pay Office	WO 22 District	Local Pay Office
Ayr	Ayr	1st Edinburgh	Edinburgh	1st Liverpool	Liverpool
	Irvine		Musselburgh		St Helens
	Arran		Haddington		Runcorn
	Kilmarnock		Dunbar		
	Maybole		Dunse	2nd Liverpool	Liverpool
	Mauchline		Berwick on		Birkenhead
	Dumfries		Tweed		Ormskirk
	Castle Douglas				
	Kirkcudbright	2nd Edinburgh	Edinburgh	1st East	Tower Hill
	Gatehouse		Galashiels	London	Braintree
	Newton		Jedburgh		Coggleshall
	Stewart		Kelso		Maldon
	Wigton		Hawick		Witham
	Glenluce		Peebles		
	Stranraer		Dalkeith	2nd East	Tower Hill
	Thornhill			London	Brentwood
	Campbeltown	1st Glasgow	Glasgow		Chelmsford
			Airdrie		Rayleigh
1st Belfast	Belfast		Hamilton		Grays
	Lisburn		Ardrishaig		Billericay
	Newtownards		Lanark		Romford
	Carrickfergus		Strathaven		
			Inverary	1st North	London
2nd Belfast	Belfast		Oban	London	War Office
	Lisburn		Biggar		St Albans
	Hillsborough				Dunstable
	Saintfield	2nd Glasgow	Glasgow		Luton
			Biggar		Hitchin
1st Cork	Cork		Campbeltown		Hatfield
	Ballincollig		Dumbarton		Barnet
	Kinsale		Lanark		
	Bandon			2nd North	London
	Clonakilty	Inverness	Fort George	London	Bishop's
	Skibereen		Inverness		Stortford
	Bantry		Nairn		Dunmow
	Dunmanway		Forres		Harlow
	Skull		Elgin		Ponders End
	Cove		Rothes		Waltham Abbey
			Grantown		Hertford
2nd Cork	Cork		Drumnadrochit	1st West	London
	Bandon		Beauly	London	Brentford
	Bantry		Fortrose		Uxbridge
	Queenstown		Dingwall &		Windsor
			Evanton		Maidenhead
1st Dublin	Dublin		Invergordon		Henley upon
	Trim		Tain		Thames
	Swords		Lochalsh		High Wycombe
	Dunshoughlin		Fort William		
			The Lewis	2nd West	London
2nd Dublin	Dublin		Glenelg	London	Aylesbury
	Bray		Fochabers		Berkhamsted
	Leixlip		Cullen		Chesham
	Lucan		Portsoy		Leighton
	Naas		Banff		Buzzard
			Fort Augustus		Tring
					Watford

WO 22 District	Local Pay Office	WO 22 District	Local Pay Office	WO 22 District	Local Pay Office
1st Manchester	Manchester Rochdale Ashton	3rd Plymouth	Plymouth Liskeard Bodmin Camelford Wadebridge St Columb St Austel Lostwithiel	Thurso	Thurso Wick Sweeny Swiney Helmsdale Golspie Dornoch Bonar Bridge
2nd Manchester	Manchester Oldham Middleton				Aultnacalgach Farr Kirk Kirkwall (Orkney)
Paisley	Paisley Greenock Rothesay Beith Dunoon	1st Portsmouth	Headquarters Ryde Haslemere Godalming Guildford Havant Midhurst Petworth Chichester		Lerwick (Shetland) Lairg Melvich Tongue Brora
1st Plymouth	Plymouth Modbury Kingsbridge Dartmouth Totnes Ashburton				
2nd Plymouth	Plymouth Callington Launceston Stratton Hartland Holsworthy Tavistock	2nd Portsmouth	Headquarters Alton Alresford Bishops Waltham Fareham Farnham Horndean Odiham Petersfield		

4.6.6 In-pensions

There are muster rolls for in-pensioners of Chelsea Hospital (the men commonly called Chelsea Pensioners) for 1702–1789 in WO 23/124–131, and for 1864–1865 in WO 23/132; a list of in-pensioners, 1794–1816, in WO 23/134; and an alphabetical register, 1837–1872, in WO 23/146.

Admission books for the years 1778–1756 and 1824–1917 are in WO 23/133, 163–172, 174–180. Arranged chronologically, these books give the regiment, name, age, service, rate of pension, cause of discharge, date of admission to pension, and decision of the Board of Chelsea Hospital. An address is also often given. An index of in-pensioners admitted between 1858 and 1933 is in WO 23/173.

Further lists of Chelsea pensioners can be found in AO 3/667 and 668. These cover the years 1779–1827 and 1842–1843 respectively.

A list of in-pensioners at the Royal Hospital, Kilmainham, between 1839 and 1922 is in WO 118/47–48. This list also includes out-pensioners.

4.6.7 Pensions: other sources

Additional information about both in- and out-pensioners at Chelsea can sometimes be found in the Board Minutes and Papers, 1784–1953, in WO 250, and in the Invaliding Board Minutes and Papers, 1800–1915, in WO

180, especially where appeals were made against decisions on eligibility for a pension and the rate at which it was to be paid. Minute books in WO 180/53–76 include appeals as well as other relevant papers. The books are a sample and unfortunately cover between 1823 and 1915.

A nominal list of out-pensioners discharged between 1821 and 1829, who had served in the tropics, for which an additional pension was payable, is in WO 23/25.

Some 6,335 personal files of soldiers (and a few sailors) who received a disability pension and who were discharged before 1914 are in PIN 71. A number of papers for widows' pensions are also included in this class. The files contain medical records, accounts of how and where illness or injuries occurred and men's own accounts of incidents in which they were involved. Also included were conduct sheets, recording the place of birth, age, names of parents and family, religion, physical attributes and marital status. These records are arranged alphabetically. The dates reflected in the descriptions of these files represent the date the individual joined the army and the date when the pension ceased. You can search PIN on the catalogue by the name of the individual.

4.6.8 Widows' pensions

Pensions to widows, children and other dependants of non-commissioned officers and men killed on active service have only been paid by the state since 1901 (retrospective to 1899). Before then, such pensions might be provided by private subscriptions or by the Royal Patriotic Fund. Annual Commissioners Reports of the Royal Patriotic Fund, printed with the Parliamentary papers, list the names of widows to whom grants were paid. PIN 96 also contains annual reports and minutes of the meetings of the Commissioners who administered the Fund from 1854 until 1904, and of their successors on the General Council of the Corporation, which then replaced the Commission, through to the end of the First World War.

One file is a record of payments made to widows and dependants from the Transvaal War Fund, which gives some detail of the recipients.

4.7 Soldiers Settling Abroad

Pensions were also paid to former British soldiers who had emigrated to the colonies. Chelsea Hospital out-pension registers, 1814–1857, for these men are in WO 120/69–70. Another register, 1845–1854, is in WO 23/31.

Lists of men who emigrated to Australia and New Zealand between 1830 and 1848 under schemes to settle soldiers there are in WO 43/542 (for Australia) and WO 43/853 (New Zealand).

A more detailed description of the sources available is in *Family Roots* by Stella Colwell.

4.8 Case Studies

4.8.1 *Private Benjamin Randell Harris of the 66th Foot, 95th Foot and 8th Royal Veterans*

As an enlisted man Benjamin Harris was unusual in that in 1848, some 34 years after he left the army, his memoirs were published as *Recollections of Rifleman Harris*. This has recently been reprinted as *A Dorset Rifleman: the Recollections of Benjamin Harris*, edited by Eileen Hathaway.

The basic facts of Harris's career recounted in his memoirs are verified by his record of service in WO 97/1133. The records of service of men discharged to pension between 1760 and 1854 are available on microfilm, with an index available on computer. The index can be searched by surname, forename or initial, regiment and place of birth. Benjamin Harris might appear to be a common name; indeed, searching the surname Harris in WO 97 on the online catalogue produces 901 entries. But adding the forename Benjamin reduces this to eight, only one of whom served in the 95th Foot. His attestation form shows that he served in the 66th Regiment of Foot, the 95th Regiment of Foot and the 8th Royal Veteran Battalion. The description book in WO 25/608 provides a physical description of Harris; a sample page can be seen in Fig. 9.

Although details relating to the career of an individual can be obtained by using other sources, only the records of soldiers discharged to pension at Chelsea Hospital can be found in WO 97. The computerized name index to WO 97 enables you to find the records of over 250,000 men discharged between 1760 and 1854.

Not mentioned in Harris's memoirs is the medal he was awarded for service in the campaign in Portugal and Northern Spain in 1808–1809. The Military General Service Medal (MGS) was not authorized until 1847 and could only be issued to survivors of campaigns fought between 1793 and 1814. Consequently, as Harris's memoirs were not published until 1848, he was alive when the medal was authorized. Private Benjamin Harris 95th Foot was awarded an MGS with clasps for Rolica, Vimiero and Corunna (WO 100/8).

The career of Benjamin Harris is typical of many of the period. It is possible to find out about many men who served in the British Army in the late eighteenth and early nineteenth centuries.

4.8.2 *Death in service: Crimean War 1854–1856: Private John Moffatt of the 55th Foot*

The majority of deaths that occurred during the Crimean War were as a result of disease rather than of enemy action. When an other rank died in service, his record of service was destroyed. As widows' pensions for other ranks did not become common until the Boer War period (1899–1902), once a soldier's estate had been settled the War Office had no need to keep his record of service as no further money would have be due to that individual.

The records in WO 97 are arranged in chronological batches, but as John

Moffatt died in service his record is not preserved in this class. The most important record classes to use when someone died in service are the Regimental Musters and Pay Lists in WO 10–WO 16, the casualty returns in WO 25 and the deaths and effects papers, also in WO 25.

The Crimean War medal roll in WO 100 is a useful place to start gathering information about an individual soldier who saw active service in the Crimean War. The medal roll for the Crimean War medal awarded to members of the 55th Foot is in WO 100/30. Private John Moffatt appears on folio 404 for his medal and clasps for the battles at Alma and Inkerman and on folio 468 for his clasp for operations at Sebastopol. The second entry notes that he was dead at the time that the medal roll was compiled.

As no record of service for John Moffatt survives, a picture of his career can only be built up by using other sources.

Description books (by regiment) of soldiers can be found in WO 25. There is, however, no surviving book for the 55th Foot.

The muster and pay lists mentioned above (WO 10–WO 16) are quarterly accounts completed by the regiment, which account for all of the manpower in the regiment over a given three-month period. The muster will tell you where the muster was taken, who was serving with the regiment (both officers and men), what each soldier was being paid, when an individual left a regiment by whatever cause and, if an individual remitted his pay, to whom the money was sent. The musters can also tell you where a regiment travelled during the reporting quarter.

As we know that John Moffatt was alive on 4 November 1855, the date of the Battle of Inkerman, the muster that covers this date can be used as a starting point. By working backwards and forwards from this date it is possible to find out when John Moffatt died and when he joined the army.

According to the muster for the period October to December 1854 (WO 12/6518), the 55th Foot were in the Crimea and serving at various locations and John Moffatt was still alive and serving with the regiment. The next muster, for the period January to March 1855 (WO 12/6519), shows that John Moffatt was sent to hospital at Scutari on 4 January; it was there that he died on 7 February 1855. This information is confirmed in the Scutari Depot Muster in WO 14/2.

Working backwards, chronologically through the musters, it is recorded that John Moffatt transferred into the 55th Foot from the 13th Light Infantry (13 LI) at Gibraltar on 26 March 1854 (WO 12/6517). The muster of this regiment for March 1854 (WO 12/3071) confirms the transfer of John Moffatt, along with a number of other men into various regiments, all heading for the Crimea. Tracing back, muster by muster, the entry of John Moffatt into the 13th Light Infantry was eventually discovered in a muster for the period January to March 1848 (WO 12/3065). He had enlisted in Belfast on 26 January 1848. His height is given, but there is no further description of the man. All that the records tell you is when and where he joined, how tall he was, where he served and when he died.

4.8.3 Service in a famous regiment: Colour Sergeant John Harding of the 2/24th Foot

The 24th Foot is one of the most well-known infantry regiments of the Victorian Army. The annihilation of over 800 British troops, mostly members of the 1/24th and 2/24th Foot (that is, the first and second battalions of the regiment), at the Battle of Isandhlwana on 22 January 1879, and the defence at Rorke's Drift by men of the same units on 22/23 January 1879, both actions during the Zulu War, have caused much heartache for researchers who believed their man was there.

John Harding was born in February, 1859 at Hillingdon, near Uxbridge in Middlesex, and enlisted into the 25th Brigade of the army at London on 27 February 1877. He was sent to the 24th Foot depot at Brecon in Wales where he became 25B/1323 Private J. Harding, 2/24th Foot.

When the regiment went to South Africa in February 1878, John Harding went with them. By the time of the Zulu War in 1879, he had been promoted to corporal. When the British Army invaded Zululand in January 1879, they did so in three columns. Men from the 1/24th and 2/24th were dispersed around all three columns. It was men of the 3rd column who fought at the Battle of Isandhlwana and defended Rorke's Drift. John Harding and 'H' company in which he served were in the column commanded by Lord Chelmsford and did not therefore see action at either Isandhlwana or at Rorke's Drift. Chelmsford's column arrived at Rorke's Drift on the morning of 23 January. On this particular day, while at Rorke's Drift, John Harding was promoted to lance sergeant (Regimental Order Book South Wales Borderers Museum O 1948 2 refers).

For a detailed study of the action at Isandhlwana and the defence of Rorke's Drift, which lists those present at both actions, see *The Noble 24th* by Norman Holme.

For his service in the Zulu War, John Harding was awarded the South African War Medal with the clasp 1877–9. Details of all the South African War Medals awarded to the 24th Foot can be found in WO 100/46. This shows the entries for the award of this medal to Private Frederick Hitch and Alfred Henry Hook, both of whom were also awarded the Victoria Cross for their gallantry at Rorke's Drift. The Register of Victoria Cross Awards, a sample of which is illustrated as Fig. 20, gives the reasons for their awards.

After the Zulu War ended, John Harding went on to see over 15 years' service in India. After promotion to sergeant and then colour sergeant, he eventually rose to the rank of regimental sergeant major (RSM). It obviously did not suit him, for within three months of his promotion he reverted to colour sergeant at his own request. This was to be the beginning of a sad decline for a man who thus far had had a successful army career.

On 5 June 1891, Colour Sergeant John Harding was tried by regimental court martial for being drunk on duty. He was found guilty and reduced to the rank of corporal. Soon after the court martial, Harding transferred into the 2nd Battalion of the Derbyshire Regiment. Alcoholism continued to plague his career until he was finally discharged from the army at Calcutta on 22 March 1898.

Such is the picture of one man's military career that can be reconstructed from one record; Harding's record of service is in WO 97/2977.

4.8.4 *Service in the army twice: Private William Oscroft*

William Oscroft was born at Arnold near Nottingham and he joined his local regiment, the Derby Regiment, on 19 August 1885. At the time of his enlistment Oscroft's occupation was hosier.

Given the regimental number of 1127 on enlistment, Oscroft's record shows that he was above average height in 1885 — his physical description gave his height as 73 inches, with good physical development.

Posted to the 1st Battalion Derbyshire Regiment on 6 October 1885 after his training, Oscroft was to serve with this battalion until 11 March 1886 when he was posted to the 2nd Battalion. It is obvious from his record that Oscroft was transferred to the 2nd Battalion to make the battalion up to full strength as it departed for India on the same day.

Seeking operational service in Sikkim in 1888, William Oscroft was awarded the India General Service Medal 1854-95 with the clasp Sikkim 1888. Oscroft was discharged from the army on 29 September 1891 after serving 6 years and 42 days.

Life as a civilian obviously did not suit William Oscroft for he rejoined the army on 16 March 1900 in the 1st Battalion Royal Northern Reserve Regiment. The Royal Northern Reserve Regiment soon became the Royal Garrison Regiment and its personnel were sent to various parts of the British Empire to relieve the regular army troops for service elsewhere.

Private William Oscroft was posted to the 1st Battalion Royal Garrison Regiment and saw service with them in South Africa, when he died on 12 September 1905.

Strangely, Oscroft's record of service is spread across WO 97 and WO 96.

4.8.5 *Service in the Boer War 1899–1902: Private Alexander Lee Stanton of the Imperial Yeomanry*

Since the advent of the camera, images of soldiers have always been very popular. Many soldiers about to travel overseas had their photograph taken so that they could be given to their next of kin. Many of these photographs can provide useful information for the genealogist. It is most unusual for such photographs to survive with the public records. The portrait of Private Stanton, an enlarged detail from a photograph of the first contingent of men of the 42nd (Hertfordshire) Company Imperial Yeomanry (COPY 1/446), reproduced as Fig. 24, is exceptional and is only with the public records because it was registered for copyright protection purposes.

The Imperial Yeomanry was formed in late 1899 as a result of the need for mounted infantry in South Africa and was recruited specifically for service overseas. Alexander L. Stanton joined the 42nd Company (Hertfordshire) Imperial Yeomanry on 22 January 1900. He appears to have been unemployed when he joined up. As service in the Imperial Yeomanry was only for one year, Stanton may have enlisted just to see if he liked army life.

After forty days' training in England, Stanton, together with the first contingent of 42nd Company Imperial Yeomanry, left for South Africa. According to his attestation papers completed when he joined the army (WO 128/20), he had been promoted to corporal by November 1900, when he was discharged from the Imperial Yeomanry to join the Commander in Chief's Bodyguard. He died of wounds received in action on 3 January 1901. As this occurred after he had left the Imperial Yeomanry, it appears that his original unit may have been the only one to retain his records. Attestation papers of the Imperial Yeomanry are available in the record class WO 128 and are arranged in service number order, with the registers in WO 129; see also section 4.2.4.

The Commander in Chief's Bodyguard was a unit raised in South Africa. Enrolment papers for South African local forces are in the class WO 126 and are arranged alphabetically by name of unit and then alphabetically by name of soldier. The nominal rolls for the South African local forces are arranged as above and are in the class WO 127. The enrolment papers for the Commander in Chief's Bodyguard are in WO 126/31–34, with Stanton's papers being in WO 126/34. The enrolment paper for Stanton is very brief but records that he joined the Bodyguard on 20 November 1900, aged 30, and that he was a scout and that he died. It is interesting to note a variation of next-of-kin details on the two attestation forms. On the Imperial Yeomanry attestation paper, Stanton's next of kin is given as his mother in Belfast. On the Commander in Chief's Bodyguard application paper, Stanton's next of kin is given as his sister in New York.

Men who saw service in the Boer War (1899–1902) were entitled to the Queen's South Africa Medal (QSA). The medal roll for the QSA for the 42nd Company Imperial Yeomanry is in WO 100/125. The roll notes that Alexander Stanton was entitled to the medal with the Cape Colony, Transvaal and Wittebergen clasps. The roll also notes that he died in South Africa and that he had served in the Commander in Chief's Bodyguard. The QSA medal roll for the Commander in Chief's Bodyguard is in WO 100/243. This roll confirms the medal entitlement and that Stanton was a corporal in that unit, with the service number 27469. It also notes his date of death as 3 January 1901, of wounds received in action near Lindley. This date does not tally exactly with the South African Field Force Casualty roll 1899–1902 (WO 108/360), which notes that Stanton died on 6 January 1901, of wounds received three days before. A copy of this roll is available as a printed work in the library.

5 ROYAL ARTILLERY

The Royal Artillery was established by Royal Warrant on 26 May 1716, as a permanent force of specialists to operate guns with a calibre bigger than a musket or rifle. The Royal Horse Artillery, which was originally part of it, was established in 1793. Until 1855, the Royal Artillery was under the control of the Ordnance Office rather than the War Office and, as a result, many of its records were kept separately. This separation is reflected in the current arrangement of the records, and much material relating to the Royal Artillery can be found in classes containing records relating to the Ordnance Office. The Royal Artillery wore blue uniforms rather than red, had a separate pay system and, until 1834, drew their pensions from the Board of Ordnance rather than from Chelsea.

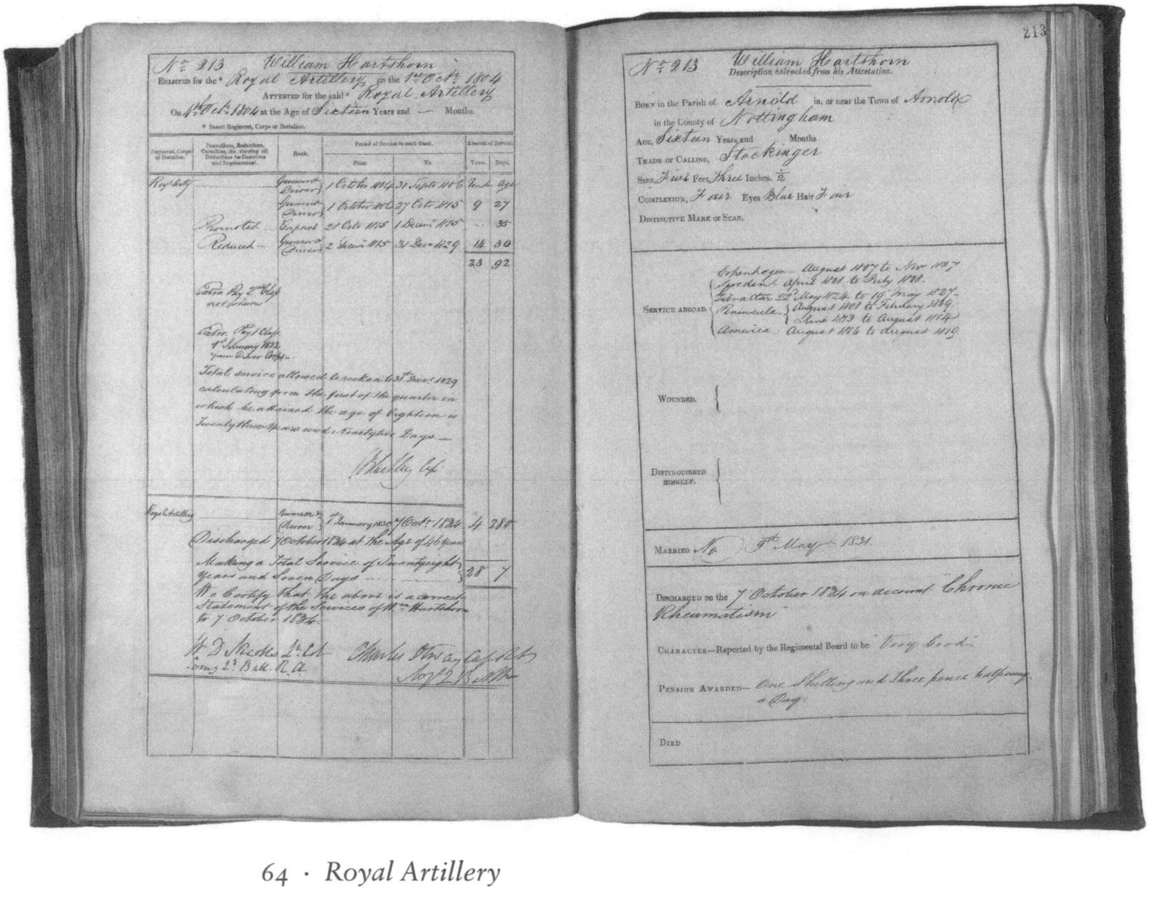
No. 213 William Hartshorn
Enlisted for the* Royal Artillery on the 1st Octr 1804
Attested for the said* Royal Artillery
On 1st Octr 1804 at the Age of Sixteen Years and — Months.
* Insert Regiment, Corps or Battalion.

Regiment, Corps or Battalion.	Promotions, Reductions, Casualties, &c.	Rank.	Period of Service in each Rank. From	To	Amount of Service. Years.	Days.
Royl Arty		Gunner & Driver	1 October 1804	31 Septr 1806	Under	Age
		Gunner & Driver	1 October 1806	27 Octr 1815	9	27
	Promoted	Corporal	28 Octr 1815	1 Decemr 1815	..	35
	Reduced	Gunner & Driver	2 Decemr 1815	31 Decr 1829	14	30
					23	92

Total service allowed to reckon to 31st Decr 1829 calculating from the first of the quarter in which he attained the age of eighteen is Twenty three years and Ninety two Days —

Discharged 7 October 1834 at the Age of 46 years
Making a Total Service of Twenty eight Years and Seven Days — 28 7
We Certify that the above is a correct Statement of the Services of Wm Hartshorn to 7 October 1834.

No. 213 William Hartshorn
Description extracted from his Attestation.
Born in the Parish of Arnold in, or near the Town of Arnold
in the County of Nottingham
Age, Sixteen Years and Months
Trade or Calling, Stockinger
Size, Five Feet Three Inches. ½
Complexion, Fair Eyes Blue Hair Fair
Distinctive Mark or Scar,
Service Abroad. Copenhagen August 1807 to Nov 1807; Sweden April 1808 to July 1808; Gibraltar 22d May 1824 to 19 May 1827; Peninsula August 1808 to February 1809, June 1813 to August 1814; America August 1814 to August 1819.
Wounded.
Distinguished himself.
Married No 9th May 1831.
Discharged on the 7 October 1834 on account "Chronic Rheumatism"
Character—Reported by the Regimental Board to be "Very Good"
Pension Awarded— One Shilling and Three pence halfpenny a Day.
Died

Fig. 14 *Royal Artillery record of service.* WO 69/90

Marriage and birth registers for the Royal Artillery between 1817 and 1827, 1860 and 1877 are in WO 69/551–582.

5.1 Officers

A published *List of Officers of the Royal Regiment of Artillery*, 1716–June 1914 is available at Kew.

Records of service of officers, 1770–1870, are included in WO 76, for which there is an incomplete name index in the Open Reading Room; see 3.5.2. Earlier lists of officers, 1727–1751, are in WO 54/684, 701. Pay lists for officers, 1803–1871, are in WO 54/946.

Other records include an incomplete series of commission books, 1740–1852, in WO 54/237–239, 244–247 and of officers for 1793 in WO 54/701. Original patents and warrants of appointment, 1670–1855, are in WO 54/939–945. Appointment papers for officers, 1809–1852, are in WO 54/917–922.

There are registers for officers receiving half pay between 1810 and 1880 in WO 23/82. For further details of half pay, see 3.6.

June's Woolwich Journal was a newspaper for the Royal Artillery at Woolwich. It contained news of officers and their movements, with other interesting information. The National Archives holds copies only for 1847 to 1850 in WO 62/48.

5.2 Other Ranks

Records of service of soldiers (gunners) in the Royal Artillery, 1791–1855, are in WO 69, although much of the series was destroyed by enemy action in 1941 when the records were being used by Chelsea Hospital. The vast majority of the records in this series were created from *c*.1830 onwards, so although the series is described as starting in *c*.1791, it means that a man's career may have started around that time but he was still serving *c*.1829/30 or later.

The records of service in WO 69 are bound in volumes and arranged by battalion or brigade and then by number. They show the name, age, description, place of birth, trade, and dates of service, of promotions, of marriage and of discharge or date and cause of death. These records are arranged under the unit in which the individual last served, which can be ascertained from indexes and posting books in WO 69/779–782, 801–839.

Soldiers' documents for men of the Royal Artillery discharged to pension between 1760 and 1854 are in WO 97, although there appear to be very few documents earlier than 1792.

Muster rolls for the Royal Artillery, 1708–1878, are in WO 10. This series is arranged in a number of different ways and it helps to know the battalion brigade or company when searching. The places where units served are

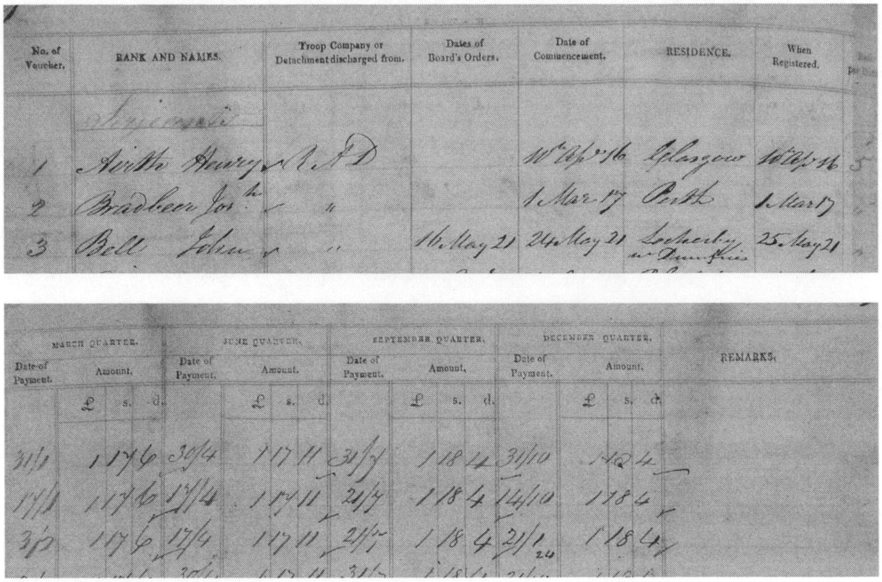

Fig. 15 *Royal Artillery: Register of Pensioners 1823.* WO 54/348

often used in the document descriptions. Except for a few rolls, mostly for the eighteenth century, battalions that served in India are not included. Some later muster rolls are in WO 16.

Entry books of discharges, transfers and casualties between 1740 and 1858 are in WO 54/317–328. Casualty returns from 1850 are in WO 25.

There is also an incomplete series of registers of deceased, discharged or deserted men, 1772–1774, 1816–1873, in WO 69/583–597, 644–647, arranged by artillery regiment. Description books for Royal Artillery battalions between 1749 and 1859 are in WO 54/260–309, and for depots between 1773 and 1874 in WO 69/74–80. Books for the Royal Irish Artillery, 1756–1774, are in WO 69/620. A number of miscellaneous pay lists and other records of the Royal Artillery, 1692–1876, are in WO 54/672–755.

Registers of pensions, 1816–1833, are in WO 54/338–452, 470–480. Registers of pensions being paid in 1834, when responsibility for them was transferred from the Board of Ordnance to the Royal Hospital, Chelsea, are in WO 23/141–145. In addition, there is in WO 116/127–185 a special series of admission books for Royal Artillery pensions between 1833 and 1913.

5.3 Royal Horse Artillery

Records of service of soldiers in the Royal Horse Artillery, 1803–1863, are in WO 69. Description books for the Royal Horse Artillery between 1776 and 1821 are in WO 69/1–6.

A number of application papers for posts in the Royal Horse Artillery between 1820 and 1851 are in WO 54/927. Baptism and marriage registers between 1859 and 1883 are in WO 69/63–73.

6   ROYAL ENGINEERS

The Corps of Engineers, consisting of officers only, was established as part of the Board of Ordnance in 1717. In 1772 a Corps of Royal Military Artificers was formed, to which other ranks were recruited. In 1811 it became the Royal Corps of Sappers and Miners. The two Corps merged in 1856 to form the Royal Engineers. Many documents relating to Sappers and Miners are described in the lists as relating to Royal Engineers.

6.1   Officers

Until 1855, engineer officers were the responsibility not of the War Office but of the Board of Ordnance. Lists of engineer officers for 1793 are in WO 54/701. Registers of the establishment of the Royal Engineers for 1851 and 1855 are in WO 54/235–236. Commission books for officers, 1755–1852, are in WO 54/240–247. Returns of officers, showing stations where they were based between 1786 and 1850, are in WO 54/248–259. Appointment papers of officers, 1815–1846, are in WO 54/923–924. Pay lists for officers, 1805–1871, are in WO 54/947.

Records of service, 1796–1922, are in WO 25/3913–3919, and include details of officers' marriages and children. An incomplete card index to these records is available in the Open Reading Room at Kew. Reports on students at the School of Military Engineering at Chatham, 1858–1914, are in WO 25/3945–3954. The register of cadets of the Royal Military Academy at Woolwich is in the class WO 149, but is held by the Royal Military Academy at Sandhurst and not at the National Archives.

There are registers of officers receiving half pay between 1810 and 1880 in WO 23/82. For further details of half pay, see 3.6.

There exists a published list of officers called the *Roll of Officers of the Corps of Royal Engineers from 1660 to 1898*. A copy is available at Kew.

Service records of officers who served in the Supply and Service Department of the Royal Engineers between 1828 and 1903 are in WO 25/3921–3922.

6.2 Other Ranks

Soldiers' documents for 1760 to 1854 are in WO 97/1148–1152, and from 1855 to 1872 in WO 97/1359–1364. For further information about soldiers' documents, see 4.2.

A register of deceased soldiers in both the Royal Engineers and the Royal Corps of Sappers and Miners, 1824–1858, is in WO 25/2972, and an abstract of effects and credits of deceased men for 1825 in WO 25/2973. Entry books of discharges, transfers and casualties for artificers, sappers and miners and Royal Engineers between 1800 and 1859 are in WO 54/329–335.

A return of sappers and miners entitled to pensions in 1830 is in WO 54/482. Registers of sapper and miner pensioners, compiled in 1834 but dating back to the Napoleonic Wars, are in WO 23/141–145; they include descriptions of individuals. Description books for sappers, miners and artificers, 1756–1833, are in WO 54/310–316.

Musters and pay lists for the Royal Corps of Sappers and Miners and the Engineers between 1816 and 1878 are in WO 11. Further details about muster rolls are in section 4.3.

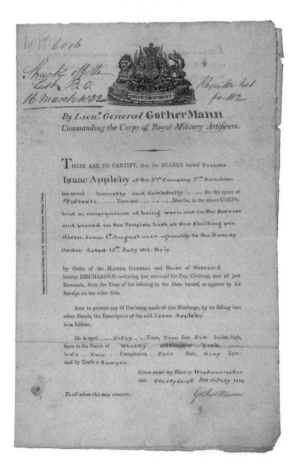

Fig. 16 *Record of service of a soldier of the Royal Military Artificers c. 1800–1830.* WO 54/329

7 MILITIA, YEOMANRY AND VOLUNTEERS

The Militia was a trained local part-time force, with its origins in the Middle Ages, for home defence in time of rebellion or invasion. Section 2.2 describes the Tudor and Stuart militia and the records it created.

The Militia Act 1757 re-established one or more regiments for each county, raised from volunteers and conscripts chosen by ballot from each parish. Until 1871, the raising and training of local militias was the responsibility of the Lord Lieutenant of the county, who also appointed officers. In peacetime, the Militia assembled at intervals for drill and manoeuvres; after 1782, they came under the ultimate authority of the Home Secretary. In wartime, however, having been mobilized (or embodied) by royal proclamation, they were subject to the orders of the commander in chief and were liable to serve anywhere in the British Isles. They were not bound to serve overseas, although in wartime individuals and even whole units might be encouraged to do so.

Other auxiliary forces formed in the late eighteenth and early nineteenth centuries were the Yeomanry, a cavalry corps; the Volunteers, raised by private or municipal enterprise for local defence; and the Local Militia. The Volunteers were dissolved in 1813 and the Local Militia in 1816, but the Yeomanry continued, mainly acting as an armed police force, until it was drastically reduced in 1859.

The Fencible Infantry and Cavalry, which were regular regiments raised for home service only, are often classed with the militia.

In 1859, as a result of local pressure and fears of a possible foreign invasion, volunteer regiments were again formed. Until 1873, they had little formal connection with the War Office. Thereafter, a small number of soldiers (including officers) or retired soldiers formed a permanent staff on each of these regiments.

After the reorganization of the Army on a territorial basis in 1881, the county militia regiments became the third battalions and the volunteer units the fourth and sometimes the fifth battalions of their local regiments. In 1908 the Militia was renamed the Special Reserve and the Volunteers and the Yeomanry became the Territorial Force. Men in the Territorial Force were only liable to serve within the United Kingdom, but individuals might volunteer to serve abroad. Those in the Special Reserve had the same liabil-

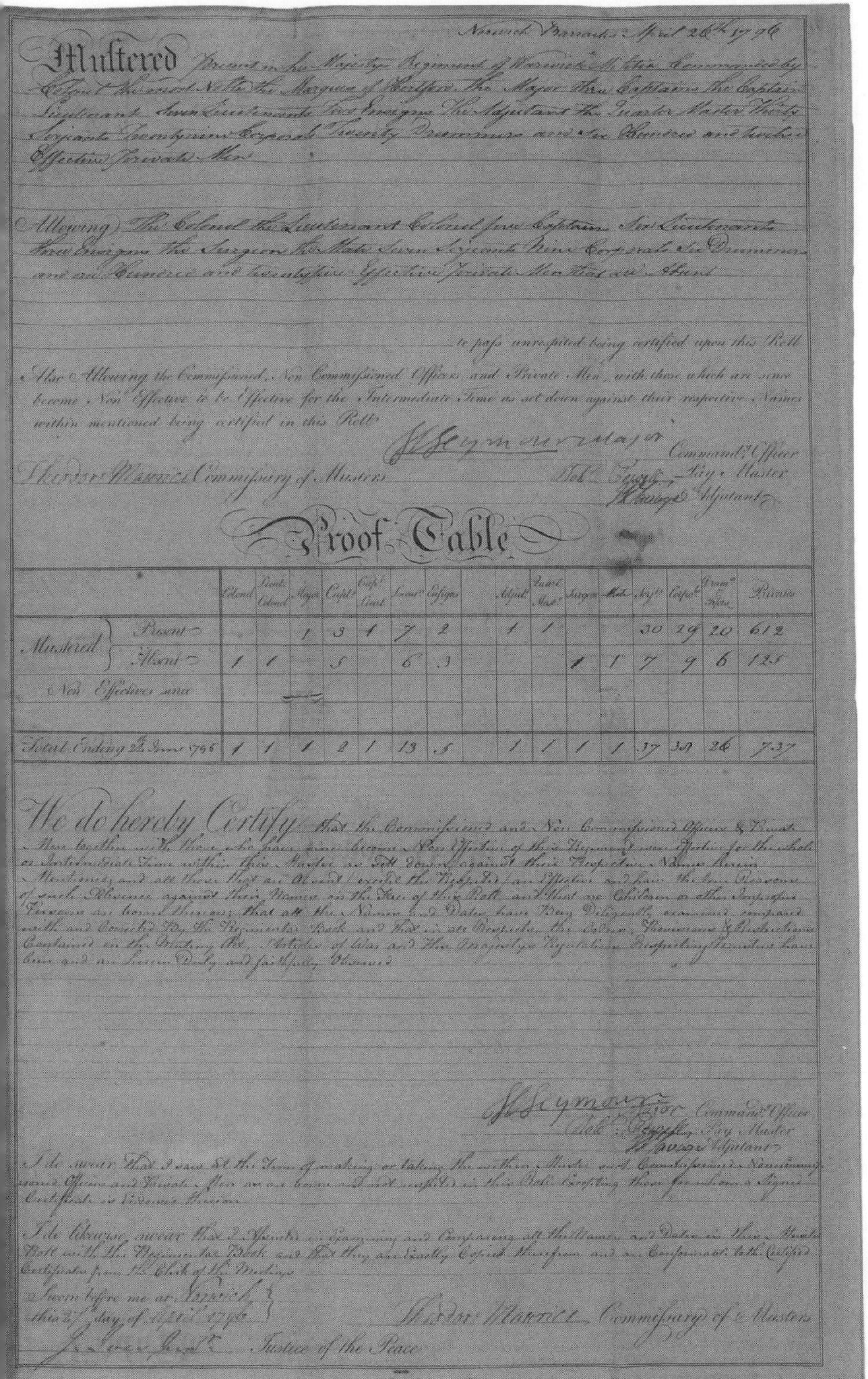

Fig. 17 *Muster for the Warwickshire Militia 1796.* WO 13/2194

Proof Table

		Colonel	Lieut Colonel	Major	Capt	Capt Lieut	Lieut	Ensign	Adjut	Quart Mast	Surgeon	Mate	Serjt	Corpl	Drumrs & Fifers	Privates
Mustered	Present			1	3	1	7	2	1	1			30	29	20	612
	Absent	1	1		5		6	3			1	1	7	9	6	125
Non Effectives since																
Total Ending 2d June 1796		1	1	1	2	1	13	5	1	1	1	1	37	39	26	737

ity as ordinary Army Reservists of being called out for permanent service at home or abroad in an emergency. Both had to undergo annual training. In 1924, the Special Reserve was renamed the Supplementary Reserve; it was not finally disbanded until 1953. In 1940 the Local Defence Volunteers, renamed the Home Guard, was formed for Home Defence. Stood down in December 1945, it was re-formed in 1952 and finally wound up in 1957.

7.1 Officers

Information about the appointment of officers to militia and volunteer units from 1782 to 1840 can be found in the Home Office Military Papers (HO 50), with related entry books in HO 51. The papers include some establishment (showing number of men) and succession (reflecting changes in manpower) books, but there is no name index and, in general, no information is given beyond the names of officers and the dates of their commissions. From 1865, the names of officers appear in the *Army List*.

Records of service of officers in a number of militia regiments are in WO 68. They date from about 1757 to 1925, but are incomplete. Provided that you know the unit in which he served, you can get a rough idea of an officer's service from the muster books in WO 13. Registers of pensions paid to militia officers, 1868–1892, are in WO 23/89–92. A selection of birth and baptismal certificates from 1788 to 1886 is in WO 32/8906–8913.

7.2 Other Ranks

The most useful records for the family historian are the attestation forms of those men who served in the militia, which are in WO 96. They range in date from *c.*1806 to 1915, but the majority are from the second half of the nineteenth century. They are arranged in regimental order of precedence, first under the name of the regular regiment of which the militia unit was part and then alphabetically by surname order. In form and content they are similar to soldiers' documents, described in 4.2.

Also included in WO 96 are the papers of a number of other part-time soldiers. The following table is a breakdown of the arrangement of WO 96.

Reference	Description
WO 96/1–1281	Infantry regiments in order of precedence, with each regiment then in alphabetical order by name.
WO 96/1282–1296	Royal Army Medical Corps (RAMC) Militia
WO 96/1297–1307	Royal Monmouthshire Royal Engineers
WO 96/1308–1460	Royal Garrison Artillery (RGA) Militia arranged in alphabetical order by county or region and then in alphabetical order by name.
WO 96/1461–1519	Royal Garrison Regiment
WO 96/1519–1522	6th Battalion North Staffordshire Regiment

The Royal Garrison Regiment existed from 1901–1908 and was formed from a number of reserve and provisional regiments, with the purpose of relieving regular army troops as garrison troops, thus freeing the regular soldiers to carry out operational service. Many of the men of the RGR were ex-regulars.

A number of soldiers' documents for men who served in militia regiments between 1760 and 1854 are in WO 97/1091–1112. They are arranged in name order, and appear to be mainly for Irish regiments. Very few of them date from before 1792.

Muster books and pay lists of the English, Scottish, Irish and Colonial Militia, and the Fencible Infantry and Cavalry, Yeomanry, Irish Yeomanry and Volunteers from 1780 to 1878 are in WO 13. They provide a means of establishing the dates of enlistment and discharge or death. When an individual appears for the first time, the entry in the muster book may show his age. For volunteer units only, payments to the professional cadre, and not the ordinary volunteers, are included. Muster books are of use only if you know which unit your ancestor belonged to.

A list of Chelsea pensioners discharged from militia and yeomanry regiments between 1821 and 1829 is in WO 23/25.

Accounts and vouchers of payments to militiamen, their families and dependents may survive with the records of the Receivers of the Land Tax (E 182), out of which such payments were made. (From 1798, for example, the families of militiamen serving in Ireland were provided with a bounty of eight pence per week per wife and child under ten.) These records are arranged topographically and are not listed in detail.

Records relating to men who served in the Imperial Yeomanry during the South African (Boer) War are described in 12.3 and in the case study of Private A. L. Stanton in 4.8.5.

7.3 Further Information

Records of individual units of Militia, Yeomanry, Volunteers, Territorials or Home Guard are more likely to be found in local record offices, often with the private papers of Lords Lieutenant and other local notables who served as officers, than in the National Archives. An example of the type of records more commonly found locally is the Bosanquet Papers (PRO 30/3), which include the minute books, orderly books and reports of the Light Horse Volunteers of London and Westminster, 1779–1831.

The main source of militia records is in WO 68. They include order books, succession books, records of officers' services, regimental histories and enrolment books.

For units based in London and Middlesex, a number of muster books are in WO 70. Records for a few provincial units are in WO 79. Records of the Tower Hamlets Militia are in WO 94. There are some general Militia accounts in WO 9 and records relating to allowances for Militia, Yeomanry

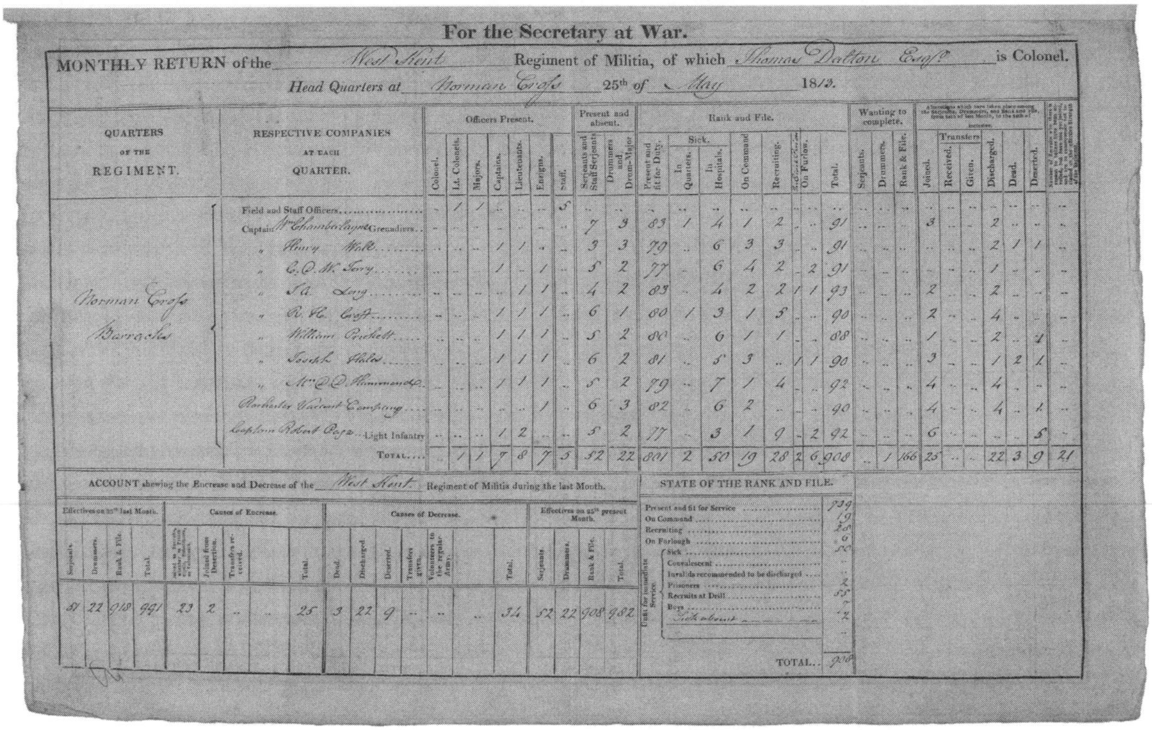

For the Secretary at War.

MONTHLY RETURN of the *West Kent* Regiment of Militia, of which *Thomas Dalton Esq.* is Colonel.

Head Quarters at *Norman Cross* 25th *of* *May* 1813.

QUARTERS OF THE REGIMENT	RESPECTIVE COMPANIES AT EACH QUARTER	Officers Present: Colonel	Lt. Colonels	Majors	Captains	Lieutenants	Ensigns	Staff	Present and absent: Serjeants and Staff Serjeants	Drummers and Drum-Major	Rank and File: Present and fit for Duty	Sick: In Quarters	Sick: In Hospitals	On Command	Recruiting	[illegible]	On Furlow	Total	Wanting to complete: Serjeants	Drummers	Rank & File	Joined	Transfers: Received	Transfers: Given	Discharged	Dead	Deserted	
Norman Cross Barracks	Field and Staff Officers	..	1	1	..	..	..	5	..	..	..	..	..	..	..	..	..	..	..	..	..	..	..	..	..	..	..	..
	Captain Wm Chamberlayne Grenadiers	..	..	..	..	..	..	..	7	3	83	1	4	1	2	..	..	91	..	..	..	3	..	..	2	..	..	..
	" Henry Walt	..	..	..	1	1	..	..	3	3	79	..	6	3	3	..	..	91	..	..	..	..	..	..	2	1	1	..
	" C. O. W. Terry	..	..	..	1	..	1	..	5	2	77	..	6	4	2	..	2	91	..	..	..	..	..	..	1	..	..	..
	" J. A. Long	..	..	..	..	1	1	..	4	2	83	..	4	2	2	1	1	93	..	..	..	2	..	..	2	..	..	..
	" R. H. Croft	..	..	..	1	1	1	..	6	1	80	1	3	1	5	..	..	90	..	..	..	2	..	..	4	..	..	..
	" William Prickett	..	..	..	1	1	1	..	5	2	80	..	6	1	1	..	..	88	..	..	..	1	..	..	2	..	1	..
	" Joseph Hales	..	..	..	1	1	1	..	6	2	81	..	5	3	..	1	1	90	..	..	..	3	..	..	1	2	1	..
	" Mr. C. O. Hammond	..	..	..	1	1	1	..	5	2	79	..	7	1	4	..	..	92	..	..	..	4	..	..	4	..	..	..
	Rochester Vacant Company	..	..	..	..	..	1	..	6	3	82	..	6	2	..	..	..	90	..	..	..	4	..	..	4	..	1	..
	Captain Robert Pope Light Infantry	..	..	..	1	2	..	..	5	2	77	..	3	1	9	..	2	92	..	..	..	6	..	..	..	..	5	..
	TOTAL	..	1	1	7	8	7	5	52	22	801	2	50	19	28	2	6	908	..	1	166	25	..	..	22	3	9	21

ACCOUNT shewing the Encrease and Decrease of the *West Kent* Regiment of Militia during the last Month.

Effectives on 25th last Month: Serjeants	Drummers	Rank & File	Total	Causes of Encrease: [illegible]	Joined from Desertion	Transfers received		Total	Causes of Decrease: Dead	Discharged	Deserted	Transfers given	Volunteers to the regular Army		Total	Effectives on 25th present Month: Serjeants	Drummers	Rank & File	Total
51	22	918	991	23	2	..	..	25	3	22	9	..	..	..	34	52	22	908	982

STATE OF THE RANK AND FILE.

Present and fit for Service	739
On Command	19
Recruiting	28
On Furlough	6
Unfit for immediate Service: Sick	50
Convalescent	..
Invalids recommended to be discharged	..
Prisoners	2
Recruits at Drill	55
Boys	7
[illegible]	2
TOTAL	908

Fig. 18 *Monthly Return for the West Kent Militia 1812.* WO 17/929

and Volunteers, 1793–1831, in PMG 73.

Many records of militia and volunteer units are preserved at local record offices. These records are described in *Militia lists and musters, 1757–1876* by Jeremy Gibson and Mervyn Medlycott. For details of other record offices, see chapter 20.

For a more detailed study of early records relating to Militia, see *Records of the Militia and Volunteer Forces 1757–1945*, revised edition by W. Spencer in the National Archives' library.

7.4 Militia Records of Service

One effect of the Cardwell reforms of the regular army in the early 1870s was to bring in a form of association, whereby militia units that were nominally from a given region or county were linked; eventually in 1881 these were combined under a new regimental title. Many of the militia records in WO 68, WO 76 and WO 79 may be listed under either the original name or the post-1881 title. If you are unable to find what you are looking for in the following list, try searching for the unit name in the online catalogue but limiting the search to WO 68, WO 76 and WO 79. The following records include description and enrolment books, bounty books and officers' records of service.

Regiment	Reference
Aberdeenshire Militia, Royal *became* 3rd Gordon Highlanders	WO 76/451–452
Amounderness Battalion, Lancashire Militia	WO 79/2
Anglesey Militia, Royal	WO 25/3920
Argyll and Bute Militia *became*	
West of Scotland Royal Field (Reserve) Artillery	WO 68/98–117
4th Battalion Argyll and Sutherland Highlanders, *formerly*	
Royal Renfrew Militia	WO 68/372–374
Armagh Militia *became* 3rd Battalion Royal Irish Fusiliers	WO 68/383–401
Armagh Light Infantry *became* 3rd Battalion Royal Irish Fusiliers	WO 68/476
Army Service Corps	WO 68/562
4th Battalion Bedfordshire Regiment, *formerly*	
Hertfordshire Militia	WO 68/375
Berkshire Militia *became* 3rd Battalion Berkshire Regiment	WO 68/472
Berwick Artillery Militia *became part of*	
South East Of Scotland Royal Field (Reserve) Artillery	WO 68/78–85
3rd Battalion Border Regiment, *formerly*	
Royal Cumberland Militia	WO 68/376
4th Battalion Border Regiment, *formerly*	
Royal Westmoreland Militia	WO 68/377
Caernarvon and Merioneth Militia, Royal, *became*	
4th Battalion Royal Welch Fusiliers	WO 68/215–217
Cambridge Militia, *became* 4th Battalion Suffolk Regiment	WO 68/140–157
3rd Battalion Cameron Highlanders, *formerly*	
Inverness and Highland Light Infantry Militia	WO 68/378
Cardigan Royal Field (Reserve) Artillery, *formerly*	
Cardigan Royal Rifles Militia	WO 68/1–2
Carlow Militia, *became* 8th Battalion King's Royal Rifle Corps	WO 68/296–305
	WO 76/289–290
Carmarthen Royal Field (Reserve) Artillery, *formerly*	
Carmarthen Royal Rifles Militia	WO 68/3–22
Cavan Militia, *became* 4th Battalion Royal Irish Fusiliers	WO 68/402–405
4th Battalion Cheshire Regiment, *formerly*	
2nd Royal Cheshire Militia	WO 68/214
Clare Royal Field (Reserve) Artillery, formerly Clare Militia	WO 68/23
3rd Battalion Connaught Rangers, *formerly* North and	WO 68/319–328
South Mayo Militia and Galway Militia	WO 79/40
5th Battalion Connaught Rangers, *formerly*	
Roscommon Militia	WO 68/475
	WO 79/41, 44&45
Cork City Artillery Militia	WO 68/368
Cork City Infantry Militia, *became* Royal Munster Fusiliers	WO 68/409
North Cork Infantry Militia, *became*	
9th Battalion King's Royal Rifle Corps	WO 68/302–312
Cornwall and Devon Miners Royal Field (Reserve) Artillery,	
became Cornwall and Devon Miners Artillery	WO 68/24–25
Royal Cumberland Militia, *became*	
3rd Battalion Border Regiment	WO 68/376
Devon Royal Field (Reserve) Artillery, *formerly*	
Devon Artillery Militia	WO 68/26–27
2nd or South Devon Militia, *became*	
3rd Battalion Devonshire Regiment	WO 68/139

Donegal Royal Field (Reserve) Artillery, *formerly*
    Donegal Artillery Militia   WO 68/28–30
Donegal Militia, *became*
    5th Battalion Royal Inniskilling Fusiliers   WO 68/221–230
Dublin City Royal Field (Reserve) Artillery, *formerly*
    Dublin City Artillery Militia   WO 68/31–32
4th Battalion Royal Dublin Fusiliers, *formerly*
    Dublin City Militia   WO 68/491
Dumfries Militia, *became*
    3rd Battalion King's Own Scottish Borderers   WO 68/508
Durham Royal Field (Reserve) Artillery, *formerly*
    Durham Artillery Militia   WO 68/33–34
Edinburgh County Militia, *became*
    3rd Battalion Royal Scots (Lothian) Regiment   WO 68/551–561
4th Battalion Essex Regiment, *formerly* West Essex Militia   WO 68/257–277
                                                      & 359–360

Fermanagh Militia, *became*
    3rd Battalion Royal Inniskilling Fusiliers   WO 68/382
Fife Royal Field (Reserve) Artillery, *formerly* Fife Militia   WO 68/–1
Forfar and Kincardine Royal Field (Reserve) Artillery, *formerly*
    Forfar and Kincardine Militia   WO 68/42–43
Galway Militia, *became* 3rd Battalion Connaught Rangers   WO 68/328
                                                    WO 79/43

Glamorgan Royal Field (Reserve) Artillery, *formerly*
    Glamorgan Artillery Militia   WO 68/44
                                                WO 69/612

4th Battalion Gloucester Regiment, *formerly*
    Royal North Gloucester Militia   WO 68/231–241
                                                WO 76/266

Haddington Artillery Militia, *became part of*
    South East of Scotland Royal Field (Reserve) Artillery   WO 68/78–85
3rd Battalion Hampshire Regiment, *formerly* Hampshire Militia WO 68/379–381
                                                WO 76/518

Hampshire and Isle of Wight Royal Field (Reserve) Artillery,
    formerly Hampshire and Isle of Wight Artillery Militia   WO 68/45–53
Hereford Militia, *became* 4th Battalion Shropshire Light Infantry WO 68/278–295
Hertfordshire Militia, *became*
    4th Battalion Bedfordshire Regiment   WO 68/375
3rd Battalion Highland Light Infantry, *formerly*
    1st Royal Lanark Militia   WO 68/503–506
                                                   & 522

4th Battalion Highland Light Infantry   WO 68/489–490
4th Battalion Royal Inniskilling Fusiliers, *formerly*
    Royal Tyrone Infantry Militia   WO 68/71 & 382
5th Battalion Royal Irish Fusiliers, *formerly* Mongahan Militia WO 68/316–318
3rd Battalion Royal Irish Regiment, *formerly* Wexford Militia   WO 68/173–174
6th Battalion Royal Irish Rifles, *formerly* Louth Militia   WO 68/3130315
Kent Royal Field (Reserve) Artillery, *formerly*
    Kent Artillery Militia   WO 68/337–340
3rd Battalion Royal West Kent Regiment, *formerly*
    West Kent Light Infantry Militia   WO 68/406
Kerry Militia, *became* 4th Battalion Royal Munster Fusiliers   WO 68/410–412
Kilkenny Militia   WO 68/456–457

King's County Militia, *became* 3rd Battalion Leinster Regiment	wo 68/408
1st or King's Own Royal Tower Hamlets Militia, *became*	
7th Battalion Rifle Brigade	wo 68/407
	& 416–421/3
	& 424–428
1st, 2nd and 3rd Batteries Lancashire Royal Field (Reserve)	wo 68/54–58
Artillery, *formerly* Lancashire Royal Field Artillery Militia	wo 76/160–162
2nd Lancashire Militia	wo 68/488
3rd Battalion Lancashire Fusiliers	wo 68/500
1st Royal Lancashire Militia	wo 68/479
Royal North Lincoln Militia, *became*	
4th Battalion Lincolnshire Regiment	wo 68/458–462
Royal South Lincoln Militia, *became*	
4th Battalion Lincolnshire Regiment	wo 68/131–138
Linlithgow Artillery Militia, *became part of*	
South East of Scotland Royal Field (Reserve) Artillery	wo 68/78–85
Londonderry Royal Field (Reserve) Artillery, *formerly*	
Londonderry Artillery Militia, *formerly*	
Londonderry Light Infantry Militia	wo 68/64–67
Royal Longford and Westmeath Militia, *became*	
on amalgamation 6th Battalion Rifle Brigade,	
prior to amalgamation were respectively	wo 68/329–336, 439
9th and 6th Battalions Rifle Brigade	and wo 76/286 & 292
Medway Division, Royal Engineers	wo 68/369
Mid-Ulster Royal Field (Reserve) Artillery, *formerly*	
Tyrone Artillery Militia	wo 68/68–72
Monmouthshire Battalion	wo 68/507
Royal Monmouth Militia	wo 25/3920
Royal Montgomeryshire Militia, *became*	
4th Battalion South Wales Borderers	wo 68/218–220
	& 450–455
Norfolk Royal Field (Reserve) Artillery, *formerly*	
Norfolk Artillery Militia	wo068/341–345
4th Battalion Norfolk Regiment, *formerly*	
2nd or East Norfolk Militia	wo 68/123–190
	& 498
West Norfolk Militia	wo 68/467–469
Northumberland Royal Field (Reserve) Artillery, *formerly*	
Northumberland Artillery Militia	wo 68/3 & 121
3rd Battalion Oxfordshire Light Infantry, *formerly*	
Royal Buckinghamshire Militia	wo 68/242–256
Oxford Militia, *became*	
4th Battalion Oxfordshire Light Infantry	wo 68/413–414
Peeblesshire Artillery Militia, *became part of*	
South East of Scotland Field (Reserve) Artillery	wo 68/78–85
Pembroke Royal Field (Reserve) Artillery, *formerly*	
Pembroke Artillery Militia	wo 68/74–75
Plymouth Division, Royal Engineers	wo 68/370
Portsmouth Division, Royal Engineers	wo 68/371
2nd or Queen's Own Royal Tower Hamlets Militia, *became*	
5th Battalion Rifle Brigade	wo 68/415
2nd Royal Regiment of Tower Hamlets Militia	wo 68/422–423
King's Shropshire Militia, *became*	
3rd Battalion Shropshire Light Infantry	wo 68/440

Sligo Royal Field (Reserve) Artillery, *formerly*	
Sligo Artillery Militia	WO 68/76–77
3rd and 4th Battalions Somerset Light Infantry, *formerly*	
1st and 2nd Somerset Militia	WO 68/158–172
3rd and 4th Battalions South Staffordshire Regiment, *formerly*	
1st King's Own Stafford Militia	WO 68/523–534
3rd and 4th Battalions North Staffordshire Regiment, *formerly*	
2nd and 3rd King's Own Stafford Militia	WO 68/470–471
Suffolk Royal Field (Reserve) Artillery, *formerly*	
East Suffolk Light Infantry Militia	WO 68/348–358
2nd Suffolk Militia	WO 68/480–482
3rd Battalion Suffolk Regiment, *formerly* West Suffolk Militia	WO 68/463–466, 492–494, 509–514, 516–521 & 549
3rd and 4th Battalions East Surrey Regiment, *formerly*	
1st and 3rd Royal Surrey Militia	WO 68/445 & WO 76/64, 65 & 68
3rd Battalion West Surrey Regiment, *formerly*	
2nd Royal Surrey Militia	WO 68/477–478
Sussex Royal Field (Reserve) Artillery, *formerly*	
Royal Sussex Artillery Militia	WO 68/86–87
Tipperary Royal Field (Reserve) Artillery, *formerly*	
1st or South Tipperary Artillery Militia	WO 68/88–95
4th Battalion Warwick Regiment, *formerly*	
2nd Warwick Militia	WO 68/361–367
Waterford Royal Field (Reserve) Artillery, *formerly*	
Waterford Artillery Militia	WO 68/96–97
3rd Battalion West Riding Regiment, *formerly*	
6th West Yorkshire Militia	WO 68/215–217
5th Battalion Wiltshire Militia	WO 76/530 & WO 79/24
Worcestershire Militia, *became*	
3rd Battalion Worcestershire Regiment	WO 76/493
East and North York Artillery Militia, *became*	
Yorkshire Royal Field (Reserve) Artillery	WO 68/121–122
3rd Battalion York and Lancaster Regiment, *formerly*	
3rd West Yorkshire Militia	WO 68/447, 473 & 499
North Yorkshire Militia, *became*	
4th Battalion Yorkshire Regiment	WO 68/175–213
1st West Yorkshire Militia, *became*	
3rd Battalion King's Own Yorkshire Light Infantry	WO 68/448, 474 & 499 (1)
2nd West Yorkshire Militia	WO 68/449 & WO 76/316
4th West Yorkshire Militia	WO 76/316
5th West Yorkshire Militia, *became*	
3rd Battalion Yorkshire Regiment	WO 68/535–536
South Yorkshire Regiment, *became*	
King's Own Yorkshire Light Infantry	WO 68/448

8

CASUALTY RETURNS
AND OPERATIONAL RECORDS

Records of units and formations engaged in particular campaigns are listed in detail in *The Records of the War Office and related departments 1660–1964* by Michael Roper. The record class SP 87 State Papers Foreign, Military Expeditions, contains correspondence of the Secretary of State, mainly with military commanders in the field, for the period 1695 to 1763. Individuals who served in particular campaigns may be traced through the awards of campaign medals—see 9.2.

8.1 Casualties

There are several series of monthly and quarterly casualty returns for both officers and ordinary soldiers, arranged by regiment, in WO 25. These returns are dated between 1809 and 1910 and many are indexed. They give name, rank, place of birth, trade, the date, place and nature of the casualty, debts and credits, and next of kin or legatee. The returns in WO 25/3250–3260 cover the period 1842–1872 and include details of men discharged or who had deserted.

A series of entry books of casualties, 1797–1817, from the Muster Master General's Office is in WO 25/1196–1358. These books give the names in alphabetical order, with details of the cause of death and any financial credits that the deceased might have had.

Nominal rolls of casualties were kept for many of the campaigns in which the Army fought during the second half of the nineteenth century. These rolls include the names of officers as well as other ranks.

Campaign	Date	Reference
Burma	1888	WO 25/3473
China	1857–1858	WO 32/8221, 8224, 8227
	1860	WO 32/8230, 8233–8234
China (Tsingtao)	1915	WO 32/4996B
Egypt	1882, 1884	WO 25/3473
New Zealand	1860	WO 32/8255
	1863–1864	WO 32/8263–8268, 8271, 8276–8280

Campaign	Date	Reference
Sierra Leone	1898	WO 32/7630–7631
South Africa	1878–1881	WO 25/3474, WO 32/7700, 7706–7708, 7727, 7819
	1899–1902	WO 108/89–91, 338
Sudan	1884–1885	WO 25/3473, WO 32/6123, 6125–6126, 8382

Several casualty lists for specific campaigns have been published, including *The Casualty Roll for the Crimea* by Frank and Andrea Cook; *'They Fell like Stones': casualties of the Zulu War, 1879* by John Young; *South Africa Field Force Casualty List, 1899–1902*, a facsimile of WO 108/338; *The Last Post being a roll of all Officers (Naval, Military and Colonial) who gave their names for Queen, King and Country in the South Africa War, 1899–1902* by Mildred C. Donner; and *To what end did they die? Officers who died at Gallipoli* by R. W. Walker.

Other records relating to casualties include registers of authorities to deal with effects, 1810–1822, in WO 25/2966–2971 (recording name, regiment, date of death, amount of effects and credits and the name and address of the person, usually next of kin, applying for them); an index to effects, 1830, in WO 25/2974; a register of effects and credits, 1830–1844, in WO 25/2975; and record book of effects 1862–1881 in WO 25/3476–3490, indexed by WO 25/3491–3501.

Papers relating to Artillery and Engineer deaths and effects, 1824–1859, are in WO 25/2972–2973, 2976–2978. WO 334 includes annual death and

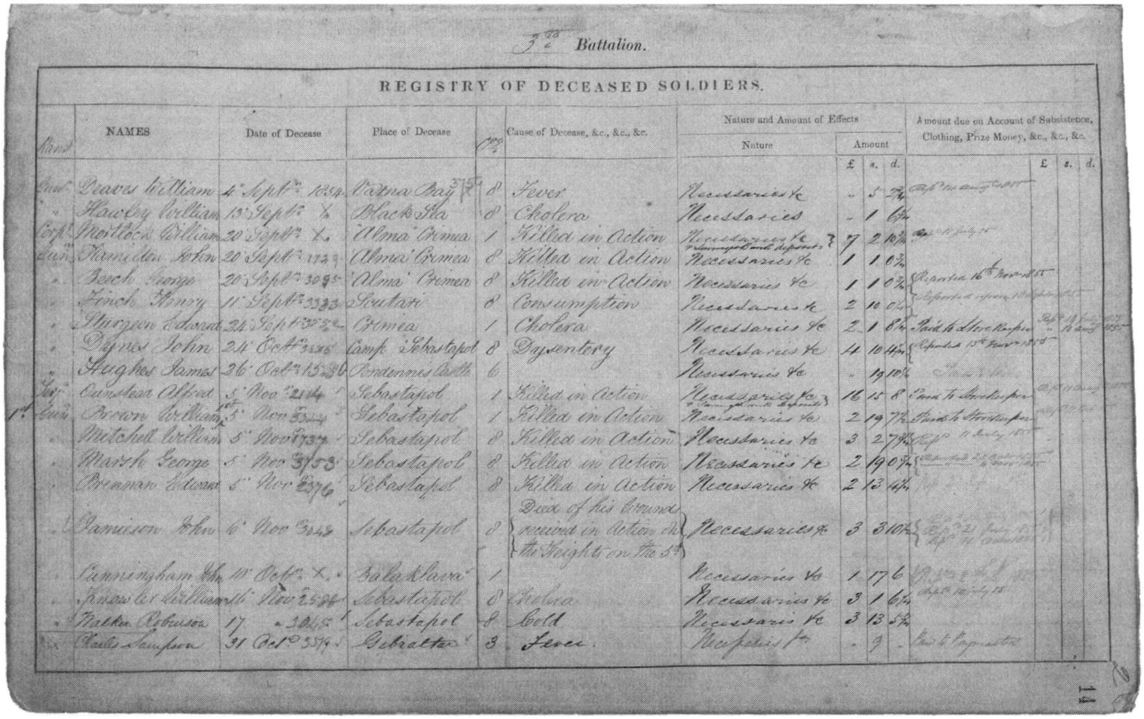
3rd Battalion.

REGISTRY OF DECEASED SOLDIERS.

Rank	NAMES	Date of Decease	Place of Decease	No.	Cause of Decease, &c., &c., &c.	Nature and Amount of Effects: Nature	Amount £	s.	d.	Amount due on Account of Subsistence, Clothing, Prize Money, &c., &c., &c.
Gunr	Deaves William	4th Septr 1854	Varna Bay	8	Fever	Necessaries &c	–	5	2¾	[illegible]
"	Hawley William	13th Septr	Black Sea	8	Cholera	Necessaries	–	1	6¼	
Corpl	Mortlock William	20th Septr	Alma Crimea	1	Killed in Action	Necessaries &c [illegible]	7	2	10¼	[illegible]
Gunr	Hamilton John	20th Septr	Alma Crimea	8	Killed in Action	Necessaries &c	1	1	0¾	
"	Beech George	20th Septr	Alma Crimea	8	Killed in Action	Necessaries &c	1	1	0¾	Reported 16th Novr 1855
"	Finch Henry	11th Septr	Scutari	8	Consumption	Necessaries &c	2	10	0¼	[illegible]
"	Sturgeon Edward	24th Septr	Crimea	1	Cholera	Necessaries &c	2	1	8¼	Paid to Storekeeper [illegible]
"	Dynes John	24th Octr	Camp Sebastopol	8	Dysentery	Necessaries &c	4	10	4½	Reported 15th Novr 1855
"	Hughes James	26th Octr	Pendennis Castle	6		Necessaries &c	–	19	10½	[illegible]
Serjt	Ourstead Alfred	5th Novr	Sebastopol	1	Killed in Action	Necessaries &c [illegible]	16	15	8	Paid to Storekeeper [illegible]
1st Gunr	Brown William	5th Novr	Sebastopol	1	Killed in Action	Necessaries &c	2	19	7½	Paid to Storekeeper
"	Mitchell William	5th Novr	Sebastopol	8	Killed in Action	Necessaries &c	3	2	7¾	Repd 11 July 1855
"	Marsh George	5th Novr	Sebastopol	8	Killed in Action	Necessaries &c	2	19	0¼	[illegible]
"	Brennan Edward	5th Novr	Sebastopol	8	Killed in Action	Necessaries &c	2	13	4½	
"	Jamieson John	6th Novr	Sebastopol	8	Died of his Wounds received in Action on the Heights on the 5th	Necessaries &c	3	3	10½	[illegible]
"	Cunningham John	10th Octr	Balaklava	1		Necessaries &c	1	17	6	[illegible]
"	Knowles William	11th Novr	Sebastopol	8	Cholera	Necessaries &c	3	1	6¼	[illegible]
"	Walker Robinson	17 "	Sebastopol	8	Cold	Necessaries &c	3	13	5½	
"	Charles Sampson	31 Octr	Gibraltar	3	Fever	Necessaries &c	–	9	–	Paid to Paymaster

Fig. 19 *Royal Artillery casualty return for the Crimean War period, 1854.* WO 69/584

disability returns for 1817–1892, which give the names of individuals. wo 69/613 contains letters concerning Royal Artillery casualties from the Battle of Elanslaagte during the Boer War (1889–1902).

8.2   Operational Records

Unlike the operational records of the First World War and subsequent conflicts, where there were procedures laid down for keeping a daily record of operational events, records concerning operational matters pre-1909 are, in many cases, of less use to the family historian and are spread across a number of different records series.

Most pre-1909 operational records take the form of despatches, usually from the senior officer commanding the battle or campaign. The despatch from the most senior commander in the field may be made up of his own report and those of his subordinate officers, all of which will give an idea of what occurred during that particular campaign or battle.

The majority of pre-1909 operational records are spread across seven different records series, each of which, as one might imagine, is arranged in a different way.

Early despatches for campaigns including operations against Napoleon, in America in 1812 and the Crimea, may be found in wo 1.

Further reports concerning operations in the Crimea may be found in wo 28.

The majority of reports and despatches for operations post-1855 can be found in the series wo 32. The wo 32 series is arranged by subject, with the subject being given a numerical or alphabetical code. The majority of operational reports and despatches can be found in either Code 46 or under 'O' for overseas, and then under the specific code given to that part of the world where the operation took place. The most effective way of searching wo 32 is by either the name of the officer commanding the operation or by the name of the war or battle you are interested in.

Detailed reports concerning some operations can be found in wo 33.

The series wo 105 and wo 108 contain reports and despatches concerning the Boer War (1899–1902).

The records of the Directorate of Military Operations and Intelligence can be found in wo 106 and this series is one worth consulting.

9   MEDALS AND AWARDS, 1793–1991

Medals and awards can be split into four basic groups: awards for gallantry or meritorious service, campaign medals, long-service medals and awards to commemorate specific events.

Apart from orders of chivalry, the earliest of which is the Order of the Garter dating from 1348, the majority of awards for campaign service or gallantry or meritorious service date from the nineteenth and twentieth centuries.

The earliest campaign medal was the Waterloo Medal, instituted in 1816, whilst the Military General Service Medal for campaigns from 1793–1814 was instituted in 1847.

Of all the awards for gallantry, the Victoria Cross was only instituted in 1856 yet this was preceded by the Distinguished Conduct Medal in 1854.

The Military Cross and Military Medal were only created during the First World War. Another First World War creation and still in use was the Most Excellent Order of the British Empire, which was created in 1917.

For a detailed guide to the medal records held at the National Archives and in the India Office Collection at the British Library, see *Medals: the Researcher's Guide* by William Spencer (TNA, 2006).

9.1   Awards for Gallantry or Meritorious Service

All awards for gallantry or meritorious service are, except in the most exceptional circumstances, announced in the *London Gazette*. The *London Gazette* is available online at *www.gazettes-online.co.uk*. It is possible to search the *London Gazette* by name, period and by award but I recommend that you keep the search simple.

Copies of the *London Gazette* are available at the National Archives on microfilm. It is also possible to search the paper indexes announcing awards for both world wars.

Although various distinctions have been bestowed upon individuals for their deeds performed during peace or wartime, it is only since the Victorian era that awards for gallantry or meritorious service have been bestowed on a more liberal and regular basis.

Apart from the highest orders of chivalry, the most frequently bestowed

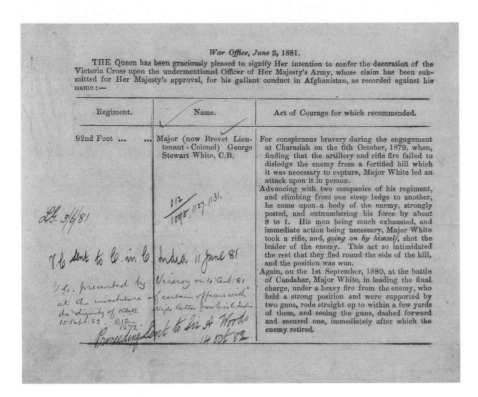

War Office, June 2, 1881.

THE Queen has been graciously pleased to signify Her intention to confer the decoration of the Victoria Cross upon the undermentioned Officer of Her Majesty's Army, whose claim has been submitted for Her Majesty's approval, for his gallant conduct in Afghanistan, as recorded against his name :—

Regiment.	Name.	Act of Courage for which recommended.
92nd Foot	Major (now Brevet Lieutenant-Colonel) George Stewart White, C.B.	For conspicuous bravery during the engagement at Charasiah on the 6th October, 1879, when, finding that the artillery and rifle fire failed to dislodge the enemy from a fortified hill which it was necessary to capture, Major White led an attack upon it in person. Advancing with two companies of his regiment, and climbing from one steep ledge to another, he came upon a body of the enemy, strongly posted, and outnumbering his force by about 8 to 1. His men being much exhausted, and immediate action being necessary, Major White took a rifle, and, *going on by himself,* shot the leader of the enemy. This act so intimidated the rest that they fled round the side of the hill, and the position was won. Again, on the 1st September, 1880, at the battle of Candahar, Major White, in leading the final charge, under a heavy fire from the enemy, who held a strong position and were supported by two guns, rode straight up to within a few yards of them, and seeing the guns, dashed forward and secured one, immediately after which the enemy retired.

Fig. 20 *The Register of the Victoria Cross.* WO 98/4

order of chivalry in the early nineteenth century was the Most Honourable Order of the Bath (1725). The records of appointments to the Order of the Bath can be found in WO 103.

The war against Russia in the Crimea brought about the creation of two gallantry awards. The Distinguished Conduct Medal (DCM) was instituted in 1854. Submissions for awards of the DCM made between 1854 and 1901 are in WO 146. Further files about the DCM can be found in WO 32 code 50S. The register of the DCM providing a name index of awards granted between 1855 and 1920 is in WO 391, available on microfilm in the Open Reading Room. Awards of the DCM granted between 1854 and 1909 are listed in *Recipients of the Distinguished Conduct Medal 1855–1909* by P.E. Abbott. Recipients of the DCM between 1914 and 1920 are listed in *Recipients of the DCM 1914–1920* by R.W. Walker. *For Distinguished Conduct in the Field: Register of The DCM 1920–1992* by P. McDermott covers the last awards up to when the DCM was abandoned.

The Victoria Cross (VC) was instituted in February 1856 and was first awarded for acts of bravery performed during the Crimean War. The first VC was awarded to Charles Lucas. Details relating to Victoria Crosses awarded between 1854 and 1914 can be found in WO 32 codes 50D and 50M. The National Archives has many books about the Victoria Cross; please ask in the library.

The register of awards of the VC covering the period 1856–1957, together with the royal warrant instituting the award and submission for awards up to 1903, is in WO 98. Entries from the register relating to men who were awarded the Victoria Cross for gallantry at Rorke's Drift in 1879 are in WO 98/4. The registers of the VC in WO 98 have been digitized and placed on DocumentsOnline.

A list of recipients of the VC 1856–1946 is in CAB 106/320. Citations for the Victoria Crosses awarded during the Second World War are in CAB 106/312. Some, but not all, recommendations for VCs awarded since 1939 are in the series WO 373.

In 1886, the Distinguished Service Order (DSO) was instituted (WO 32/6278) as an award for distinguished service during campaigns and for acts of gallantry. Details about the DSO can be found in WO 32 code 52D. Details of all awards of the DSO granted between 1886 and 1923 can be found in *Register of the DSO* by Sir O'Moore Creagh and Miss E. Humphries, a copy of which is available in the Library. The register of the DSO is in the series WO 390 and covers the period 1886–1945.

Recommendations for awards made during the Boer War can be found in WO 108 and some in WO 105.

Awards created and awarded during the First World War are covered in *First World War Army Service Records* by W. Spencer (TNA, 4th ed. 2008).

Recommendations for awards for gallantry or meritorious service for the period 1938–1991 can be found in the record class WO 373. This class, which is available on microfilm, is arranged by operational theatre in which the award was won and then in *London Gazette* date order. Awards for meritorious service that were announced in the 'Half Yearly' lists, the New Year or Birthday Honours can also be found in WO 373. Awards for service in Malaya, Korea and other post-Second World War conflicts can also be found in WO 373. Awards for 'Combat Gallantry' include the VC, DSO, Military Cross (MC), DCM and Military Medal (MM). Awards for 'Non-Combat Gallantry' include the George Cross and George Medal. Awards for meritorious service include the CBE, OBE, MBE and BEM.

WO 373 is slowly being digitized and placed on DocumentsOnline. It is possible to search by name of recipient and by award. So far, only awards from the Second World War have been digitized. It is currently still possible to use the microfilm copies of WO 373.

Those seeking information about nurses who were awarded the Royal Red Cross (RRC) or Royal Red Cross 2nd Class (ARRC) during the Second World War can find the surviving recommendations in WO 373. The register of the Royal Red Cross for the period 1883 to 1994 can be found in WO 145.

9.2 Campaign Medals, 1793–1913

Although many commanding officers of various campaigns were given a medal to commemorate that particular campaign or battle, the modern era of campaign medals did not start until 1816, with the authorization of the Waterloo Medal for services the previous year. The Waterloo Medal is important in modern medallic history, as it was the first medal given to all men, irrespective of rank; it was the first medal to be stamped by machine and, as long as their next of kin applied for it, the first to be given to the families of men who died in the battle.

Although a number of other medals were awarded for campaigns around the globe, the next important medal to be instituted after the Waterloo Medal was the Military General Service Medal 1793–1814 (MGS). Authorized in 1847, the MGS was only issued to survivors of a number of battles that took place in the wars against France. As the medal was only issued to survivors who were still alive in 1847, it is not common.

Details of all British campaign medals awarded for campaigns between 1793 and 2003 can be found in *British Battles and Medals* by J. Hayward, D. Birch and R. Bishop, a copy of which is available in the library.

9.2.1 *Medal rolls*

After a campaign or battle was over, many campaign medals were authorized to be given to participating troops. In order to find out who was present at a particular campaign or battle, a roll of all those present, or not, had to be taken. Once the roll was taken, a medal roll in the format laid down by the Army Order (WO 123) announcing the award was created. The medal rolls for all of these medal issues can be found in the record class WO 100 and are available on microfilm in the Open Reading Room. An example is illustrated as Fig. 21. The WO 100 class list is arranged in chronological order of campaign or battle. Each medal roll is arranged in regimental

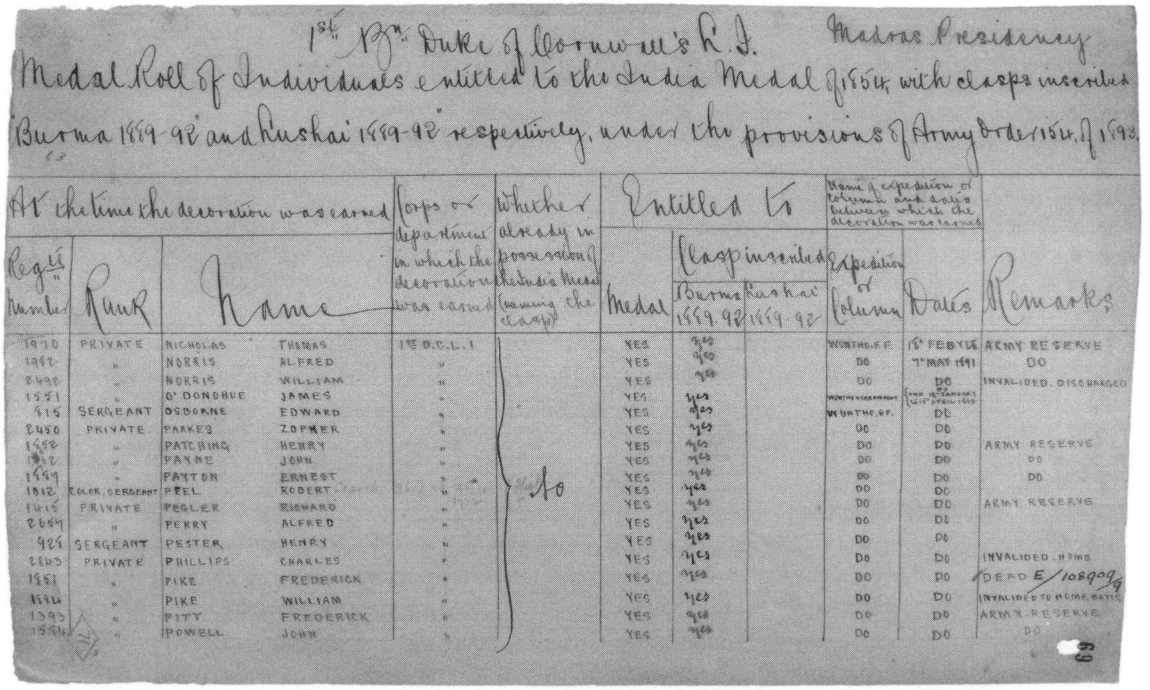

1st Bn. Duke of Cornwall's L.I. Madras Presidency

Medal Roll of Individuals entitled to the India Medal of 1854, with clasps inscribed "Burma 1889-92" and "Lushai 1889-92" respectively, under the provisions of Army Order 154, of 1893.

Regtl Number	Rank	Name		Corps or department in which the decoration was earned	Whether already in possession of the India Medal (naming the clasps)	Medal	Clasp inscribed Burma 1889-92	Clasp inscribed Lushai 1889-92	Expedition or Column	Dates	Remarks
1970	PRIVATE	NICHOLAS	THOMAS	1st D.C.L.I		YES	yes		WUNTHO. F.F.	15th FEBY 91	ARMY RESERVE
1982	"	NORRIS	ALFRED	"		YES	yes		DO	7th MAY 1891	DO
2492	"	NORRIS	WILLIAM	"		YES	yes		DO	DO	INVALIDED. DISCHARGED
1551	"	O' DONOHUE	JAMES	"		YES	yes		[illegible]	[illegible]	
815	SERGEANT	OSBORNE	EDWARD	"		YES	yes		WUNTHO. F.F.	DO	
2450	PRIVATE	PARKES	ZOPHER	"		YES	yes		DO	DO	
1552	"	PATCHING	HENRY	"		YES	yes		DO	DO	ARMY RESERVE
1912	"	PAYNE	JOHN	"		YES	yes		DO	DO	DO
1599	"	PAYTON	ERNEST	"		YES	yes		DO	DO	DO
1012	COLOR. SERGEANT	PEEL	ROBERT	"	No	YES	yes		DO	DO	
1415	PRIVATE	PEGLER	RICHARD	"		YES	yes		DO	DO	ARMY RESERVE
2659	"	PERRY	ALFRED	"		YES	yes		DO	DO	
925	SERGEANT	PESTER	HENRY	"		YES	yes		DO	DO	
2843	PRIVATE	PHILLIPS	CHARLES	"		YES	yes		DO	DO	INVALIDED. HOME
1951	"	PIKE	FREDERICK	"		YES	yes		DO	DO	DEAD E/108909/9
1584	"	PIKE	WILLIAM	"		YES	yes		DO	DO	INVALIDED TO HOME BATTN
1393	"	PITT	FREDERICK	"		YES	yes		DO	DO	ARMY RESERVE
1584	"	POWELL	JOHN	"		YES	yes		DO	DO	DO

Fig. 21 *Typical War Office medal roll from 1893 showing the sort of information such a document can capture.* WO 100/75

order of precedence—that is, the most senior regiment first, and then usually by rank and within these in alphabetical order.

A number of medal rolls have been published over the years; please ask in the library to see what is available. Apart from the War Office records, other sources relating to medals include the records of the Royal Mint, most notably the Waterloo Medal book, which is in MINT 16/112.

The campaign medal rolls for the First World War are in the record class WO 329, with a card index, available on microfiche, in the record class WO 372. For a full explanation of these rolls, see *First World War Army Service Records by* W. Spencer (TNA, 4th ed. 2008) and section 16.4.

Post-World War One campaign medal rolls for operations in Afghanistan in 1919, other parts of India and the North-West Frontier up to 1924, Iraq, Persia and Kurdistan are available in WO 100. More post-1925 medal rolls will eventually be added to WO 100.

9.2.2 *Other sources on campaign medals*

Apart from the records mentioned above, a number of other record classes contain lists of names relating to campaigns and their subsequent medal issue. These include:

Campaign	Reference
Kurdistan (1925)	WO 32/3564
New Zealand (1861, 1863)	WO 32/8258, 8270
Nubia, Sudan (1926–1927)	WO 32/3537
Rhodesia (1898)	WO 32/7840, 7842–7843
Sierra Leone (1898)	WO 32/7629, 7632, 7635
Somaliland (1903–1904)	WO 32/8428, 8440
South Africa (1878–1879)	WO 32/7682, 7764
South Africa (1899–1903)	WO 32/7960, WO 108/136–179
Sudan (1884–1886, 1896–1898)	WO 32/3539
Tsingtao, China (1914–1915)	WO 32/4996B

9.3 Long-service Medals

In 1833, a Long Service and Good Conduct Medal was instituted for soldiers who had served 18 years in the Army. Medal rolls for this medal between 1831 and 1953 are in WO 102. The majority of the rolls in WO 102 are available on microfilm, but WO 102/17 and WO 102/18 have been digitized and are available only via DocumentsOnline.

Awards of long-service medals to officers in colonial forces, 1891–1894, are in WO 32/8293–8298. WO 102 also contains some rolls for medals issued to men serving in militia and colonial forces.

In 1846 a Meritorious Service Medal was authorized for sergeants and warrant officers who had performed good service other than in battle. Awards for meritorious service between 1846 and 1919 are in WO 101. A register of annuities paid to recipients of the meritorious or long-service awards, 1846–1879, is in WO 23/84. Rolls for the Volunteer Officers' Decoration, 1892–1932, are in WO 330.

Awards of the Territorial Force Efficiency Medal (TFEM), Territorial Efficiency Medal (TEM) and the Efficiency Medal (Territorial) were announced in Army Orders, some of which can be found in WO 123. Awards of the TFEM and TEM can also be found on DocumentsOnline, where they will be found amongst the First World War Medal Index Cards.

9.4   Medals Commemorating Specific Events

A number of different medals have been awarded to members of the British Army over the last hundred years, such as medals commemorating the coronation or jubilee of a sovereign, or for marksmanship. Unfortunately, rolls for most of these medal issues are not preserved amongst the records in the National Archives. Those that are can be found in WO 100 and WO 32 code 50A.

The medal roll for the 1911 Coronation Medal is in WO 330/1 and 2.

Medal rolls for the 1935 Jubilee, 1937 Coronation, 1953 Coronation and 1977 Jubilee are available on the open shelves in the library. Each roll is arranged in alphabetical order.

9.5   Foreign Medals Awarded to British Soldiers

Since the Crimean War, and in a number of instances prior to that, foreign governments have sometimes awarded decorations to British servicemen. In most cases, the award of foreign decorations has been dealt with by the Treasury Department of the Foreign Office. Although a number of awards were announced in the *London Gazette*, in many cases it is the records in FO 83, FO 371 and FO 372 that need to be consulted. If you wish to use these Foreign Office classes, you may need to seek further advice from staff in the Open Reading Room.

10 COURTS MARTIAL

Officers and ordinary soldiers who committed crimes in accordance with the Army Act, Mutiny Act or under the Articles of War could be tried by their peers and superiors for such offences. The crimes were many and varied and could extend from murder to losing kit or equipment. Depending upon the offence and the operational circumstances at the time, an individual could be tried by a different level of court martial.

There were three different types of court martial for which the National Archives holds records: general courts martial, general regimental courts martial (before 1829) and district courts martial (after 1829). General courts martial conducted during wartime and in the theatre of operations were called Field General Courts Martial and many such trials led to the execution of the defendant.

Although the three above mentioned levels of courts martial are amongst the records held at Kew, there was a lower level, which is probably mentioned more frequently and that is regimental court martial. Regimental courts martial were conducted by the commanding officer of a unit where the offence was relatively minor and for which the commanding officer has the appropriate powers of punishment.

10.1 Officers

Tracing the courts martial of commissioned officers is relatively straightforward, since they could be tried only by general court martial. WO 93/1B is an index to trials of officers, 1806–1904. WO 93/1A is an index to general courts martial between 1806 and 1833.

There are three main types of record relating to individual trials: papers, proceedings and registers.

Papers were compiled at the time of the court martial and are arranged in date order. They are in WO 71/121–343 and cover the period between 1688 and 1850, with one file for 1879. Other papers for trials between 1850 and 1914 were destroyed by enemy bombing in 1940. Papers for some special cases, mainly senior officers, are listed individually between 1780 and 1824 in WO 71/99–120, as are special returns for Ireland, 1800–1820, which are in WO 71/252–264.

When papers reached the Judge Advocate General's Office, their contents were entered into the volumes of proceedings. They were kept in two series, depending on whether the sentence was confirmed at home by the sovereign or abroad by a colonial governor or overseas commander. These records are in WO 71/13–98 and continued in WO 91. Until the mid-nineteenth century, the proceedings report the trials in detail, but later volumes give only the charges, findings and sentences in the form in which they were handed to the sovereign. They also contain copies of warrants for the holding of courts martial and correspondence concerning the confirmation of sentences. Registers of warrants are in WO 28. The commander in chief's submissions upon sentence are in WO 209.

The Judge Advocate General's Office also compiled registers of courts martial, giving the name, rank, regiment, place of trial, charge, finding and sentence. Registers of courts martial confirmed abroad are in WO 90 and those confirmed at home are in WO 92. Records of field general courts martial date only from the South African War (1899–1902) and are combined in registers with district courts martial, for 1900 and 1901 only, in WO 92. Later registers, between 1909 and 1963, are in WO 213.

10.2   Other Ranks

NCOs and ordinary soldiers could be tried by general regimental courts martial (before 1829) and district courts martial (after 1829), as well as by general courts martial. As a result, it is more difficult to find the records of individual cases. Only registers, rather than full proceedings, were compiled in the Judge Advocate General's Office. Registers of general regimental courts martial between 1812 and 1829 are in WO 89; those of district courts martial between 1829 and 1971 are in WO 86. Both classes contain trials confirmed both at home and abroad, except those for London, 1865–1875, which are in WO 87, and India, 1878–1945, in WO 88. There are no records of minor offences tried by regimental courts martial, apart from the details that may be recorded on a soldier's regimental conduct sheet, found with his record of service.

For general courts martial, the records are as described for officers above.

10.3   Other Sources

Records relating to individual cases are closed for 75 years from the date of the last entry in each piece. However, purely summary records of a more recent date are open. WO 93/40 gives particulars of death sentences carried out between 1941 and 1953. Nominal rolls of courts martial of all ranks of Australian and Canadian forces, 1915–1919, are in WO 93/42–45. A list of death sentences carried out in the British Army during the First World War is in WO 93/49. Nominal rolls of courts held in the Prisoners of War camp at Changi, 1942–1944, are in WO 93/46–48. Statistics for army and air force courts martial, 1914–1954, are in WO 93/49–59.

Registers of courts martial conducted during the Crimean War can be found in WO 28/126–128.

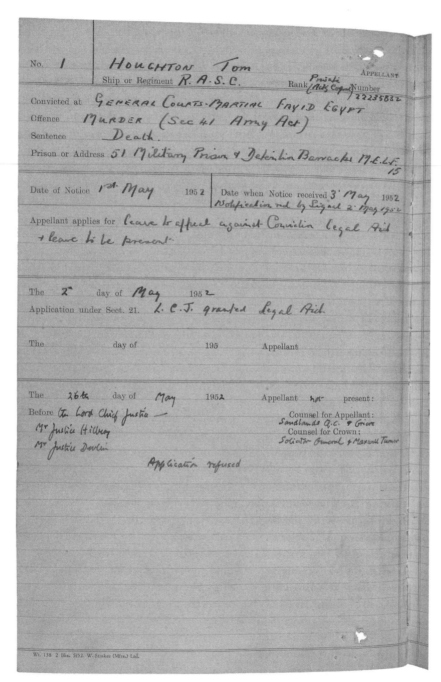

Fig. 22 *The Register of Courts Martial Appeal Cases 1952–1957.* J 152/1

10.4 Appeals

Records concerning appeals against the findings or sentence of a court martial were heard by the Supreme Court and the associated records can be found in J 152 and J 135.

J 152 contains the Courts Martial Appeal Court Registers of Appeal and these record the names of appellants, summary details of their original trial and sentence, whether leave to appeal was granted, and, if so, its outcome. They also indicate the reference assigned by the office to the relative case file. These registers cover the period 1952–1984.

J 135 contains correspondence and papers of the court registrar, arising from the submisssion by the convicted person or his legal representative of notice of appeal. In most cases, the files are accompanied by a transcript of the original proceedings and, where leave to appeal is granted, its outcome is noted. The files in J 135 cover the period 1952–1996. It is possible to search J 135 by name of appellant on the catalogue but please note the records are closed for 30 years from the date of appeal.

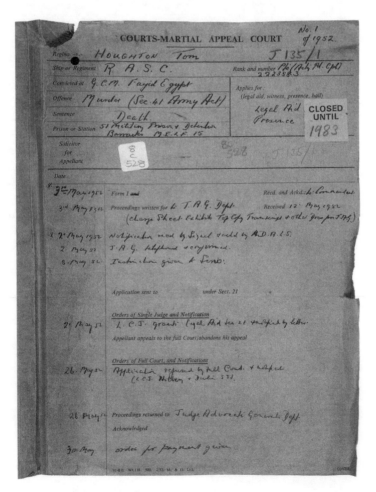

Fig. 23 *Court Martial Appeal file 1952.* J 135/1

11 THE BRITISH ARMY IN INDIA AND THE INDIAN ARMY

The British Army in India and the armies of the East India Company and the Indian Army frequently cause the family historian problems. Before 1861, it was possible for British men to join the British Army and see service in India and it was also possible for them to join the armies of the East India Company as an other rank or as an officer. Later it was possible for a British man to join the Indian Army as an officer or to be transferred in and a British Army NCO could also be transferred in or attached to the Indian Army. After the Indian Mutiny 1857–1858, fewer European men directly joined the Indian Army as an ordinary soldier until the twentieth century—and then usually only as a specialist.

Until 1859, the East India Company had its own army consisting of separate regiments of European and Indian troops led by European officers. The Company administered India through three Presidencies—Bengal, Madras and Bombay—each of which had its own army. In 1861, the European regiments became part of the British Army and the Indian troops became the Indian Army under the control of the viceroy in Delhi.

Service records for officers and soldiers of the East India Company armies and the Indian Army are, for the most part, held by the British Library, Asia, Pacific and Africa Collections. These include muster rolls and casualty returns for the Bengal Army (1716–1861); the Madras Army (1762–1861) and the Bombay Army (1708–1865); records of pension funds, such as the Lord Clive Fund (from 1770) and registers of births, marriages and deaths. The Library also holds entry papers for officer cadets between 1789 and 1860. These papers include baptismal certificates and educational qualifications. Also kept by the Library are registers of recruits, 1817–1860, and embarkation lists, 1753–1861.

A very brief description of the records held by the British Library is given in chapter 20.

By far the most detailed guide to all of the India Office holdings relating to the armies of the East India Company and the Indian Army is *Guide to the records of the India Office military department* by A. Farrington. This guide covers not only the records concerning individuals, but also those relating to operations.

Another useful guide is *Researching Ancestors in the East India Company Armies* by Peter A. Bailey.

The British Library, Asia, Pacific and Africa Collection also holds published lists of East India Company army officers—*Indian Army Lists* and the *East India Register and Directory*, which was published annually from 1803. Some examples of the *India List*, *Indian Army List*, *Bengal Army List* and *Madras Army List* are available in the library at Kew.

For more information about the India Office records and the online resources available via the British Library website, see *www.bl.uk/collections/asiapacificafrica.html*.

11.1   East India Company and Indian Army

A few records relating to the East India Company and Indian Army are held by the National Archives. Lists of officers of the European regiments, 1796–1841, are in WO 25/3215–3219.

Registers of service of officers holding a commission on 1 November 1871 are in the papers of the Army Purchase Commission in WO 74, together with a series of applications from the officers of Indian establishments (the number of men who could be paid for by India) 1871–1891, to which certificates of service are attached. Papers and applications are indexed by regiment, but not by name of applicant. There is a name index for WO 74 in the Open Reading Room.

Discharges prior to 1854 for men who had seen service in the armies of the East India Company can be found in WO 97 and WO 121. When searching use the term 'east india' as well as the soldier's name by combining them by using AND.

Registers and indexes of East India Company Army pensions, 1849–1876, and Indian Army pensions, 1849–1868, are in WO 23/17–23. A register of pensions paid to former soldiers serving with the East India Company between 1824 and 1856 is in WO 25/3137. Lists of deserters from the Company's army between 1844 and 1851 are in WO 25/2933.

War diaries of Indian Army formations during the First World War are in WO 95. War diaries for the Second World War are in WO 169–WO 179 and include Indian Army units

British Library records relating to the armies of the East India Company and the Indian Army are almost as vast and just as complex as the War Office records held at the National Archives. The period and status of an individual will dictate which India Office records you will need to look at. Although there are, of course, variations, the following is a basic guide as to where to start:

L/MIL/9/1–106 relate to the recruitment of soldiers into the East India Company from 1753 to 1861.

L/MIL/9/107–332 relate to the entry of officer cadets from 1775 to 1940.

Other records in L/MIL/9 relate to surgeons, veterinary surgeons, nurses, temporary appointments between 1919 and 1921 and appointments to the Indian Army Reserve of Officers 1917–1918.

The records in L/MIL/10 relate to service in the Bengal Army.
The records in L/MIL/11 relate to service in the Madras Army.
The records in L/MIL/12 relate to service in the Bombay Army.
The records in L/MIL/14 relate to service in the Indian Army.

Many of the records in L/MIL/10–14 have been indexed. There are, for example, indexes of soldiers' papers in L/MIL/10–12 and an index of officers' records of service in L/MIL/14 on the open shelves in the Asia, Pacific and Africa reading room at the British Library.

Discharge papers and other records concerning soldiers of the Bengal Army for the period 1820–1882 can be found in L/MIL/10/301–326.
Discharge papers and other records concerning soldiers of the Madras Army for the period 1851–1874 are in L/MIL/11/277–282.
Discharge papers and other records concerning soldiers of the Bombay Army for the period 1856–1876 can be found in L/MIL/12281–288.

Not only did a large number of British men become officers in the Indian Army, a large number of British Army NCOs volunteered or were transferred to the unattached or miscellaneous lists of the Indian Army. Information concerning these NCOs can be found in the above-mentioned records.

The records of the unattached lists usually list the NCOs in alphabetical order and are further arranged by the department the individual was employed by. Further information includes original regiment/corps, date of joining the list, date of attestation and remarks.

Bengal Army unattached list returns for c.1866–1907 are in L/MIL/10/253–300.
Madras Army unattached list returns for 1853–1907 are in L/MIL/11/232–276.
Bombay Army unattached list returns for c.1855–1907 are in L/MIL/12/198–280.
Indian Army unattached list returns for 1908–1944 are in L/MIL/14/144–194.

A large number of the records in L/MIL/9–12 are listed on the Access to Archives website and can be searched by name via *www.a2a.org.uk*.

11.2 British Army in India

Service records of officers and men serving with the British Army in India, as in other parts of the world, are described in chapters 3 and 4.

A list of British officers who served in India between 1796 and 1804 is in wo 25/3215. Records for soldiers discharged on return from India before 1806 will be found in the depot musters of their regiments (wo 67). Between 1863 and 1878, the discharges of men returning from India are recorded in the musters of the Victoria Hospital, Netley (wo 12/13077–13105); between 1862 and 1889, similar information is in the muster rolls of the Discharge Depot at Gosport (wo 16/2284, 2888–2915). Except for a few eighteenth-century artillery rolls, there are no musters of artillery and engineers in India, but musters of infantry and cavalry regiments in India between 1883 and 1889 are in wo 16/2751–2887.

11.3   Other Sources

Registers of the deaths of officers in the Indian services for the Second World War are held by the British Library in the Asia, Pacific and Africa Collections.

L/MIL/14/142 contains the casualty list for British Officers of the Indian Army for the period 1914–1921 and L/MIL/14/143 does the same for 1939–1948.

Registers of garrison churches, and other churches used by soldiers and their families, are held by the diocesan authorities in India. Births, marriages and deaths for officers and men of the British Army in India appear in the Chaplain's Returns. Details of these records are given in chapter 20.

The National Army Museum holds Hodson's Index, a very large card index of British Officers in the Indian Army, the Bengal Army and the East India Company Army, but not the British Army in India. Many of the entries go beyond bare facts to include colourful stories of life. Civilians and government staff are included if they had seen army life. Details of the holdings of the National Army Museum are given in chapter 20.

Useful books are *Lists of Officers of the Bengal Army* by V.C.P. Hodgson, *Armies of the Raj* by Byron Farwell, which is a social history of the Indian Army, and *Ubique*, which contains war services of officers of the Bengal Army up to immediate post-Mutiny period.

12 COLONIAL AND DOMINION FORCES

Many colonial regiments were raised in the eighteenth and nineteenth centuries for a variety of reasons. However, the two key reasons were, one, because British troops could not tolerate the climate and, two, the proximity of available manpower. For example, the West India Regiment was raised to see service in both the West Indies and in West Africa because troops of European origin could not cope with the climate.

The Canadian Mounted Rifles were raised specifically for service in that country and much of the manpower for that regiment came from the region and in many cases were former British Army soldiers or people who originally came from Britain.

Published histories of such units are noted in *Regiments and Corps of the British Empire and Commonwealth, a critical bibliography* by R. Perkins. References to individual officers and men may also occasionally be found in the appropriate records of the Colonial Office and its predecessors.

Soldiers' documents for men who served in colonial regiments between 1760 and 1872 are in WO 97. Microfilmed copies of these records for regiments raised, or primarily serving, in Canada are held by the National Archives of Canada, 395 Wellington Street, Ottawa, KIA ON3 Canada.

The national archives of former colonies may hold other records relating to troops and militia forces stationed there—see 12.3.

Muster books of certain colonial regiments are in WO 12 and those of colonial militia are in WO 13. Many men from the colonies, especially those of Canadian origin, served with the 100th Foot. Half-pay returns for officers who had served in Canadian forces between 1783 and 1813 are in WO 24/748–762.

Returns of NCOs and men serving with colonial units in 1806 are in WO 25/1070–1121. Admission books for pensions payable in the colonies, 1817–1875, are in WO 23/147–152. There is an admission book for native and colonial pensioners, 1880–1903, in WO 23/160. Other registers of pensions paid to colonial soldiers are in WO 22. Casualty lists for colonial regiments between 1797 and 1817 are in WO 25/1345–1357, 2183–2207, 2242–2295, with indexes in WO 25/2689–2713, 2734–2753. Further indexes to casualty returns, 1850 to 1910, are in WO 25/3465–3471.

12.1 Records of Individual Colonial Regiments

There are description books for officers in the following regiments:

Unit	Date	Reference
Cape Mounted Rifles	1825–1865	WO 25/636–637
Ceylon Rifles	1809–1872	WO 25/638–641
Royal Canadian Rifles	1841–1868	WO 25/632–633
West India Rangers	1804–1816	WO 25/663
West India Regiments	1826–1869	WO 25/646–650, 652, 660

In addition, returns of officers' services compiled in 1829 and 1872 for a number of regiments are in WO 25/805, 824, 840, 854 and 869. Further details about these records are in section 3.5.

Lists, registers and admission books for negro and Cape Mounted Rifle Corps pensioners, 1837–1879, are in WO 23/153–157, 159. Another admission book for men serving in the Ceylon Regiment and the Gun Lascars between 1868 and 1876 is in WO 23/158.

Lists of soldiers employed by the Royal African Company between 1756 and 1815 are in T 70/1454–1456. T 70 also contains a great deal of information about garrisons in West Africa.

For the period up to 1739 the printed *Calendars of State Papers Colonial*, which are indexed by personal name, contain many references to individual officers and men. Colonial Office records for the relevant country may contain some references to individual regiments and those who served in them, such as the design of a proposed uniform for a soldier in the Cape of Good Hope Regiment (CO 48/3)—Cape of Good Hope (Cape Colony) Original Correspondence.

12.2 North America

Lists of men who served in certain provincial volunteer forces in North America, 1746–1747, 1775–1783, are in WO 28/1, 4–5. Further muster rolls for militia units in the colonies of Connecticut, Massachusetts, New Hampshire and Rhode Island between 1759 and 1763 are in T 64/22. A list of officers who served in provincial forces during the American War of Independence 1775–1782 is in T 64/23. Certificates of birth, baptism, marriage and death for a number of officers in Loyal American and Canadian units between 1776 and 1881 are in WO 42/59–63. Lists of men who served with the North and South Carolina militia are in T 50.

Some muster rolls of provincial loyalist troops in the American War of Independence are preserved in the National Archives of Canada, 395 Wellington Street, Ottawa, K1A 0N3 Canada.

12.3 South Africa, 1899–1902

Fig. 24 *Trooper A Stanton, 42nd (Herts) Company, Imperial Yeomanry 1900.*
COPY 1/446

A large number of regiments were created during the Boer War, some in the UK such as the Imperial Yeomanry and some in South Africa. The Scottish Horse, although created in South Africa, were in fact an Imperial Yeomanry unit and their records are discussed elsewhere.

Enrolment papers for men who served in locally recruited volunteer forces during the South African War (1899–1902) are in WO 126 and WO 127. The enrolment forms are in the series WO 126 and the nominal rolls are in the series WO 127.

These records are arranged in alphabetical order by name of unit, with each individual unit then arranged in alphabetical order by name of soldier. Many of these units were called Town Guards or District Mounted troops and, as such, the enrolment papers for men of such units are in alphabetical sequence by individual's name, rather than by unit name followed by the individual's name.

South Africa Local Forces Unit Name	WO 126 Piece(s)	South Africa Local Forces Unit Name	WO 126 Piece(s)
Ashburner's Light Horse	WO 126/1	Imperial Bearer Corps	WO 126/51
Bechuanaland Rifles	WO 126/1	Imperial Hospital Corps	WO 126/52–54
Bethune's Mounted Infantry	WO 126/2–3	Imperial Light Horse and	
Border Horse	WO 126/4	Imperial Light Infantry	WO 126/55–65
Border Scouts	WO 126/5	Imperial Yeomanry Scouts	WO 126/66
Brabant's Horse	WO 126/6–14	Johannesburg Mounted Rifles	WO 126/67–73
Bushmanland Borderers	WO 126/15	Kaffarian Rifles	WO 126/74
Canadian Scouts	WO 126/16–17	Kimberley Horse	WO 126/74–75
Cape Colonial Forces		Kitchener's Fighting Scouts	WO 126/76–82
(Colonial Defence Force)	WO 126/18	Kitchener's Horse	WO 126/83–88
Cape Colony Cyclist Corps	WO 126/19–22	Marshall's Horse and	
Cape Medical Staff Corps	WO 126/23	Uitenhage Volunteer Rifles	WO 126/89–90
Cape Peninsular Regiment	WO 126/24–27	Menne's Scouts	WO 123/9
Cattle Rangers	WO 126/28	Midland Mounted Rifles	WO 126/91–92
[Number not used]	WO 126/29	Namaqualand Border Scouts	WO 126/93
Colonial Scouts	WO 126/30	Natal Volunteer	
Commander in Chief's		Ambulance Corps	WO 126/93–94
Bodyguard	WO 126/31–34	National Scouts	WO 126/95
Damanat's Horse	WO 126/35–38	Nesbitt's Horse	WO 126/95–98
Dennison's Scouts		Orange River Scouts	WO 126/98
(Western Border Rifles)	WO 126/39	Orpen's Light Horse	WO 126/99
Driscoll's Scouts	WO 126/40–43	Pietersburg Light Horse	WO 126/100
Duke of Edinburgh's Own		Prince of Wales's Light Horse	WO 126/101–104
Volunteer Rifles (Colonial		Protectorate Regiment	WO 126/105
Light Horse)	WO 126/44	Railway Pioneer Regiment	WO 126/106–111
Eastern Province Horse	WO 126/45	Rand Rifles	WO 126/112–114
French's Scouts	WO 126/45	Rhodesian Regiment	WO 126/115–116
Frontier Light Horse	WO 126/46–47	Robert's Horse	WO 126/117–120
Gorringe's Flying Column	WO 126/48	Ross' Battery and	
Herschel Native Police	WO 126/48–50	Loch's Horse	WO 126/121

South Africa Local Forces Unit Name	WO 126 Piece(s)	South Africa Local Forces Unit Name	WO 126 Piece(s)
Scottish Horse	WO 126/122–126	Thorneycroft's Mounted Infantry	WO 126/142–144
Scott's Railway Guards and Cape Railway Sharpshooters	WO 126/127–129	Town Guards and District Mounted Troops	WO 126/145–163
Settle's Scouts	WO 126/129	Warren Mounted Infantry	WO 126/164
South African Light Horse	WO 126/130–138	Western Light Horse	WO 126/165
South African Mounted Irregular Forces	WO 126/139–140	Western Province Mounted Rifles	WO 126/166–167
Steinaecker's Horse	WO 126/141		

A large number of these South African Local Force units changed their names during the war. One of the most effective ways to identify not only the enrolment forms and nominal rolls, but also the medal rolls for the Queen's South Africa Medal and King's South Africa Medal, is to use the alphabetical list for such records which is incorporated into the WO 100 paper catalogue.

Casualties are recorded in WO 129/8–11 and WO 108/338. Details are also available in *South African Field Force Casualty List, 1899–1902,* which is available at Kew.

A case study of a man who served in the Imperial Yeomanry, a unit which was created as a consequence of the Boer War, is in section 4.8.5.

Records of men who served in Natal volunteer regiments or the militia between 1884 and 1912 are held by the Natal Archives Depot, Private Bag, X9012, 3200 Pietermaritzburg, South Africa.

12.3   Records from 1902 to 1953

This section only goes up to 1953 because many of the former colonies gained their independence at around this time and the responsibility for the records relating to military matters of these former colonies was passed back to them.

Records relating to members of colonial and dominion forces can sometimes be found among relevant records of the Colonial and Dominions Offices.

The Commonwealth Forces History Trust, 37 Davis Road, London W3 7SE, may be able to help people interested in the history or records of colonial and dominion army units.

Original correspondence relating to the King's African Rifles, which was formed in 1902 from the armed forces of various East African dependencies, is in CO 534, with registers in CO 623 and CO 624. Original correspondence for the Niger and West Africa Force, formed in 1897, is in CO 445, with registers in CO 581 and CO 582. From 1927 correspondence about various colonial forces is in CO 820.

War diaries of colonial and dominion forces for the First World War are in WO 95. Casualty records and medal rolls for Canadian forces in the South African and First World Wars are held by the Canadian Department of Veteran Affairs, Honours and Awards, 284 Wellington Street, Ottawa, KIA OP4, Canada.

War diaries for colonial forces for the Second World War are in WO 169–WO 178. With the exception of Australia and Southern Rhodesia, war diaries for forces of the dominions are in WO 179. War diaries for Southern Rhodesian Forces are in WO 333. Australian war diaries are held by the Australian War Memorial, GPO Box 345, Canberra, ACT 2601 Australia. See *www.awm.gov.au*.

CO 820/50/1–12 contains nominal rolls for British and European officers and other ranks serving with local forces in certain non-African colonies.

During the Korean War (1950–1953), the Commonwealth Division included several Australian and Canadian units. The war diaries for all these units are in WO 281.

Australia

Service records for men who served in the Australian armed forces after 1899 are held by the National Archives of Australia, PO Box 7425, Canberra BC ACT 2610. Tel: 1300 886 881; Fax: (02) 6212 3499; E-mail: servicerecords@naa.gov.au.

It is possible to search for many Australian records of service via the National Archives of Australia website at *http://naa12.naa.gov.au/scripts/ResearcherScreen.asp*.

An extensive collection of material relating to all branches of the Australian fighting services is held by the Australian War Memorial, GPO Box 345, Canberra, ACT 2601, Australia. The War Memorial is unable to undertake genealogical research, but can supply the names of professional researchers to do the work for you. Their holdings are described in *Roll call! A guide to genealogical sources in the Australian War Memorial* by Joyce Bradley *et al*. For further information, visit *www.awm.gov.au*.

Canada

Service records for Canadians who served during the two world wars are held by Personnel Records Unit, National Archives of Canada, 395 Wellington Street , Ottawa, Ontario KIA ON3. See also *www.archives.ca*.

New Zealand
PRE-1920 RECORDS
Naval, army and air force service records for New Zealanders from 1899 are held by: Archives New Zealand, PO Box 12–050, Wellington, New Zealand. Website: *www.archives.govt.nz*.

Records held by the National Archives of New Zealand, PO Box 6148, Te Aro, Wellington, include nineteenth-century material relating to British imperial troops, pensioner settlers, local militia and volunteer corps military settlers of the 1860s. More recent records include material on conscription, reservists and war diaries. These records are described in more detail in *Family History at the National Archives* (Wellington, New Zealand, 1990).

POST-1920 RECORDS
Personnel Archives, NZ Defence Force, Trentham Camp, Private Bag 905
Upper Hutt, New Zealand, Fax: 04 527 5275.

South Africa
Service records for South African servicemen are held by the following:

1881–1902
   The National Archives of South Africa,
   Postal address: Private Bag X236, PRETORIA 0001
   Street address: 24 Hamilton Street, Arcadia, PRETORIA
   Telephone: +27 (0)12 441 3200
   Fax: +27 (0)12 323 5287
   Fax to e-mail: 086 529 6416
   E-mail: Archives@dac.gov.za
   For further information and research see:
   www.national.archives.gov.za

The National Archives of South Africa holds a few military records but of particular interest are the personal files of the South African Constabulary which many British soldiers joined at the end of the South African War (1899–1902), usually for a short time before returning to England or going to another colony. These records are described in more detail in R. T. J. Lombard, *Handbook for Genealogical Research in South Africa* (Pretoria, 1990).

The records of personnel from the First World War onwards are held by the South African Defence Force Archives. The SA Defence Force Archives are not open to the public, but you may write to obtain information on First and Second World War Service Records. There are two addresses:

   Street Address: Schweickerdt Building, 20 Visagie Street,
   PRETORIA 0001
   Telephone: +27 (0)12 339-4600
   Fax: +27 (0)12 339-4631
   Email: sandfdoc@mweb.co.za
   Postal Address: Documentation Service Directorate, Private Bag X 289,
   Pretoria, SOUTH AFRICA 0001.

You may need permission from the person concerned or from the eldest living relative to obtain information from these records.

The Commonwealth Forces History Trust, 37 Davis Road, London W3 7SE, may be able to help people interested in the history or records of colonial and dominion army units.

13 FOREIGN TROOPS IN BRITISH PAY

There have often been foreign troops in British pay and serving under British Command. There are a number of reasons for this but perhaps the most obvious is the development of the British monarchy and its connection with Germany and Hanover in particular. Many of the records described elsewhere in this guide include information about foreign troops in British pay. In particular many foreigners, especially Germans, served with the 60th Foot.

Hessian troops, who had already been conscripted into their own army in the German state of Hesse were hired by the British to act as auxiliaries during operations against the American revolutionaries.

13.1 Records from 1775 to 1816

Hessian troops
Muster rolls of Hessian troops in British pay in North America, 1776–1794 and 1796–1797, are in AO 3/55, 58–59. Pay lists between 1775 and 1795 are in T 38/812–814. An index of names is available at Kew. Nominal rolls of Hessian troops may also be found in WO 12, WO 28/12, CO 5/139–140, 182–184 and HO 50/452.

The records for the Hessen-Cassel, Hessen-Hanau and Waldeck forces are held in the State Archive in Marburg, Germany:

Hessisches Staatsarchiv Marburg
Friedrichsplatz 15
35037 Marburg
Germany
Tel: (49) 06421 25078
Fax: (49) 06421 161125
www.staatsarchiv-marburg.hessen.de

For written enquiries, write to:
Hessisches Staatsarchiv Marburg
Postfach 540
35037 Marburg
Germany

Other information may be held by the Institut für Archivwissenschaft, Archivschule Marburg, D-3550 Marburg an der Lahn, Germany.

Napoleonic Wars

Muster rolls of French royalist forces in British pay during the Napoleonic Wars are amongst the Bouillon papers in HO 69. Musters and pay lists for officers in the French Emigrant Engineers and Artillery are in WO 54/702.

Some birth, baptism, marriage and death certificates for officers in French, Greek, Swiss and Italian Corps are in WO 42/64–65. They cover the period between 1776 and 1881, but are mostly from the Napoleonic War period.

Statements were taken in June 1806 of the period of service of all NCOs and men in certain French refugee units, with those for the Chasseurs Britanniques in WO 25/1099 and for Dillon's and Meuron's Regiments in WO 25/1116–1117. A list of men discharged from foreign regiments between 1783 and 1810 is in WO 25/1121.

Casualty returns

Casualty returns for foreign troops between 1809 and 1816 are in WO 25/2267–2271, 2289–2292, with indexes in WO 25/2753, 2892. Muster rolls of foreign regiments are in WO 12. Those for units of foreign artillery are in WO 10.

Histories of foreign regiments in the British army, 1793–1802, are given in the *Journal of the Society for Army Historical Research* vol. 22 (1943–1944).

13.2   King's German Legion

Soon after the resumption of the Napoleonic Wars in 1803, attempts were made to recruit foreign troops to serve in the British Army. The Hanoverian Army had been disbanded under the terms of the Treaty of Amiens in 1802 and special efforts were made by the British to recruit former members of this Army. Virtually all members of the King's German Legion came from Hanover. The Legion fought in the Baltic, in Spain and in southern France. In 1815 it took part in the Battle of Waterloo. It was disbanded in 1816 and many of the officers and men joined the re-formed Hanoverian Army.

Former officers of the Legion were asked to supply details of their service in 1828. These records, arranged alphabetically, are in WO 25/749–779. There is an incomplete card index, arranged by name, in the Open Reading

Room. Some birth, baptism, marriage and death certificates for officers are to be found in WO 42/52–58.

Soldiers' documents for men who served in the Legion are in WO 97/1178–1181. A register of recruits for the Legion, 1803–1808, is in WO 25/3203. Statements taken in June 1806 of the period of service of all NCOs and men serving with the Legion are in WO 25/1100–1114. A list of men discharged from the Legion between 1783 and 1810 is in WO 25/1121.

Casualty returns for the Legion are in WO 25/2272–2288, with indexes in WO 25/2752, 2888–2891. Muster rolls are in WO 12/11747–11948. Muster rolls for artillery units attached to the Legion are in WO 10. Lists of all the men of the Legion present at the Battle of Waterloo are in WO 12/11949. An index to names is available in the Open Reading Room.

A register of pensioners from the Legion, 1801–1815, is in WO 23/135. Lists of men discharged to pension in 1816 are in WO 25/3236–3237 and WO 116/25. They give the reason for discharge, age and place of birth of individuals. An alphabetical list of men in these volumes is kept at Kew. Registers of payments made between 1843 and 1867 to soldiers who had served in the Legion are in PMG 7.

Many records of the Legion are held by the Niedersächsische Hauptstaatsarchiv, Am Archiv 1, D-3000 Hannover 1, Germany.

See also *www.kgl.de*.

13.3 Records from 1815 to 1854

Discharge documents for men who served in the Foreign Veterans Battalion (a battalion of aged soldiers taken from other regiments of foreign troops in British pay), 1815–1861, are in WO 122, together with reports of medical boards on individuals in these regiments, 1816–1817. A statement of the service by officers in foreign legions from about 1817 is in WO 25/3236–3237.

Registers of half pay given to officers who had served with foreign regiments, 1819–1824, are in WO 24/763–766. Other registers of half pay and pensions to former officers who had served in foreign regiments between 1822 and 1885 are in PMG 6.

13.4 The Crimean War

At the outbreak of the War in 1854, foreign mercenary troops were recruited for service in the Crimea. (See *Mercenaries for the Crimea* by C.C. Bayley.) They formed the British, German, Swiss and Italian Legions. Muster rolls, service records and attestation forms for the British German and Swiss Legions are in WO 15 (none have survived for the Italian Legion). At the end of the War the Legions were disbanded and many men emigrated to the Cape of Good Hope. WO 15 also contains a list of officers and men of the British German Legion who settled in the Cape in 1856. The families who emigrated are listed in *Aided immigration from Britain to South Africa, 1857–1867* by Esme Bull.

Returns of half pay made to officers of foreign regiments between 1858 and 1876 are in WO 23/79–81. Registers of payments to widows of officers between 1855 and 1858 are in WO 23/113, and between 1858 and 1868 in WO 23/88.

13.5 Second World War

After the collapse of Poland in 1939, a number of Polish soldiers escaped and fought in Polish units attached to allied armies during the war. War diaries for some Polish units are in WO 169 and WO 170.

Because of the political situation in Poland, many of these soldiers and their families did not wish to return home after the war had ended. A Polish Resettlement Corps was set up in 1946 to ease the transition of Poles to civilian life in Britain and abroad. The records of the Corps are in WO 315 and contain many items of interest to the family historian. A number of the files are in Polish, however, and some have either been retained by the Ministry of Defence or are closed for 75 years.

Service records of Free Poles are retained by the Ministry of Defence at the following address. The MOD will undertake a search only on receipt of a written request from the next of kin.

Polish Correspondence Section
Room 28B
RAF Northolt
West End Road
Ruislip
Middlesex
HA4 6NG

Email: polishastdisoff@northolt.raf.mod.uk
Email: polishdisoff@northolt.raf.mod.uk

14 RECORDS OF SUPPORT SERVICES

The term 'support services' is a late twentieth-century term used to describe those elements of an army which sit directly behind—and often within—that part of the army which is in direct contact with an opponent. For every one person at the sharp end, there are nine people behind enabling the one at the front to do his job.

The contribution of personnel employed in the support services to the success of the army must never be underestimated. Many of them did not start their army careers in the support services, but were extremely brave and served in very specialized units, or with the special forces.

14.1 Barrackmasters

Barrackmasters were responsible for the construction and maintenance of barracks. A separate Barrackmaster General's Department was established under War Office control in 1793. In 1808 the department was transferred to the Treasury, and then in 1822 to the Board of Ordnance. On the transfer of the Board to the War Office in 1855, the department was disbanded.

Barrackmasters are listed in the monthly *Army Lists*. WO 54 includes appointment papers and testimonials for barrackmasters between 1808 and 1852, and for barrackmaster sergeants, 1823–1855 (WO 54/715–716, 756–823, 928–929). Some papers about the appointment of barrackmasters and their staff between 1835 and 1879 also appear in the registers of the Commissariat Department in WO 61/7–11. Pay and allowance books, 1797–1824, are in WO 54/704–713. Returns of service of barrackmasters in the British Isles, 1830–1852, are in WO 54/734, 742. An alphabetical list of barrackmaster sergeants, 1771–1824, is in WO 54/948.

14.2 Chaplains

Until the end of the eighteenth century, chaplains were employed on a regimental and garrison basis. In 1796 a chaplain general was appointed and chaplains were allocated, one to a brigade or to three or four regiments. The first Presbyterian chaplains were appointed in 1827, Roman Catholics in 1836, Wesleyans in 1881, and Jewish chaplains in 1892.

Registers of certificates of service of chaplains, 1817–1843, are in WO 25/256–258. Lists of payments to chaplains, 1805–1842, are in WO 25/233–251. Lists of chaplains receiving retired pay, 1806–1837, are in WO 25/252–253 and many relate to those who saw service in the eighteenth century. Information about the appointment of chaplains and their conditions of pay and service is in the out-letter books of the War Office Accounts Department, 1810–1836, in WO 7/60–65, and in the in-letters of the Chaplain General's Department, 1808–1828, in WO 7/66–72.

Short biographies of chaplains are in *Crockford's Clerical Directory* and the *Catholic Directory*. Chaplains are British Army officers and so are included in the *Army Lists*.

Further records are held by Ministry of Defence Chaplains, Netheravon House, Salisbury Road, Netheravon, Wiltshire SP4 9SY.

14.3 Civilian Employees

Many thousands of men and women in dozens of different occupations have always been employed to help run the Army. Unfortunately, very few records of their employment have survived. Senior civil servants at the War Office are listed in the *Imperial Calendar* and the *War Office List* published between 1861 and 1964. The *List* often includes brief biographies of certain individuals. It is available in the Open Reading Room at Kew.

Registers of pensions and superannuation payable to civilian employees, 1820–1892, are in WO 23/93–104. Pay books, rolls of names and other papers for civilians employed by the War Office between 1803 and 1919 are in WO 25/3957–3991.

Records of the War Office Boy Messenger Friendly Society and War Office School are in WO 371 and WO 32. The Society was set up in 1906 and continued until the outbreak of the First World War in 1914: a list of its members is in WO 371/3.

14.4 Commissariat

The Commissariat Department was responsible for the victualling of the Army and was set up in 1793. Before then, a decentralized system of supply by civilian contractors, or the appointment of special Commissariat Generals for specific campaigns, provided for the Army's needs. The colonel and other officers of a regiment would provide their men with food and clothing, the cost of which would be deducted from their wages. Ireland had its own Commissariat Department, the records of which, spanning 1797 to 1852, are in WO 63. In 1816 the Commissariat Department came under the control of the Treasury, but was transferred back to the War Office in 1854. Treasury Board papers in T 1 and letter books in T 64 may refer to individual Commissariat officers in this period. Commissariat officers were normally civilians but were subject to military discipline and wore uniform.

There are registers of full pay, half pay and pensions awarded to Commissariat Officers between 1810 and 1856 in WO 61/61–93, with lists of pensions granted to widows, 1814–1826, in WO 61/96–97. Registers of half pay awarded to officers between 1834 and 1885 are in PMG 5. Description and succession (movement of manpower) books for officers between 1855 and 1869, especially those in the Military Train (which was responsible for supplying the Army while abroad), are in WO 25/580–602, 824. Returns of officers' services for the Military Train in 1868 and 1869 are in WO 25/824/2.

Registers in WO 61/1–16 cover the appointment of men to the department between 1798 and 1889. Establishment lists, in WO 61/25–60, give the names of men employed in Spain and Portugal in 1809, and at various stations at home and abroad between 1816 and 1868. Records of Commissariat establishments in Spain and Portugal, 1810–1813 are in AO 11/20.

Applications for employment as clerks in the Commissariat, 1812–1813, 1825–1854 are in WO 61/104–105. Letters relating to civilian appointments in the Commissariat, 1798–1855, are in WO 58/1–47. Registers of appointments and other papers relating to the employment of civil staff by the Commissariat, 1789–1879, are in WO 61.

14.5   Invalids and Veterans

From the late seventeenth century a number of companies of invalids were formed. They consisted of soldiers partly disabled by wounds, and veterans who, from old age and length of service, had been rendered incapable of the duties of an active campaign but were able to undertake lighter duties. Invalid companies were engaged in garrison duty both at home and in the colonies. The first companies were raised in 1690. From 1703, responsibility for raising and administering the companies was placed with the Royal Hospital Chelsea and a Royal Corps of Invalids was formed. It was disbanded when invalids fit for service became part of the new Royal Garrison Regiment and the remainder went on to the strength of the newly formed Veteran Battalions. These battalions were used extensively to maintain civil peace at home. Between 1842 and 1846, they were re-formed as the Enrolled Pensioners. In 1867 the Pensioners were merged into the Second Class Army Reserve, available for home service.

Description and succession (movement of manpower) books for officers serving with the Garrison Battalions between 1809 and 1815 are in WO 25/567, 571–573, 578. Other description books for Veteran Battalions between 1813 and 1826 are in WO 25/605–625. Records of officers serving with the Royal Garrison Regiment between 1901 and 1905 are in WO 19.

Soldiers' documents for men serving in Veteran Battalions between 1804 and 1854 are in WO 97. A register of men in the Garrison and Veteran Battalions, 1845–1854, is in WO 23/27. There is a series of certificates of service in Invalid and Veteran Battalions, 1782–1833, in WO 121/137–222. Casualty returns for both the Veteran and Garrison regiments, 1809–1830, are in WO 25/2190–2195, 2216–2243.

Muster returns for companies and battalions are in WO 12. Monthly returns for companies stationed at garrisons, 1759 to 1802, which sometimes include lists of officers, are in WO 17/793–802.

A brief history of the invalids may be found in Michael Mann's article, 'The Corps of Invalids', *Journal of the Society for Army Historical Research*.

14.6 Medical Services

From 1660, each regiment had a surgeon (commissioned) and each regiment of foot also had a surgeon's mate (warranted). There was also a Surgeon General and a Physician General, who were replaced in 1810 by the Army Medical Department. In 1855 NCOs and men serving in hospitals were formed into the Medical Staff Corps, known from 1857 as the Army Hospital Corps. The regimental system was abolished in 1873 and all medical officers became part of a common Army Medical Department staff. In September 1884 the Department and the Army Hospital Corps were linked together in close association, and they finally merged to form the Royal Army Medical Corps in 1898.

There is a series of records of service of officers of the Medical Department, 1800–1840, in WO 25/3896–3912, which includes details of the professional education of surgeons. Returns of medical staff in Great Britain, 1811–1813, are in WO 25/259–260, with returns of pay, 1813–1818, at home, in the Peninsula and in France in WO 25/261–263. Pay lists for Staff medical officers, clerks and apothecaries, 1799–1847, and regimental surgeons and assistants, 1790–1847, are in WO 25/3897–3902, with an index in WO 25/3903. Service records for officers of the Medical Department between 1800 and 1840 are in WO 25/3904–3911, with an index in WO 25/3912. They include details of medical education received. Indexed volumes of candidates for commission as surgeons, 1825–1867, are in WO 25/3923–3943. Confidential reports on medical officers in 1860 and 1861 are in WO 25/3944. A useful reference is R. Drew's *List of Commissioned Medical Officers of the Army, 1660–1960*, available in the library.

There are few records of military hospitals and medical units other than for the two world wars. Some returns of patients at Lisbon, 1812–1813, and in Ordnance hospitals, 1809–1852, are in WO 25/260, 265, and sick returns sent in to the Army Medical departments, 1817–1892, including annual death and disability returns which name individuals, are in WO 334.

Soldiers' documents for the Army Hospital Corps, 1855–1872, are in WO 97/1698 and the Royal Army Medical Corps medal book, 1879–1896, is in WO 25/3992.

Appointment papers for the Ordnance Board Medical Department, 1835–1847, are in WO 54/926. Returns of officers and men serving with the department between 1835 and 1850 are in WO 54/234 and 926.

Medically qualified individuals, who saw temporary service in the RAMC during the First World War, had their own discrete series of records known to the War Office as the '25 Series'. These records no longer survive.

14.7 Nursing Services

Florence Nightingale's hospital at Scutari during the Crimean War (1854–1856) was the first to use women as nurses for British soldiers. Prior to this, most nursing duties were carried out by male orderlies seconded by their regiments to serve in regimental hospitals.

In 1861, six women nurses and a superintendent were employed by the Army Hospital Corps to serve at Woolwich and Netley. An Army Nursing Service was formed in 1881 and efforts were made to increase the numbers of female nurses in the Army. An Army Nursing Reserve was established in 1897. Both the Reserve and the Service were reorganized after the South African War (1899–1902) as Queen Alexandra's Imperial Military Nursing Service (QAIMNS). The present title of Queen Alexandra's Royal Army Nursing Corps (QARANC) was assumed in 1949.

Testimonials for nurses who wished to serve with Florence Nightingale during the Crimean War are in WO 25/264. Lydia Notley's application to serve as a nurse is illustrated in Fig. 25. She had worked as a nurse in London for 15 years and was recruited but then discharged as 'considered too stout [to] sustain her health in the East'.

Nominal and seniority rolls for nurses in the voluntary National Aid Society and the Army Nursing Service, 1869–1891, are in WO 25/3955. An indexed register of candidates for appointment as staff nurses, 1903–1926, is in WO 25/3956.

Few nurses qualified for a pension because they rarely served enough years to receive one. Pension records for nurses appointed before 1905 are in WO 23/93–95, 181. Registers of pensions for QAIMNS nurses, 1909–1928, are in PMG 34/1–5 and First World War disability pensions for nurses are in PMG 42/1–12.

In 1883, Queen Victoria instituted the Royal Red Cross to be awarded to military nurses. A register for its award from 1883 to 1990 is in WO 145. The Queen's and King's South Africa Medals were awarded to nurses for service during the South African War, 1899–1902, and the medal rolls are in WO 100.

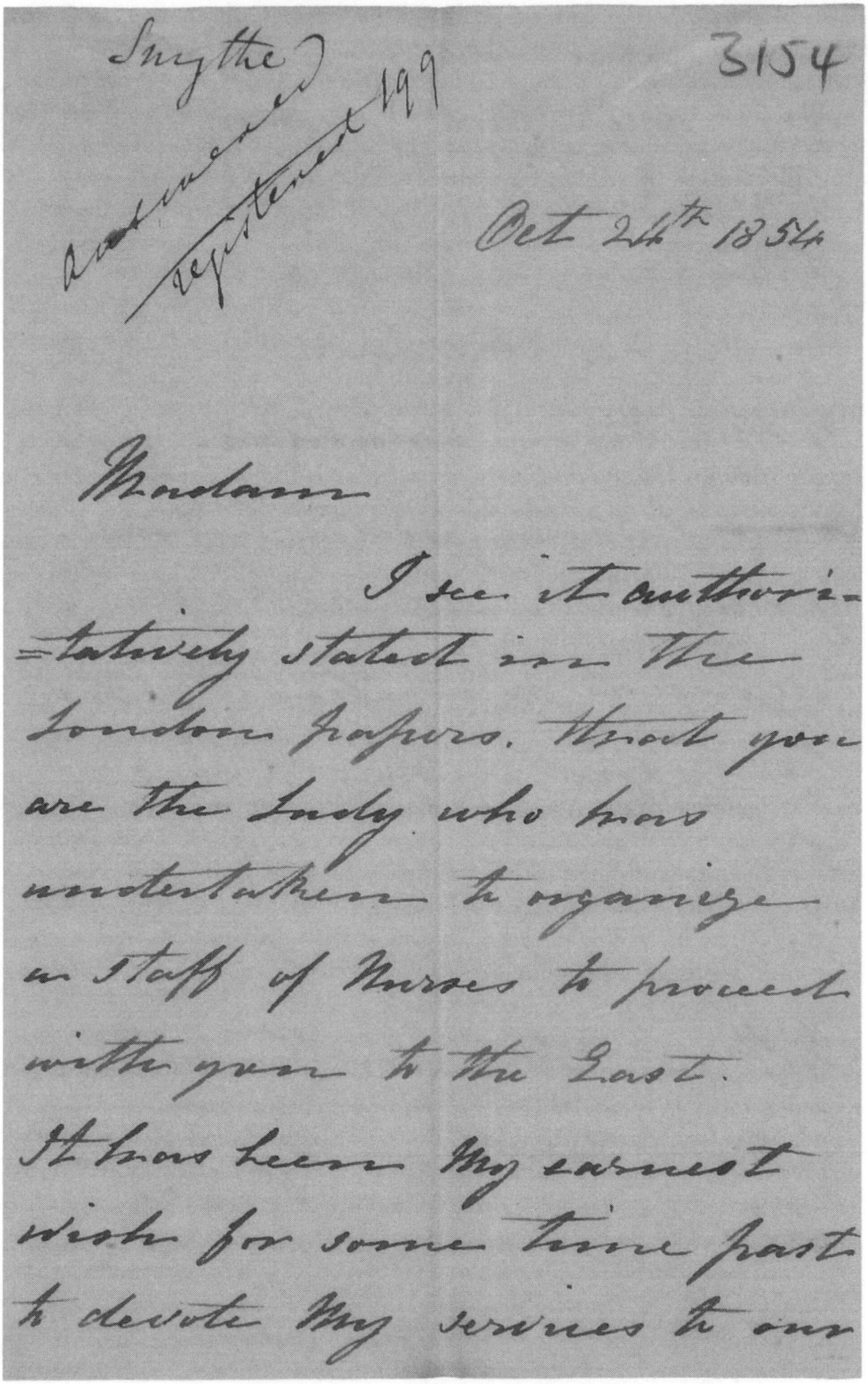

Smythe

answered
registered 199

3154

Oct 24th 1854

Madam

I see it authoritatively stated in the London papers that you are the Lady who has undertaken to organize a Staff of Nurses to proceed with you to the East. It has been my earnest wish for some time past to devote my services to our

Fig. 25 *Nurse's letter offering her services during the Crimean War.* WO 25/264

14.8 Ordnance Office

The Ordnance Office was run separately from the War Office until 1855. It was responsible for the supply of guns, ammunition and warlike stores to the Army. It also controlled the Royal Artillery and the Royal Engineers. A brief administrative history of the Office is in *The Guide to the Public Records* Part 1, section 705 and Michael Roper's *Records of the War Office*. Records relating to the Royal Artillery and the Royal Engineers are described in chapters 5 and 6 respectively.

Registers of employees of the Board of Ordnance, 1811–1847, are in WO 54/511–671. Appointment papers for barrackmasters, clerks and other people employed by the Board between 1819 and 1855 are in WO 54/756–903, 927. Miscellaneous correspondence relating to people employed by the Office is in WO 44/695–700.

Registers of Ordnance pensions being paid in 1834, when responsibility was transferred to the Royal Hospital Chelsea, are in WO 23/141–145.

The monthly Orders of the Army Ordnance Corps, 1901–1919, are in WO 111. These include a great deal about promotions, awards, deaths, discharges and courts martial.

14.9 Ordnance Survey

Between 1790 and 1805, map-making was carried out by civilians working under the direction of Royal Engineer officers. In 1805 the civilians were formed into the Corps of Military Surveyors and Draughtsmen. The Corps was disbanded in 1817 and the previous system reinstated. A card index containing the names of men who served either in the Corps or as civilians is held by the National Archives' Map Department at Kew. The index is based on information in WO 54/208 and other documents, and contains details of appointments and promotions. From 1824 a number of survey companies, initially from the Royal Corps of Sappers and Miners and later from the Royal Engineers, were set up to help with the work of the Survey. It became known as the Ordnance Survey in 1841. The records of these men can be found in exactly the same way as those of other servicemen.

A list of Royal Engineer officers who served in the Survey between 1791 and 1927 is in OS 1/1. A register of soldiers who died while serving with 13 Survey Company between 1829 and 1859 is in OS 3/300. This gives information about the cause of death and disposal of personal effects. OS 1/1/4 contains a list of all Royal Engineers serving with the Survey on 1 July 1890. A register of marriages of men in 16 Survey Company between 1901 and 1929, together with the birth dates of any children, is in OS 3/341. OS 3/275–277 contains seniority lists between 1935 and 1942.

14.10 Royal Marines

Marines were raised in 1664 as land soldiers to serve on ships. Royal Marines were never under the control of the Army, but were always the responsibility of the Royal Navy. As a result, there are very few records relating to the Marines in War Office classes. Marine records of interest to genealogists in Admiralty (ADM) classes are fully described in Garth Thomas's *Records of the Royal Marines* (PRO Readers' Guide No 10, 1994).

14.11 Schools and Colleges

The Duke of York's Royal Military School was founded in 1802 as The Royal Military Asylum for Children of Soldiers of the Regular Army at Chelsea, moving to Dover in 1909. It assumed its present name in 1892. Admission and discharge books for children from 1803 to 1923 are in WO 143/17–25, with an index of admissions, 1910–1958, in WO 143/26. An apprenticeship book for the period 1806 to 1848 is in WO 143/52. Summaries of offences committed by boys, 1852–1879, are in WO 143/53–58. A record of admissions to the School, 1906–1956, is in WO 143/70. Girls were admitted to the female branch until 1840, but this was abolished in 1846.

At first many of the children were not orphans, but the majority of later entrants appear to have lost at least their father and quite frequently both parents. Children appear to have been admitted between the ages of two and ten, and were discharged in their mid-teens. Most of the girls not claimed by their parents were apprenticed, often as servants: the boys went into the Army, or were apprenticed if they were not fit for military service. The admission and discharge registers, 1803–1923, are very informative: they are arranged by date of admission (WO 143/17–26), although one of the boys' registers, for 1804–1820, is in alphabetical order. The information for the girls is the fuller: number, name, age, date of admission, from what regiment, rank of father (P, T, S, etc, for private, trooper, sergeant), parents' names and, if living, parochial settlement, when dismissed, and how disposed of (that is, whether they died, were retained by parents while on leave, apprenticed). The boys' admission register gives the same information with the exception of parents' names. The discharge registers give more information on the child's future—apprenticeship, service in a regiment, etc.

A similar school, the Royal Hibernian Military School, was set up in Ireland in 1769. It was amalgamated with the Duke of York's School in 1924. Many of its records were destroyed by enemy action in 1940. An index of admissions to the School drawn up in 1863, with retrospective entries to *c*.1835 and annotations to approximately 1919, is in WO 143/27.

Records of the Royal Military Academy, Woolwich, which was established in 1741 to train engineer and artillery officers, and the Royal Military College, which was founded in 1799 to train cadets and regimental officers (WO 99, WO 149–WO 151), are available to the public at Sandhurst, where the two institutions were merged in 1947. They may be consulted by arrangement with the Commandant. See *www.sandhurst.mod.uk/tour/archives.htm* for further information.

14.12 Military Intelligence

An Intelligence Branch was established by the War Office in 1873, becoming the Military Intelligence Division in 1887 and Directorate of Military Operations in 1904. Intelligence papers from earlier periods may also survive; the Scovell Papers (WO 37), for example, contain intercepted correspondence and intelligence papers collected by General Scovell as Commander of the Corps of Guides and chief cypher officer in the Peninsular War, and are more fully described in Michael Roper's *Records of the War Office*.

Records concerning military intelligence can be found in WO 106 and WO 208.

A Secret Service Bureau was established in 1909 and records of the counter-intelligence service, which subsequently became MI5, covering the period 1909–1919, are now available in the record class KV 1. These include accounts of payments to members of staff in KV 1/11–12, 69–70 and lists of staff in KV 1/52, 59. Many of its wartime employees were women. These records have been published on CD-ROM, *MI5: The First Ten Years* (PRO, 1998). There are other records in the KV series; of these KV 2, the personal files, are probably the most interesting. KV 2 can be searched by name on the catalogue.

15 PRISONERS OF WAR AND WAR CRIMES

There are few records for men in the British Army who were prisoners before 1914. WO 40/2 contains a list of British and American Prisoners of War (PoWs) drawn up in 1781 with a view to exchange. Other lists are in T 64. Lists and accounts of British PoWs in France and elsewhere for the period between 1793 and 1814, transmitted by the agent for prisoners in Paris, are among the registers of PoWs in ADM 103. They appear, however, to cover largely naval and civilian internees. A list of PoWs at Valenciennes between 1805 and 1813 is in WO 25/2409.

British PoWs taken in the Crimea and by the Boers between 1899 and 1902 are listed in the *London Gazette*, but these lists are incomplete and generally name only officers, arranged under regiments. *The South African Field Force Casualty Roll, 1899–1902*, lists the names and regiments of men captured by the Boers.

15.1 First World War

AIR 1/892 contains lists of British and dominion PoWs held in Germany, Turkey and Switzerland in 1916. A list of British and Dominion Army PoWs in German camps, especially the one at Giessen, in July 1915 is in ADM 1/8420/124.

Interviews and reports of the Committee on the Treatment of British Prisoners of War between 1915 and 1919 are in WO 161/95–101 and these records have been digitized and placed on DocumentsOnline, where it is possible to search by name. Relative to the number of British POWs, there are very few reports in WO 161 and you are most likely not to find a report.

There is a substantial amount about PoWs in the General Correspondence of the Foreign Office (FO 371) and a specific class of records dealing with PoWs (FO 383), although few files relating to individuals survive. The records in FO 383 have been indexed by name and place and it is possible to search for individuals within this series by doing a name search on the Catalogue and by specifying FO 383.

A list of officer PoWs was compiled by the military agents Cox and Co.

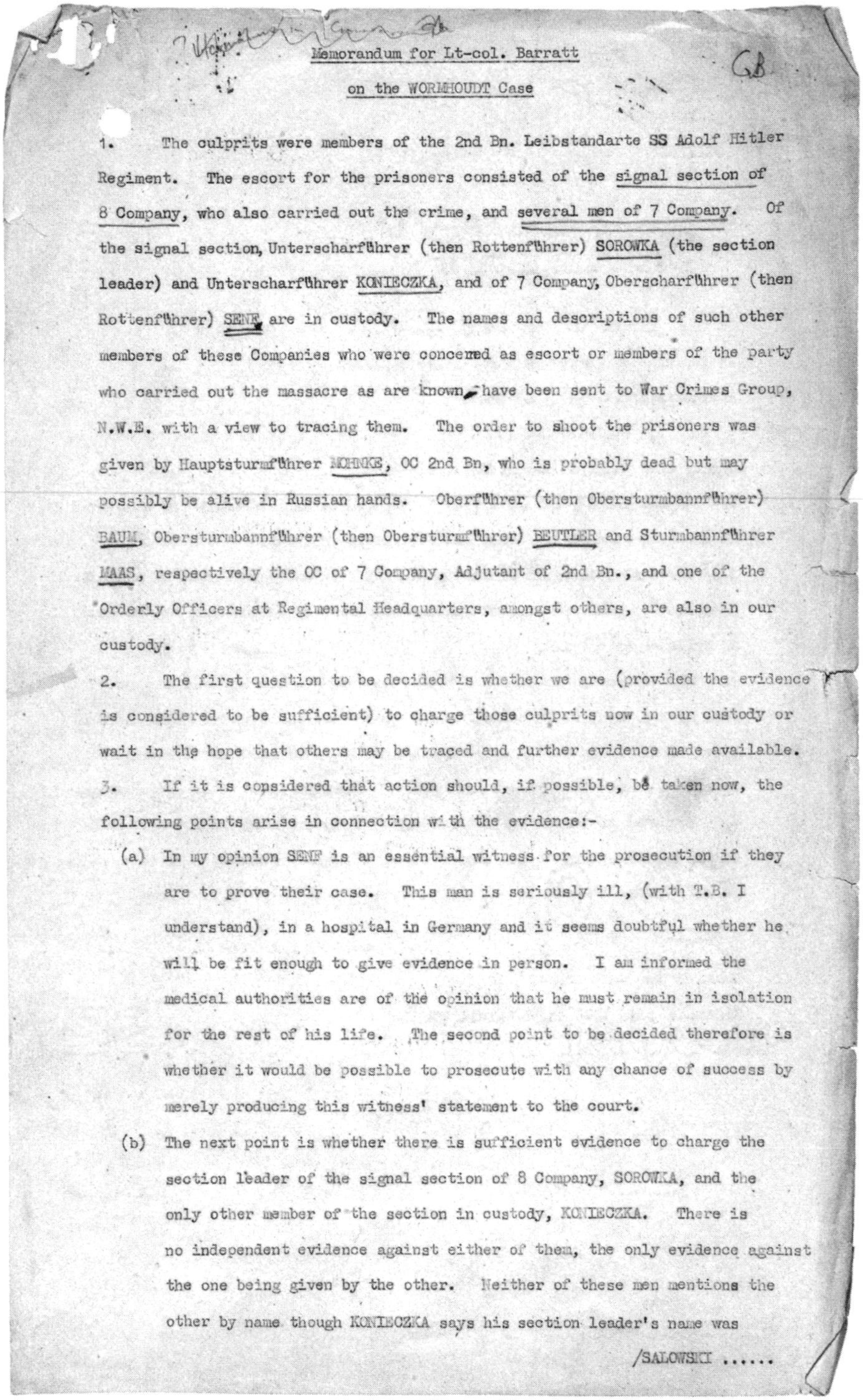

Memorandum for Lt-col. Barratt

on the WORMHOUDT Case

1.   The culprits were members of the 2nd Bn. Leibstandarte SS Adolf Hitler Regiment.   The escort for the prisoners consisted of the signal section of 8 Company, who also carried out the crime, and several men of 7 Company.   Of the signal section, Unterscharführer (then Rottenführer) SOROWKA (the section leader) and Unterscharführer KONIECZKA, and of 7 Company, Oberscharführer (then Rottenführer) SENF are in custody.   The names and descriptions of such other members of these Companies who were concerned as escort or members of the party who carried out the massacre as are known have been sent to War Crimes Group, N.W.E. with a view to tracing them.   The order to shoot the prisoners was given by Hauptsturmführer MOHNKE, OC 2nd Bn, who is probably dead but may possibly be alive in Russian hands.   Oberführer (then Obersturmbannführer) BAUM, Obersturmbannführer (then Obersturmführer) BEUTLER and Sturmbannführer MAAS, respectively the OC of 7 Company, Adjutant of 2nd Bn., and one of the Orderly Officers at Regimental Headquarters, amongst others, are also in our custody.

2.   The first question to be decided is whether we are (provided the evidence is considered to be sufficient) to charge those culprits now in our custody or wait in the hope that others may be traced and further evidence made available.

3.   If it is considered that action should, if possible, be taken now, the following points arise in connection with the evidence:-

(a)   In my opinion SENF is an essential witness for the prosecution if they are to prove their case.   This man is seriously ill, (with T.B. I understand), in a hospital in Germany and it seems doubtful whether he will be fit enough to give evidence in person.   I am informed the medical authorities are of the opinion that he must remain in isolation for the rest of his life.   The second point to be decided therefore is whether it would be possible to prosecute with any chance of success by merely producing this witness' statement to the court.

(b)   The next point is whether there is sufficient evidence to charge the section leader of the signal section of 8 Company, SOROWKA, and the only other member of the section in custody, KONIECZKA.   There is no independent evidence against either of them, the only evidence against the one being given by the other.   Neither of these men mentions the other by name though KONIECZKA says his section leader's name was

/SALOWSKI ......

Fig. 26 *A typical example of a narrative gathered during the investigation of a Second World War war crime.* WO 309/21

in 1919 called a *List of Officers taken prisoner in the various Theatres of War between August 1914 and November 1918*. It was reprinted in 1988 and is available in the library.

Army officers captured during the First World War had to submit a report on the circumstances of their capture when they were repatriated at the end of the war. Many of these reports can be found in their records of service. For further details, see 16.1.2.

15.3   Second World War

WO 392 contains lists of all British and Dominions Prisoners of War (PoWs) held by the Germans and Italians from 1939 to 1945, including the Merchant Navy. A series of three volumes, entitled *Prisoners of War*, containing the names and service details of 169,000 British and Dominions PoWs in German hands on 30 March 1945, can be consulted in the library.

A list of Indian Army PoWs is on the open shelves in the Asia, Pacific and Africa reading room at the British Library.

Information concerning PoWs in Japanese hands is more comprehensive than that for PoWs held by the Germans and Italians. The main source is the card index WO 345. This consists of 57,000 cards of Allied PoWs and civilian internees, arranged alphabetically. Registers of Allied PoWs and civilians held in camps in Singapore can be found in WO 367. WO 347 consists of the hospital records for Allied PoWs held in Asia.

Perhaps the most important PoW records for the Second World War are the records in WO 344, Liberated Prisoner of War Interrogation Questionnaires. This series consists of approximately 140,000 questionnaires completed by mainly British and Commonwealth Prisoners of War of all ranks and services, plus a few other Allied nationals and Merchant seamen. This series is arranged in two collections; prisoners held by the Germans (including those formerly held by the Italians) and prisoners held by the Japanese (see Fig. 33). Each series is then arranged in alphabetical order.

As well as giving personal details (name, rank, number, unit and home address), these records can include the date and place of capture, the main camps and hospitals in which the PoW was imprisoned, work camps, serious illnesses suffered while a prisoner and medical treatment received, interrogation after capture, escape attempts, sabotage, suspicion of collaboration by other Allied prisoners, and details of bad treatment by the enemy to themselves or others. In addition, individuals were given the opportunity to bring to official notice any other matters, such as courageous acts by fellow prisoners or details of civilians who assisted them during escape and evasion activities. Consequently, additional documentation is sometimes attached.

A further alphabetical list of British PoWs in Japan and Japanese occupied territory can be found in WO 392/23–26, while other nominal lists are in FO 916 and CO 980. Escape and Evasion Reports for the Far East can be found in AIR 40/2462 and WO 208/3493–3494. The Interrogation Reports of liberated PoWs from the Far East are in WO 203/5193–5199, 5640 and WO 208/3499.

Information about individuals may occasionally be found among War Office files in WO 32 (code 91), and WO 219/1402, 1448–1474. The War Diary of MI9, the division of Military Intelligence that dealt with escaped prisoners of all services, is in WO 165/39, and its papers are in WO 208. Medical reports on conditions in PoW camps, with some reports on escapes, are among the Medical Historians Papers in WO 222/1352–1393. Further reports and lists of men sometimes occur in the Judge Advocate General's war crimes papers in WO 235, WO 309, WO 310, WO 311, WO 325, WO 331, WO 344, WO 356 and WO 367.

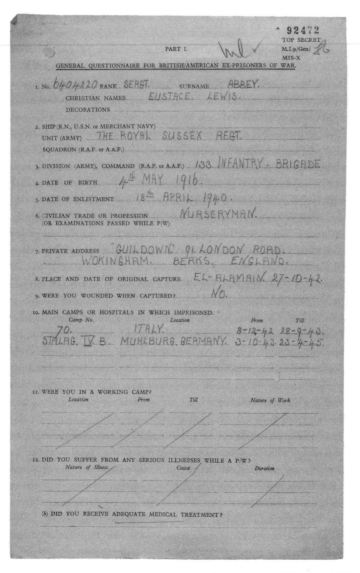

Fig. 27 *Second World War returning PoW Questionnaire.* WO 344/1/1

The International Committee of the Red Cross in Geneva keeps lists of all known PoWs and internees of all nationalities for both world wars. Searches are only made in response to written requests and an hourly fee is charged. Contact the International Council of the Red Cross, Archives Division, 19 Avenue de la Paix, CH-1202, Geneva, Switzerland. Enquiries within the United Kingdom concerning these lists should be sent to: The Director, International Welfare Department, British Red Cross Society, 9 Grosvenor Crescent, London SW1X 7EJ.

15.4   Korea

Lists of British and Commonwealth PoWs of all services, between January 1951 and July 1953, are in WO 208/3999. The Historical Records and Reports on the Korean War in WO 308/54 also contain a list of Commonwealth prisoners compiled in January 1954. General correspondence covering PoWs is in WO 162/208–264, WO 32/19273 and DO 35/5853–5863.

The records in WO 162/208–264 are arranged by the name of the person who completed the questionnaire. The reports were used to find out about any other prisoners.

15.5   War Crimes

Although war crimes may not have affected all service personnel and civilians in both world wars, and in subsequent operations, they remain in the consciousness of many. There are numerous files concerning war crimes covering the investigation of crimes and the prosecution of the perpetrators.

The majority of war crimes files can be found in the series WO 235, WO 309–311 and WO 325.

The records in WO 235 cover war crimes committed all over the world and the best way to search these files is by the name of the defendant(s).

WO 309 contains files concerning crimes committed in North West Europe and WO 310 contains files concerning crimes perpetrated in South East Europe. The files in WO 311 are a general collection created and kept by the Judge Advocate General's Department and these files cover various aspects of war crimes.

War crimes files concerning crimes committed and perpetrated in South East Asia can be found in the series WO 325.

Further information about war crimes can be found in Research Guide Military Records Information 27. An index of war crimes, covering places where such crimes were committed, the names of perpetrators or specifically named incidents such as the Wormhoudt murders, is kept behind the enquiry desk in the Open Reading Room.

Fig. 28 *Second World War War Crimes Investigation: Judge Advocate General's department document listing.* WO 311/34

Register No.   0103/4999/P.W.2.   Minute Sheet No.

S E C R E T

Military Department,
J.A.G.'s Office.

Reference our Loose Minute 0103/4999/P.W.2. dated 19th April, 1945.

1.   Attached is a further series of documents we have recently received from various sources in respect of war crimes against prisoners of war.

2.   These documents have been numbered and classified into German and Italian cases.

3.   The following is a summary of the war crimes concerned.   Suitable references have been made on the documents in those cases where previous action has been traced.

GERMAN CASES	NO.	REFERENCE TO DOCUMENTS
Shooting of French parachutists	1	G SAS 505 - 19/4/45 from 1 B.A.C.
Shooting of 2 American PW.	4	Appr. F to E and E. Report No.451.
Chaining of PW.	8	M.I.9./S/PG(Poland) 1570 - 12/11/43.
Shooting of PW.	9	M.I.9.(b)/47114 - 30/10/42.
Illtreatment of P.M.Desgranges.	10	M.I.9./S/PG(G)1296.
Illtreatment of A.C.I.Gewelber	13	M.I.9./S/PG(G)1917 - 19/5/44.
Shooting of Brig. Clifton	15	M.I.9./REP/C/3/194.
Illegal employment of PW.	17	P.W.2. Interrogation.
Nominal roll of staff of Stalag XX B.	19	Report No.PW1S(H)/LDC/627.
Shooting of PW.	20	M.I.9./UDF/PW/Int/U.K./1821 - 7/3/45.
List of German personalities.	21	AIS/ME/361
Shooting of L/Cpl. Dent	26	P.W.2. Interrogation
Beating of PW.	29	} MFIU PW Intell. Bull 1/57 - 12/4/45.
Shooting of PW	29	}
Illtreatment in E.28	32	AIS/CMF/SKP/4615

Italian Cases:

Illtreatment of PW.	2 & 3	M.I.9./S/PG(It)1935
Shooting of Stewart and Atkinson.	5	} C.S.D.I.C./M.E.)/SKP/346 - 23/3/45.
Illtreatment of Sgt. Pavlidis	5	}
Illtreatment of Ross & Buchan	6	Report No.I.24 - 6/11/43
Shooting of PW.	7	DC/N)16/86/42 - 7/1/43
Illtreatment of Sgt. Barker	11	Report I.31 - 27/11/43
PW stoned by Italian civilians.	12	CSDIC/AFHQ/NA/E.3 - 30/12/43
Illtreatment of PW.	14	CSDIC/AFHQ/SKP/108 - 11/6/44.
Assault on Playne and Cooke	16	MI9/REP/IT/349 - 11/2/44.
Shooting of Tpr. Aarons.	18	P.W.2. Interrogation
Illtreatment of Naval PW.	22	P.W.2.Interrogation
Beating of Robson	23	P.W.2.Interrogation
Treatment of PW in Camp 21.	24	P.W.2.Interrogation
Manacling of PW.	25	K.W.24/5 - 12/2/43 from F.O.
Beating of Lt. Millar	27	M.I.9./S/PG(G)1716.
Shooting of PW	28	I.S.9./WEA/2/17/810/2576.
Illtreatment of Gnr. Whitehead	30	P9/11 - 21/9/44 from I.S.9. (Med.)
Shooting of Cpl. Cymonds	31	AIS/CMF/SKP/4581-7 - 26/3/45.

P.W.2.
Curzon Street House.
MAYfair 9400/Ext.618.
26 April, 1945.

for D.A.A.G.

(5243) Wt 10554/5806 400m 5/40 BPL 51/6860 J4750   [P.T. Over

16 FIRST WORLD WAR

The exact number of men who served as other ranks during the First World War is difficult to calculate. At the outbreak of the war, the British Army numbered approximately 250,000 including all ranks, regulars and reserves. Interestingly, this figure is very close to the total number of commissions granted during the war. Sources state that some 5.4 million men served in the British Army on the Western Front and some 3.6 million served in other theatres. However, many men served in more than one operational theatre and some in three or more.

The best introduction to records in the National Archives relating to an individual's service in World War I is *First World War Army Service Records* by W. Spencer (TNA, 4th ed. 2008). This includes illustrations of the types of document you are likely to find, which include attestation papers, discharge papers, medical records and casualty forms. You may also find *World War I Army Ancestry* by Norman Holding and Iain Swinnerton useful. Holding has also written *More Sources of World War I Army Ancestry* and *The Location of British Army records: a National Directory of World War I Sources*.

A valuable introduction to the organization of the Army in the First World War is *British Army Handbook, 1914–1918* by Andrew Rawson, (Sutton, 2006). The best single-volume guide to the battlefields of France and Flanders during the First World War is *Before Endeavours Fade* by Rose Coombs.

16.1 Service Records

Although millions of men saw service in the British Army during the First World War, not all of the records are available. Many records of service were destroyed by enemy action in 1940, but others are still retained by the Ministry of Defence. The following sections describe what is available.

16.1.1 *Other ranks*

The majority of service records for other ranks who were discharged from the Army by the end of 1920 were destroyed by enemy bombing in September 1940. The records relating to some 2.75 million men do survive in the records series WO 363 and WO 364. However, between the two records series there is a certain amount of duplication and indeed there are cases of men having more than one record in the same series.

The records described here only relate to men who were discharged or died between 1914 and 1920. They may include records relating to regular soldiers who first joined the Army in the late nineteenth century, but they will not contain the records of those who continued to serve after 1920 or who transferred to one of the other services, taking their service record with them. It has been estimated that you have about a 40 per cent chance of finding the service records of a particular soldier who served in the First World War.

To find a surviving service record, it is useful to know the man's full name, his rank, service number and regiment. If you do not have this information, you can get it from the First World War Medal Index cards described in section 16.4. Bear in mind that he may have served in more than one regiment and had more than one service number, and that there may be several individuals with exactly the same forenames and surnames.

The surviving First World War service records are preserved in two record classes, both of which are available only on microfilm.

The records in WO 364, sometimes known as the 'Unburnt Records', are a collection of some 750,000 individual records of service. If your soldier survived and received a pension, start with WO 364. Alphabetically arranged, they relate to those discharged on medical or other grounds and to regular soldiers who were discharged at the end of their period of service and were awarded a pension. Men who had signed up for the duration normally only received a gratuity on demobilization, not a pension, unless they were awarded one on medical grounds.

The records of approximately 2,000,000 individuals are being transferred into the record class WO 363. The records in WO 363 include men who completed their service as well as those who were killed or who died of wounds, or were executed. Unlike WO 364, which is arranged in a number of logical alphabetical sequences, WO 363 is arranged initially by first letter of the surname A–Z; then you need to look at the paper name indexes in order to find out which reel of microfilm contains the name you are searching for. You may find that the surname you are looking for in WO 363 is spread across a number of reels of microfilm, not necessarily in numerical order.

WO 364 and WO 363 have, or are being, digitized and put onto the *www.ancestry.co.uk* website, where it is possible to search by name, place or birth, regiment and regimental number (WO 363 only) and year of birth. While being able to search for a specific individual by computer is a great advance, the Ancestry website requires skilled use to extract the information you seek.

Although there is a separate series for records of service for Royal Flying Corps (RFC) other ranks (see below), the records of other ranks of the RFC may also be found in WO 363 or WO 364, especially if they were discharged before 1 April 1918.

The records of service of members of the Household Battalion can be found in WO 400/286–301. These records cover the period 1916–1919 and the majority relate to men who died in service or who were invalided from the army.

16.1.2 Officers

The records of service of some 217,737 officers who saw service during the First World War, including all branches of the Army and the Royal Flying Corps, are in the record classes WO 339 (with an index in WO 338) and WO 374.

WO 374 is the smaller class, containing some 77,829 records, and mostly relates to those who were commissioned into the Territorial Army or had a temporary commission. It is arranged alphabetically and the class list gives a full list of names. Many of the original War Office references for the papers in this series take the form of the first letter of the surname and the first vowel of the surname of the officer, and then a number. These references are known as 'Vowel' references and you may find them in the indexes in WO 338. A vowel reference for an officer called Green would thus be 'GE 123'—the G being the first letter of the surname and the E being the first vowel.

WO 339 contains the service records of 139,908 officers, arranged by 'long number'. You must identify this 'long number' by using the alphabetical index of names in WO 338, which is seen on microfilm. Service records should be found here if the officer ceased serving before 1922 and was a pre-war regular officer, was commissioned into the Special Reserve of officers or was given an Emergency Commission in the regular Army.

The service records of a few notable individuals, such as Sir Douglas Haig and Wilfred Owen, are in WO 138.

For further information about the records described in sections 16.1.1 and 16.1.2, together with details about other records relating to the First World War, see 3.5.3 and *First World War Army Service Records* by W. Spencer (TNA, 4th ed. 2008).

16.1.3 Records of service after 1920

The records of those men who saw service after 1920 (other ranks) and 1921 (officers) are not yet in the public domain. The contact point for further information is:

Ministry of Defence
Army Personnel Centre
Historic Disclosures
Mailpoint 400
Kentigern House
65 Brown Street
Glasgow G2 8EX

Further information can be obtained from *www.veterans-uk.info*.

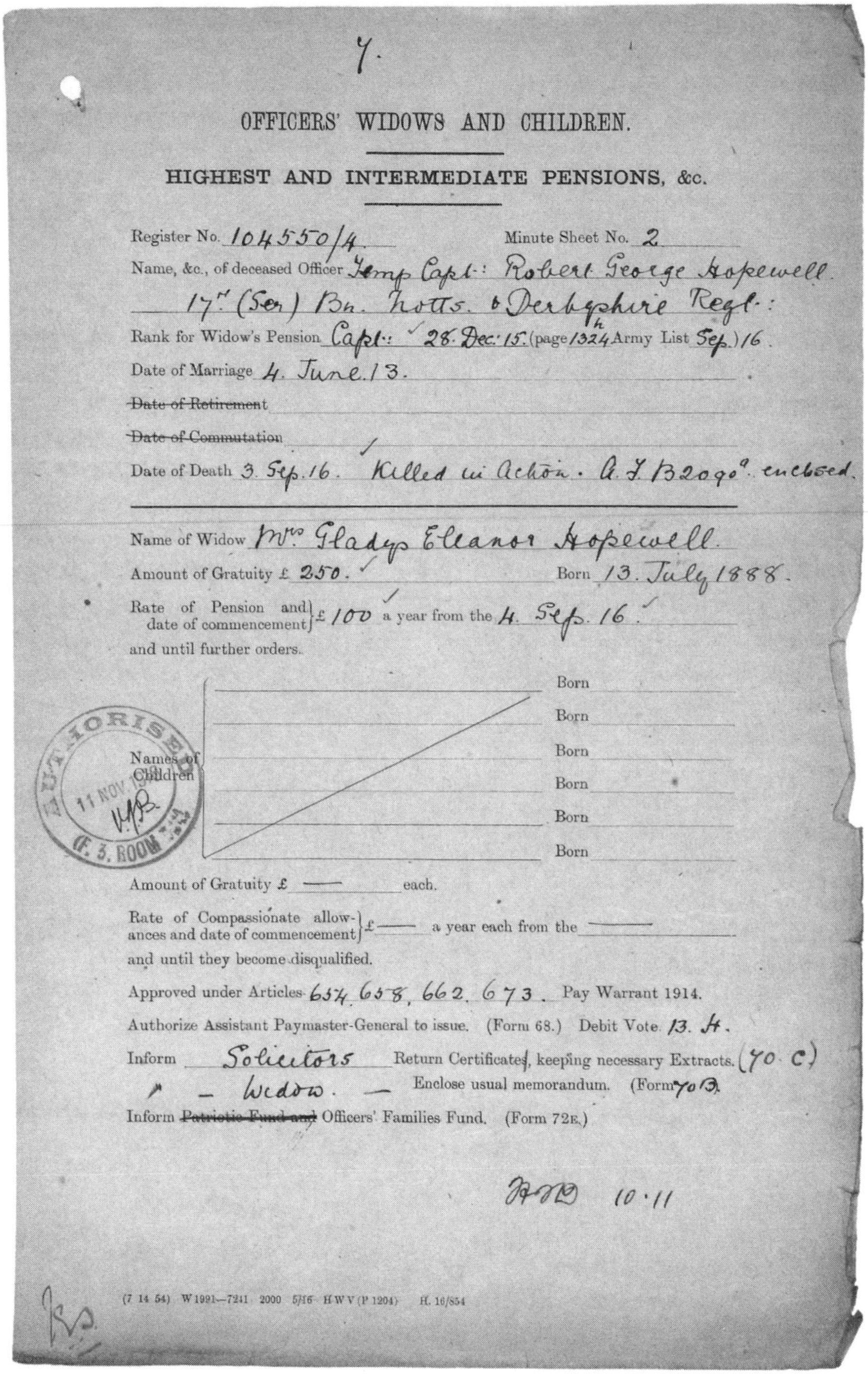

OFFICERS' WIDOWS AND CHILDREN.

HIGHEST AND INTERMEDIATE PENSIONS, &c.

Register No. *104550/4*   Minute Sheet No. *2*

Name, &c., of deceased Officer *Temp Capt: Robert George Hopewell*
17ᵗ (Ser) Bn. Notts. & Derbyshire Regt:

Rank for Widow's Pension *Capt: 28. Dec. 15.* (page *1324* Army List *Sep.) 16.*

Date of Marriage *4. June. 13.*

~~Date of Retirement~~

~~Date of Commutation~~

Date of Death *3. Sep. 16.   Killed in Action. A.F.B2090ᵃ enclosed.*

Name of Widow *Mrs Gladys Eleanor Hopewell.*

Amount of Gratuity £ *250.*   Born *13. July 1888.*

Rate of Pension and date of commencement £ *100* a year from the *4. Sep. 16.*
and until further orders.

Names of Children		Born
		Born
		Born
		Born
		Born
		Born

Amount of Gratuity £ ———— each.

Rate of Compassionate allowances and date of commencement £ ——— a year each from the ————
and until they become disqualified.

Approved under Articles *654. 658. 662. 673.* Pay Warrant 1914.

Authorize Assistant Paymaster-General to issue. (Form 68.) Debit Vote *13. 4.*

Inform *Solicitors* Return Certificates, keeping necessary Extracts. *(70. C)*
  " — *Widow.* — Enclose usual memorandum. (Form *70 B.*)

Inform ~~Patriotic Fund and~~ Officers' Families Fund. (Form 72E.)

10. 11

(7 14 54) W1991—7241. 2000 5/16 H W V (P 1204) H. 16/854

Fig. 29 *Pension sheet found in the file of a First World War officer who was killed in action.* WO 339/37823

16.2 Casualty Records

A list, arranged by regiment, of men who died during the war, was published in *Soldiers Died in the Great War* (80 vols, HMSO, 1921). There is a similar volume for officers who died during the war. Microfilmed copies of these publications are kept in the Open Reading Room.

Soldiers Died in the Great War has been turned into a CD-ROM, access to which is available via electronic resources on the internal TNA website. It is possible to search by name, regimental number, date of death, unit and operational theatre.

Another good source for the names of dead officers is the *Cross of Sacrifice* series by S. and B. Jarvis, which covers all the armed services. Copies are available in the library.

A roll of honour for men of the London Stock Exchange who served in the forces is kept in the library. Lists of employees of the Midland Railway who were either wounded or killed in action are in RAIL 491/1259. A similar roll of honour for men of the London, Brighton and South Coast Railway is in RAIL 414/761 and for the North Eastern Railway in RAIL 527/993.

French and Belgian death certificates for British soldiers who died in hospitals or elsewhere outside the immediate war zone between 1914 and 1920 are in RG 35/45–69. They are arranged by first letter of surname and can be informative, but are in French or Flemish.

A list of men killed or wounded during the Easter Rising in Dublin in 1916 is in WO 35/69.

The Commonwealth War Graves Commission records all soldiers who died, or who were reported missing in action, during the war. It is possible to search by name the Commission's 'Debt of Honour' database via *www.cwgc.org*. Their records indicate the unit with which the soldier was serving and his place of burial. Their address is: Commonwealth War Graves Commission, 2 Marlow Road, Maidenhead SL6 7DX.

16.3 Medical and Disability Records

A selection of case files, covering a cross-section of disability pensions awarded after the First World War, is in PIN 26. PIN 26 is arranged in a number of different sequences and by different sub-series; it is, however, possible to search the series by name on the catalogue. Many of the reasons for discharge are listed in the piece description for each file, the most common being GSW (Gun Shot Wound) and VDH (Valve Disease of the Heart). A full list of these abbreviations can be found in the paper PIN 26 catalogue.

MH 106 contains a specimen collection of admission and discharge registers from hospitals, casualty clearing stations and the like. The class also contains some medical cards for individuals, including the Queen Mary's Auxiliary Army Corps (see 16.8).

Ledgers showing the payment of disability retired pay during and after

```
Reference: 4/MC/186.                                    12th May, 1953.

                            John Reginald Christie

                       Extracts from Medical War Records.


Army Form W.3162.
35th General Hospital, France.    Serial No. in A. & D. Book: 13295.    Ward 1.
Regt. or Corps:                   2/6 Nottinghamshire & Derbyshire Regiment.
Troop, Battery or Coy:            4 M.B. Depot.
Regimental No:                    106733.
Rank:                             Private.
Name:                             Christie, J.
Age:                              20.
Total Service:                    16 months.
Service with Field Force:         3 months.
Date of admission:                28. 6.18.
Date of transfer to E.D.          29. 7.18.
No. of days under treatment:      32.

Disease: Catarrhal Laryngitis.
Date of onset of disease:  3 weeks.
Treatment: Mist. expectorant - three times a day.  Inhalations of Menthol.
10.7.18 - Rept.
Treatment: Mist. expectorant - three times a day.  Inhalations of Menthol.
Hoarseness   ?        after 1 month.
Some pharyngitis.
Stoke War Hospital, T.8098.  30.7.18 to 8.8.18 - Shell Gas.
Transferred to Kings Lancashire Military Convalescent Hospital, Blackpool.

Army Form W.3243A.
Kings Lancashire Military Convalescent Hospital, Blackpool:  "C" Division.
Serial No. in A. & D. Book:  T.F.6093.
Regiment:                         2/6 Nottinghamshire & Derbyshire Regiment.
Troop, Battery or Company:        D.
Regimental No:                    106733.
Rank:                             Sig.
Name:                             Christie, J.R.
Age:                              19.
Total Service:                    1 year 6 months.
Service with Field Force:         6 months.
As a transfer from 8.8.18 - Stoke War Hospital.
Date of discharge to duty: 27.8.18.
No. of days under treatment:      19.

Disease:   Shell Gassed.
Improved - Physical Training.     Furlough, and duty.
```

Fig. 30 *Statement of service for John Christie provided by the Ministry of Pensions.* PIN 26/16679

the First World War are in PMG 42. This series only covers the period 1917–1920 and is arranged by date of award and in alphabetical order.

Ledgers for supplementary allowances and special grants to officers, their widows and dependents between 1916 and 1920 are in PMG 43. Those for pensions to relatives of deceased officers for a similar period are in PMG 44. Widows' pensions in PMG 45 are arranged by date the pension was authorized and in alphabetical order by name.

Paymaster General children's allowances are in PMG 46 and arranged by date of grant and in alphabetical order by name of officer. Pay to relatives of missing officers between 1915 and 1920 are recorded in PMG 47.

16.4 Medal Rolls

The medal rolls for 1914 Star, 1914–1915 Star, British War Medal, Victory Medal, Territorial Force War Medal, and Silver War Badge are in WO 329. These campaign medals were awarded to officers and other ranks of the Army, including nurses, and to the Royal Flying Corps.

The card index for WO 329 is in the record class WO 372, which is on microfiche in the Open Reading Room and is also available on Documents-Online. Known as the Medal Index Cards, this index covers all those who received First World War Campaign medals and the Silver War Badge. These cards are arranged by name first and then each name is arranged in regimental order of precedence.

A Medal Index Card records the surname and forename(s) or initial(s) of the recipient. It also records the rank(s), regiment/corps, regimental number(s), first operational theatre and the date they arrived in that theatre and the medals they earned. Alongside the names of the medals earned there should be the original Army Medal Office roll references. These references need to be converted in WO 329 references before you can order the actual medal roll(s). There is guidance on how to do the conversion in the Open Reading Room.

The rolls themselves give the unit in which the man served, his service number, the theatres of war he served in, and the medals to which he was entitled. In most cases, the card index contains as much information as the medal roll. For those who received a British War Medal and Victory Medal only, it may be worthwhile looking at the roll as, in the case of an infantry regiment, it may tell you which battalion the man served in.

Card indexes are also available in the Open Reading Room to recipients of the following gallantry medals: Distinguished Conduct Medal (DCM), Meritorious Service Medal (MSM), and Military Medal (MM), and to individuals Mentioned in Despatches (MiD). The cards give a reference to the *London Gazette* in which the award was gazetted. Sometimes a full citation was printed in the *Gazette* for the Distinguished Conduct Medal. Very rarely a citation is given in full for the award of the Military Medal, and in most cases they were for awards to women or for awards announced in late 1919 or early 1920. Copies of the *London Gazette* are in ZJ 1.

All of the above-mentioned card indexes have been digitized and placed on DocumentsOnline and it possible to search for an index card for the campaign medals and Silver War Badge as well as for the DCM, MM, MSM and MiDs. Searching of these cards can be done by name, number or regiment. See Chapter 21 for further advice.

Supplements to the Monthly *Army Lists* contain lists of recipients of medals, but give no date or reason for the award. Lists of foreign awards to individuals are also included. Some records of these awards are in FO 371 and FO 372. Complete lists of all recipients of medals are given in the Supplements to the Monthly *Army Lists* during 1919.

16.5 War Diaries

From 1907, units on active service were required by the Field Service Regulations Part II to keep a daily record of events. These records were called War Diaries or, occasionally, Intelligence Summaries. The diaries contain daily reports on operations, intelligence reports and other pertinent material. A substantial number of maps, once included in these diaries, have been extracted and are now in WO 153. Many diaries are difficult to read because they were often scribbled in pencil in haste, using abbreviations that are now difficult to decipher, or they may be the third copy of a triplicate.

Most war diaries are in WO 95. Certain diaries containing particularly confidential material are in WO 154, the most frequent being information relating to discipline and courts martial.

WO 95 is arranged into the different operational theatre sections and then in a strict hierarchy, with GHQ coming first.

The WO 95 sections are:

I	France and Flanders
II	Italy
III	Gallipoli and Dardanelles
IV	Egypt, Palestine and Syria
V	Salonika, Macedonia, Turkey, Black Sea, Caucasus and South Russia
VI	Mesopotamia, Iraq and North Russia
VII	East Africa, West Africa and Cameroon
VIII	India and East Persia
IX	North Persia and Siberia
X	Colonies: Aden, Bermuda, Ceylon, Hong Kong, North China, Gibraltar Malta, Mauritius and Singapore
XI	Home Forces

It is possible to search WO 95 by unit on the catalogue. Many units served in more than one operational theatre, so you may get more than one result. In order to ascertain which diary you require, look at the date descriptions very carefully.

Some of the diaries in WO 95 have been digitized and are available on DocumentsOnline.

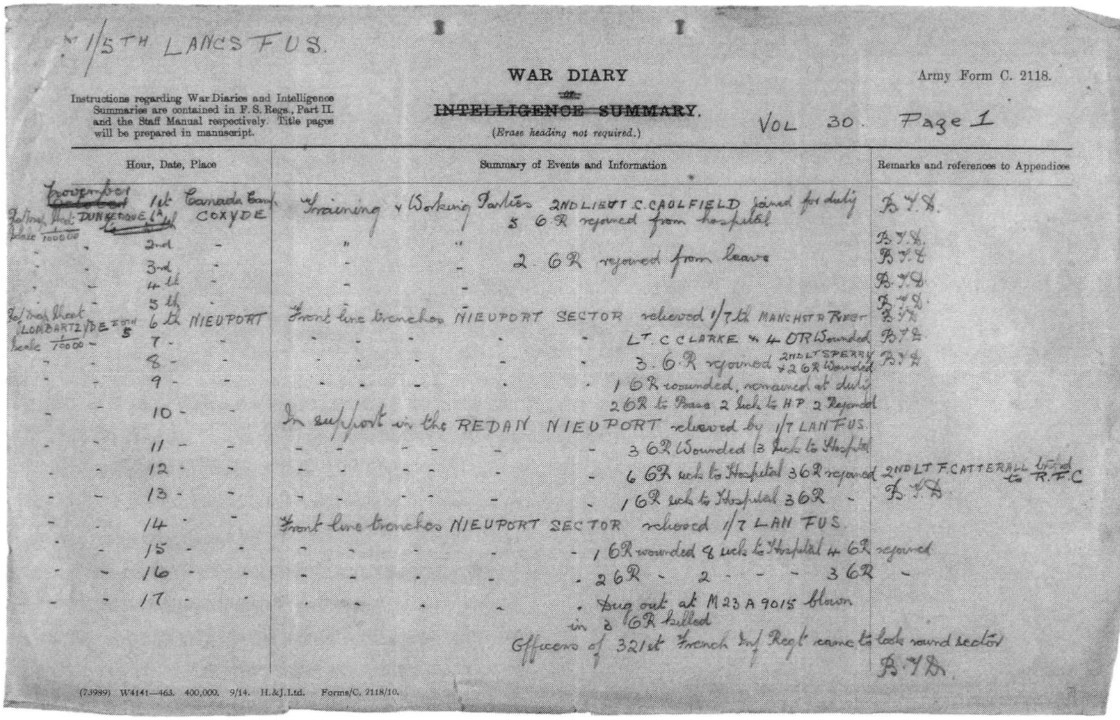
1/5TH LANCS FUS.

WAR DIARY or ~~INTELLIGENCE SUMMARY.~~ (Erase heading not required.)

Army Form C. 2118.

Instructions regarding War Diaries and Intelligence Summaries are contained in F. S. Regs., Part II. and the Staff Manual respectively. Title pages will be prepared in manuscript.

VOL 30. Page 1

Hour, Date, Place	Summary of Events and Information	Remarks and references to Appendices
November 1st Canada Camp COXYDE	Training & Working Parties 2ND LIEUT C.CAULFIELD joined for duty 5 OR rejoined from hospital	B.Y.D.
2nd	" "	B.Y.D.
3rd	2 OR rejoined from leave	B.Y.D.
4th	-	B.Y.D.
5th		B.Y.D.
6th NIEUPORT	Front line trenches NIEUPORT SECTOR relieved 1/7th MANCHSTR Regt	B.Y.D.
7	LT. C CLARKE & 4 OR Wounded	B.Y.D.
8	3 OR rejoined 2ND LT SPERRY & 2 OR Wounded	B.Y.D.
9	1 OR wounded, remained at duty 2 OR to Base 2 sick to HP 2 Rejoined	
10	In support in the REDAN NIEUPORT relieved by 1/7 LAN FUS.	
11	3 OR Wounded 13 sick to Hospital	
12	6 OR sick to Hospital 3 OR rejoined	2ND LT F.CATTERALL transd to R.F.C
13	1 OR sick to Hospital 3 OR -	B.Y.D.
14	Front line trenches NIEUPORT SECTOR relieved 1/7 LAN FUS.	
15	1 OR wounded 8 sick to Hospital 4 OR rejoined	
16	2 OR - 2 - - - 3 OR -	
17	Dug out at M23A 9015 blown in 3 OR killed. Officers of 321st French Inf Regt came to look round sector	B.Y.D.

(73989) W4141—463. 400,000. 9/14. H.&J.Ltd. Forms/C. 2118/10.

Fig. 31 *Typical First World WarWar Diary.* WO 95/2654

The diaries are those of most British and colonial units serving in theatres of operations between 1914 and 1922.

Provided that the unit is known, these war diaries can be a useful way of fleshing out the career of a man during the war. It is unusual, however, for a war diary to mention individuals, unless they are officers or NCOs. The example illustrated as Fig. 31 records the wounding in action of Lieutenant C. Clarke. Periods of combat are also likely to be described only in brief, and deaths of men or examples of gallantry may not be mentioned. You can trace where a unit served through the Orders of Battle in WO 95/5467–5493 or by consulting the published *Order of Battle* by Becke, which is available in the Open Reading Room.

16.6   Royal Flying Corps

From 1914 until the creation of the Royal Air Force on 1 April 1918, the Royal Flying Corps (RFC), which had been established in 1912, was part of the Army. Many men were recruited into the RFC from other parts of the Army. A selection of RFC squadron, and other unit, records is in AIR 1. They can contain a great deal of valuable information about individuals, especially officers and aircrew, but only a relatively small number survive.

The records of service of RFC airmen with service numbers 329, 000 or lower can be found in AIR 79. If they went on to see service in the Second World War, their records are still held by the RAF at:

RAF Disclosures Section
Room 221b
Trenchard Hall
RAF Cranwell
Sleaford
Lincolnshire
NG34 8HB
Tel: 01400 261201
Ext 6711
Ext 8161/8159 (Officers)
Ext 8163/8168/8170 (Other ranks).

Records of RFC officers can be found in WO 339 and WO 374; see 16.1.2 for further details. Records of RFC officers who went into the RAF and who did not see service after 1922 can be found in the class AIR 76, which is available in the Open Reading Room.

Records of RFC units and formations will also be found in AIR 23, AIR 25 and AIR 27–AIR 29, with a small selection of early flying log books in AIR 4.

There is a muster roll of other ranks serving in the RFC on 1 April 1918 in AIR 1/819. Another copy is in AIR 10/232–237. There are several series of casualty reports from the Western Front for the period April 1916 to November 1918 in AIR 1/843–860, 914–916 and 960–969. Medals awarded to RFC personnel are in WO 329. For further details, see 16.4. Officers are also listed in the *Army Lists*.

Casualty record cards for men of the RFC, killed or wounded during the war, are held by the RAF Museum, Hendon, London NW9 5LL. For further information about these records, see *www.rafmuseum.org.uk/london/research/index.cfm*.

16.7   Conscientious Objectors

After the introduction of conscription in 1915–1916 men could appeal against Army service through the Military Service Tribunals. Most records of these tribunals were destroyed after the war. Records for the Middlesex Service Tribunal were preserved, however, and now are in MH 47, and records of a few other Tribunals are held at local record offices.

16.8   Women in the War

As the war progressed, women came to do a number of the jobs previously done by men, such as driving, although they did not take part in actual combat. Correspondence about the employment of women in the Army is to be found in WO 32 (code 68) and WO 162/30–73. These papers contain very little of a genealogical nature.

The Women's Army Auxiliary Corps (WAAC) was formed in 1917 and became the Queen Mary's Auxiliary Army Corps in May 1918. An incomplete nominal roll for the Corps is in WO 162/16. A list of women motor drivers employed in the Women's Army Auxiliary Corps during the war is in WO 162/62. Recommendations for honours are in WO 162/65. War diaries for the Corps in France between 1917 and 1919 are in WO 95/84–85. The records of service of members of the WAAC are on microfilm in the record class WO 398. The series is arranged in alphabetical order and has been digitized and placed on DocumentsOnline where you can search by name.

The records in WO 398 are quite similar to the records of British Army other ranks and in many cases the forms are identical. The records contain basic biographical information, when and where born, where the individual served and how they were employed.

Many women served as nurses or otherwise helped in hospitals or elsewhere in the medical services. Records of nurses are described in section 14.7 above. Lists of nurses arriving in France during the war are given in WO 95/3982.

The records of service of nurses from the First World War who served in the Queen Alexandra's Imperial Military Nursing Service (QAIMNS), Queen Alexandra's Imperial Military Nursing Service Reserve (QAIMNSR) or the Territorial Force Nursing Service (TFNS) can be found in the series wo 399. The service is arranged in two alphabetical sequences: the QAIMNS and QAIMNSR together and then the TFNS. It is possible to search WO 399 by name on the Catalogue.

The records in WO 399 contain basic biographical information about each nurse, where she trained, where she served, when her service military started and ended. Unlike the other First World War records of service, the nurses' records contain quite detailed and illuminating personal reports about the subject individual.

Some medical sheets for members of the Voluntary Aid Detachment (VAD) and Queen Mary's Auxiliary Ambulance Corps during the First World War are in MH 106/2207–2211. Registers of disability and retired pay between 1917 and 1919 are in PMG 42/1–12.

Records of the VAD are held by the British Record Cross at: British Red Cross Museum and Archives, 44 Moorfields, London EC2Y 9AL. Tel: 020 7877 7058, *www.redcross.org.uk.*

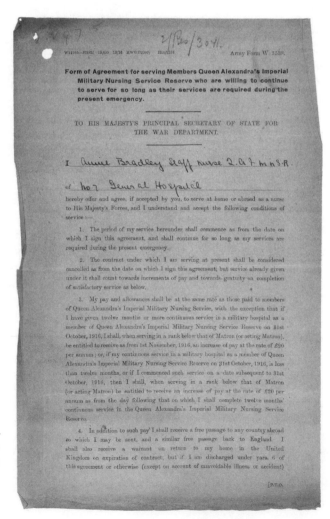

Fig. 32 *Queen Alexandra's Imperial Military Nursing Service: Form of Agreement to serve from the First World War.* WO 399/8499

17 SECOND WORLD WAR

The events of the Second World War affected more people than those of the First World War. More people were involved in the war effort and more of the civilian population were on the receiving end of enemy action, for example through air raids or war crimes.

Frustratingly for researchers, the records of service of military personnel who participated in the Second World War are still retained by the Ministry of Defence and consequently the majority of records in the public domain relate to operations, war crimes, awards for gallantry and meritorious service, and casualties.

17.1 Service Records

The records of service of officers who served after 1921 and other ranks who were discharged after 1920 are still retained by the Ministry of Defence. Only the subject individual and their next of kin may apply for copies. The contact points are:

Ministry of Defence
Army Personnel Centre
Historic Disclosures
Mailpoint 400
Kentigern House
65 Brown Street
Glasgow
G2 8EX

Further information can be obtained from *www.veterans-uk.info*.

17.2 Casualty Returns

Retrospective registers of deaths from enemy action in the Far East between 1941 and 1945 are in RG 33/11, 132, with an index in RG 43/14. The Army Roll of Honour for men and women who died during the war is in WO 304. This roll has been digitized and is available on CD-Rom and can be accessed via the online and published resources section from the internal TNA user's website. It is possible to search the digitized version of WO 304 by name, number or unit.

The Commonwealth War Graves Commission records all service personnel and many civilians who died, or who were reported missing in action, during the Second World War. For details, see 16.2.

17.3 War Diaries and other operational records

These usually give a much fuller description of the units' activities than their counterparts of the First World War. They often include a detailed narrative of the operations of the unit, together with daily orders, maps and other miscellaneous material. It is unusual for the diaries to contain details about the deaths of, or acts of bravery by, individual men, especially those serving in the ranks. Lists of officers are frequently included.

The war diaries are arranged as follows:

Theatre of operation/force	Class
British Expeditionary Force (France,1939–1940)	WO 167
Central Mediterranean Forces (Italy and Greece, 1943–1946)	WO 170
Dominion Forces	WO 179
GHQ Liaison Regiment	WO 215
Home Forces	WO 166
Madagascar	WO 174
Medical services (hospitals, field ambulances etc)	WO 177
Middle East Forces (Egypt, Libya, invasion of Sicily and Italy)	WO 169
Military missions	WO 178
North Africa (Tunisia and Algeria, 1941–1943)	WO 175
North West Expeditionary Force (Norway, 1940)	WO 168
North West Europe (France, Belgium, Holland and Germany, 1944–1946)	WO 171
South-East Asia (India, Burma, Malaya)	WO 172
Special Services	WO 218
Various smaller theatres	WO 176
War Office Directorates	WO 165
West Africa	WO 173

Orders of Battle in WO 212 show where units served. A published copy is available at the Open Reading Room desk.

17.4 Home Guard

The National Archives currently holds few papers about the Home Guard, or Local Defence Volunteers as it was first known.

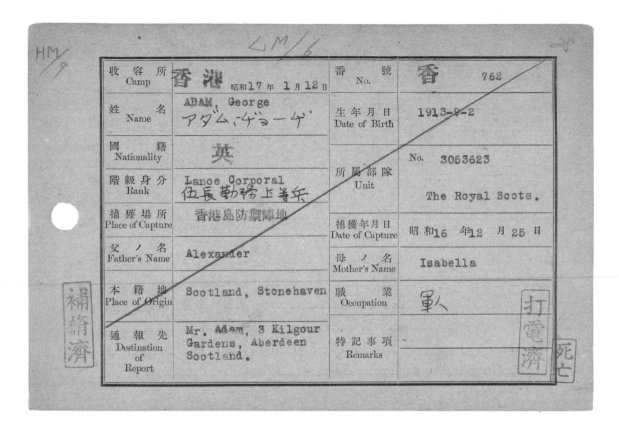

収 容 所 Camp 香港 昭和17 年 1 月 12 日
番 號 No. 香 762

姓 名 Name ADAM, George アダム、ヂョーヂ
生 年 月 日 Date of Birth 1913-8-2

國 籍 Nationality 英

階 級 身 分 Rank Lance Corporal 伍長勤務上等兵
所 屬 部 隊 Unit No. 3053623 The Royal Scots.

捕 獲 場 所 Place of Capture 香港島防禦陣地

父 ノ 名 Father's Name Alexander
捕 獲 年 月 日 Date of Capture 昭和16 年12 月25 日

本 籍 地 Place of Origin Scotland, Stonehaven
母 ノ 名 Mother's Name Isabella

通 報 先 Destination of Report Mr. Adam, 3 Kilgour Gardens, Aberdeen Scotland.
職 業 Occupation 軍人

特 記 事 項 Remarks

Fig. 33 *Japanese (created) PoW record card from the Second World War.* WO 345/1

A surviving complete run of the *Home Guard List,* listing all of the officers serving in the Home Guard, is available in the Open Reading Room. Each of these volumes contains lists, by region, of the officers in each unit of the Home Guard and each list has a name index. The date alongside the name of each officer is the date of commission in that rank, as announced in Home Guard Orders and these can be found in WO 123/464.

The *Home Guard List* is arranged under the following regional headings:

Anti Aircraft Command (October 1944 only)
Eastern Command
London District
Northern Command
Scottish Command
Southern Command
South Eastern Command
Western Command

Each entry in the *Home Guard List* can tell a lot about a unit and where in a given region they were based and served. This information can then be put to use looking for records in WO 199 or in local archives.

A manuscript list of Home Guard officers almost identical to the lists mentioned above and compiled in 1944 is in WO 199/3212–3217.

WO 199 also contains other records about the Home Guard. Of these, perhaps the most important are the unit histories. Many of the unit histories contain not only narrative but some photographs too.

Unit	Dates	Reference
2nd Battalion Anglesey	1940–1945	WO 199/3311
Ayrshire	1940–1945	WO 199/3312
2nd Battalion Bedfordshire	1940–1945	WO 199/3313
6th (Bracknell) Battalion Berkshire	1940–1945	WO 199/3314
B (Sandhurst) Company		
11th Battalion Berkshire	1940–1945	WO 199/3315
35th Battalion Cheshire	1940–1945	WO 199/3316
7th Denbigh and Flint	1940–1945	WO 199/3317
3rd Derbyshire	1940–1945	WO 199/3309
9th Derby/Notts Anti-Aircraft	1942–1945	WO 199/3310
6th Devonshire	1940–1945	WO 199/3318
10th (Torbay) Devonshire	1940–1945	WO 199/3319
2nd Dumbarton	1940–1945	WO 199/3320
101st (Dumbarton)		
Anti-Aircraft Rocket Battery	1940–1945	WO 199/3321
1st Dumfriesshire	1940–1945	WO 199/3322
3rd (13th GPO) City of Dundee	1940–1945	WO 199/3323
2nd Durham	1940–1945	WO 199/3324
9th City of Edinburgh	1940–1945	WO 199/3325
102nd (City of Edinburgh)		
Anti-Aircraft Rocket Battery	1940–1945	WO 199/3326
3rd Essex	1940–1945	WO 199/3327
19th Essex	1940–1945	WO 199/3328
196th (102nd Essex)		
Anti-Aircraft Rocket Battery	1940–1945	WO 199/3329
1st, 6th, 7th, 9th, 10th, 12th and 13th		
City of Glasgow	1940–1945	WO 199/3330
2nd City of Glasgow	1940–1945	WO 199/3331
3rd City of Glasgow	1940–1945	WO 199/3332
14th (City of Bristol) Gloucestershire	1940–1945	WO 199/3333
3rd (Basingstoke) Hampshire	1940–1945	WO 199/3334
A (Winchester City) Company,		
5th Hampshire	1940–1945	WO 199/3335
Electricity Company, 17th (Portsmouth)		
Hampshire	1940–1945	WO 199/3336
18th (Portsmouth Dockyard) Hampshire	1940–1945	WO 199/3337
23rd Hampshire	1940–1945	WO 199/3338
29th (Gosport) Hampshire	1940–1945	WO 199/3339
32nd (Connaught) Hampshire	1940–1945	WO 199/3340
71st (Hants and Isle of Wight)		
Heavy Anti-Aircraft Battery	1940–1945	WO 199/3341
3rd Huntingdonshire	1940–1945	WO 199/3342
5th (Wingham) Kent	1940–1945	WO 199/3343
16th (Kent) Anti-Aircraft Regiment	1940–1945	WO 199/3344
19th Kent	1940–1945	WO 199/3202
19th (Farningham) Kent	1940–1945	WO 199/3345

Unit	Dates	Reference
20th (Sevenoaks) Kent	1940–1945	WO 199/3346
22nd (Tunbridge Wells) Kent	1940–1945	WO 199/3201
42nd County of Lancaster	1940–1945	WO 199/3347
101st (Leicestershire) Anti-Aircraft Rocket Battery	1940–1945	WO 199/3348
6th (Silvertown) City/County of London	1940–1945	WO 199/3349
19th (South Suburban Gas Co) City/County of London	1940–1945	WO 199/3350
40th (GLCC) City/County of London	1940–1945	WO 199/3352
44th (London Transport) City/County of London	1940–1945	WO 199/3353
48th (LCC) City/County of London	1940–1945	WO 199/3354
59th (Taxi) City/County of London	1940–1945	WO 199/3355
2nd (Newport) Monmouthshire	1940–1945	WO 199/3356
10th Monmouthshire	1940–1945	WO 199/3357
101st (Monmouthshire) Anti-Aircraft Rocket Battery	1940–1945	WO 199/3358
101st (Northamptonshire) Anti-Aircraft Rocket Battery	1940–1945	WO 199/3359
2nd (Bicester) Oxfordshire	1940–1945	WO 199/3360
4th (Bullingdon) Oxfordshire	1940–1945	WO 199/3361
102nd (Renfrewshire) Anti-Aircraft Rocket Battery	1940–1945	WO 199/3362
1st Scottish Border	March 1944	WO 199/3207
2nd Scottish Border	December 1944	WO 199/3208
7th Somerset	1940–1945	WO 199/3363
2nd Company, 7th Somerset	1940–1945	WO 199/3364
8th (Burton) Staffordshire	1940–1945	WO 199/3206
13th North Staffordshire	1940–1945	WO 199/3365
11th Suffolk	1940–1945	WO 199/3366
4th (Guildford) Surrey	1940–1945	WO 199/3367
8th (Reigate) Surrey	1940–1945	WO 199/3368
53rd Surrey	1940–1945	WO 199/3369
58th Surrey	1940–1945	WO 199/3370
63rd (Richmond) Surrey	1940–1945	WO 199/3371
West Sussex Group	1940–1945	WO 199/3203
Sussex Recovery Company	1940–1945	WO 199/3373
111th (39th GPO) Sussex	1940–1945	WO 199/3372
26th (Worth Forest) Sussex	1940–1945	WO 199/3205
A Sector, 2nd and 7th Warwickshire	1940–1945	WO 199/3374
31st and 32nd (Birmingham City Transport) Warwickshire 1	1940–1945	WO 199/3375
45th (Birmingham) Warwickshire	1940–1945	WO 199/3376
1st (Bradford) West Riding	1940–1945	WO 199/3377
16th (GPO) West Riding	1940–1945	WO 199/3378
A company, 4th Wiltshire	1940–1945	WO 199/3379
9th Wiltshire	1940–1945	WO 199/3380
4th (Evesham) Worcestershire (part 1)	1940–1945	WO 199/3381
4th (Evesham) Worcestershire (part 2)	1940–1945	WO 199/3382
12th (Warley) Worcestershire	1940–1945	WO 199/3382
1st Zetland	Jan.–Mar. 1942	WO 199/3209

Perhaps the most secretive organizations under the Home Guard title were the Auxiliary Units. The basic purpose of Auxiliary Units was to act as saboteurs behind the German lines, had Germany actually invaded Great Britain. Nominal rolls of the Auxiliary Units can be found in WO 199 as follows:

WO 199/3388	Scotland and Northumberland
WO 199/3389	Northern and Eastern Counties and Hereford and Carmarthen Areas
WO 199/3390	Dorset, Kent and Somerset Areas
WO 199/3391	Southern Counties

WO 900/49 contains an example of a Home Guard daily report book.

Many surviving records concerning the Home Guard may also be held by local record offices. You may be able to locate many of these records by using *www.a2a.org.uk*.

The records of service of Home Guard personnel in the form of attestation papers on an Army Form W 3066 are still retained by the Ministry of Defence but are administered by TNT Archive Service, Tetron Point, William Nadin Way, Swadlincote, Derbyshire, DE11 0BB, Tel: 01283 227 911/912/913, Fax: 01283 227 942. The surviving records are arranged by the county and in many cases the specific battalion the individual served in, with each collection arranged in alphabetical order. TNT will release information only to next of kin, and can help only if the battalion of the person sought is given.

L. B. Whittaker has recently compiled *Stand down: Orders of battle for the units of the Home Guard of the United Kingdom, November 1944*, which may be of use in tracing units.

17.5 Campaign Medals

No medal rolls for the Second World War have yet been transferred to the National Archives Office. Surviving records about the issue of Second World War campaign medals to individuals are still held by the Ministry of Defence. Only the closest next of kin of recipients, or indeed the recipients themselves, will be provided with information.

MOD Medal Office
Building 240
RAF Innsworth
Gloucester
GL3 1HW
JPAC Enquiry Centre:
Tel: 0141 224 3600
Veterans Freephone: 0800 085 3600

Some medal records for colonial forces can be found in CO 820. See *Medals: the Researcher's Guide*, William Spencer (TNA, 2006) for further details.

17.6 Women in the War

As in the First World War, women played a major role in the Army, undertaking many duties that would normally be done by men. Correspondence about the employment of women in the Army is to be found in WO 32 (code 68) and WO 162/30–73. These papers contain very little of a genealogical nature.

Many women served in the Auxiliary Territorial Service (ATS) and their records of service are still held by the MOD; see 17.1. A few war diaries for

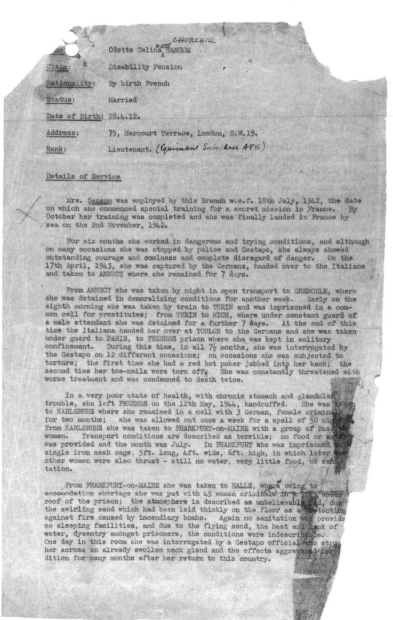

Fig. 34 *Service details found in a Second World War Ministry of Pension disability pension file.*
PIN 93/1

the ATS are to be found in WO 166. Many members of the ATS served alongside men in a large number of artillery units based in the UK and consequently if you know the identity of such units, you could look for their war diary.

A large number of women served as nurses during the war and, while their records are still retained by the Ministry of Defence, there are a number of sources available for consultation. War diaries for hospitals and medical units are in WO 177. Many medical units also submitted reports, usually of a technical nature, to the War Office and these are in WO 222.

One of the greatest employers of women during the Second World War was the Women's Land Army, with over 80,000 being employed at its peak in 1943. The records of service of the Women's Land Army are in the series MAF 421 and are available on microfiche and are arranged in alphabetical order. The government has recently acknowledged the contribution made by the Women's Land Army and is to award surviving members with a badge. Details can be found on *www.defra.gov.uk*.

17.7 Special Operations Executive

Records of the Special Operations Executive (SOE) are in the record classes HS 1–HS 20 and many contain detailed information on operations carried out by army personnel and foreign nationals serving with the SOE.

Of all the SOE records, the personal files in HS 9 are perhaps the most interesting. Arranged in alphabetical order, it is possible to search HS 9 on the online catalogue under the real name or known alias(es) of an SOE agent. The records not only contain personal information about the individual, they usually contain photographs of the person. If the subject individual was captured, there may be detailed reports about their subsequent fate. Some of the files in HS 9 contain some quite harrowing stories.

Further information about these records may be found in John Cantwell's *The Second World War. A Guide to Sources* (PRO Handbook No 15, 1998 revised edition).

Fig. 35 *Typical example of an ID Photograph found in an SOE Agent's personal file.* HS 9/1458

18 OTHER TWENTIETH-CENTURY CAMPAIGNS

After the First World War many regular soldiers looked forward to returning to normal soldiering. Outside of the two world wars normal soldiering consisted of garrison duties at home and abroad and taking part in colonial policing duties, suppressing restless people in the British Empire.

Apart from operations in India, the British Army also served in Iraq, Persia, Somaliland, Palestine both before and after the Second World War, in Malaya, Korea, Borneo, Northern Ireland and the Falklands. Places are being added to this list every year and researchers will eventually be looking into actions in new places such as Kosovo, and old and familiar places such as Afghanistan.

It is believed that 1968 is the only year when a British soldier has not been killed while taking part in operations, since well before 1900.

Many of the following records are quite brief, apart from the war diaries for the Korean War. Records concerning operations conducted between the two world wars do not cover all participating units.

18.1 War Diaries

Apart from the two world wars, the British Army has taken part in a number of operations during the last 120 years. The main source of interest for family historians will be the war diaries of participating units. References are:

Campaign	Class
Abyssinia (1935–1936)	WO 191
Egypt (1935–1936)	WO 191
India (1930–1937)	WO 191
Korea (1950–1953)	WO 281
Palestine (1936–1938, 1945–1948)	WO 191
Shanghai (1927–1932)	WO 191
Suez (1956)	WO 288

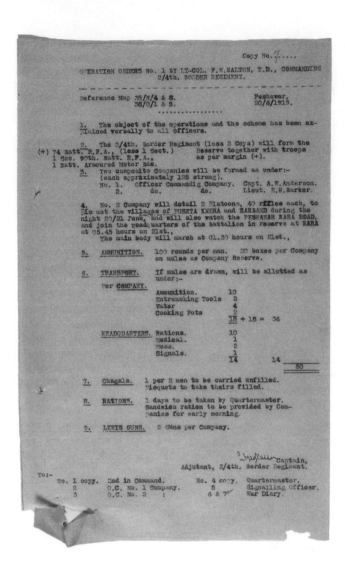

Fig. 36 *Inter War Years: Operational record for the 2/4 Border Regiment during the 3rd Afghan War 1919.* WO 95/5392

18.2 Quarterly Historical Reports

Between 1946 and 1950, army units compiled quarterly Historical Reports. They are similar in format to war diaries, but are not as detailed. The references are:

Area	Class	Area	Class
British Army of the Rhine	WO 267	Far East	WO 268
British Element Trieste Force	WO 264	Gibraltar	WO 266
British Troops Austria	WO 263	Home Forces	WO 271
Caribbean	WO 270	Malta	WO 265
Central Mediterranean Forces	WO 262	Middle East	
East and West Africa	WO 269	(including Palestine)	WO 261

Quarterly Historical Reports were replaced by the Unit Historical Record in 1950 and these are in WO 305. These reports cover the period 1957–1981 and in many cases cover operations in Northern Ireland after 1969. The arrangement of WO 305 is such that it is not arranged by particular campaigns but rather in chronological order and by unit. As with most of the operational records, it is possible to search for them by unit or by organization identity and this is probably the most effective way of locating records.

Operation Record Books for the Army Air Corps from 1957–1977 are in WO 295. The series currently contains 51 different records and the most effective way to locate a record is to search for the unit by name.

18.3 Other parts of the world, including India and Burma

Apart from the operational records in WO 191 mentioned above, other records concerning operations conducted in India and Burma and in other parts can be found in WO 32, WO 33 and WO 106. The best way to search these series is to use the place where the operation took place as a search term. Terms such as Burma, Waziristan, India, Palestine and Dervishes will all produce results.

Fig. 37 *Inter War Years: Unit War Diary. Essex Regiment in India 1930–31.* WO 191/54

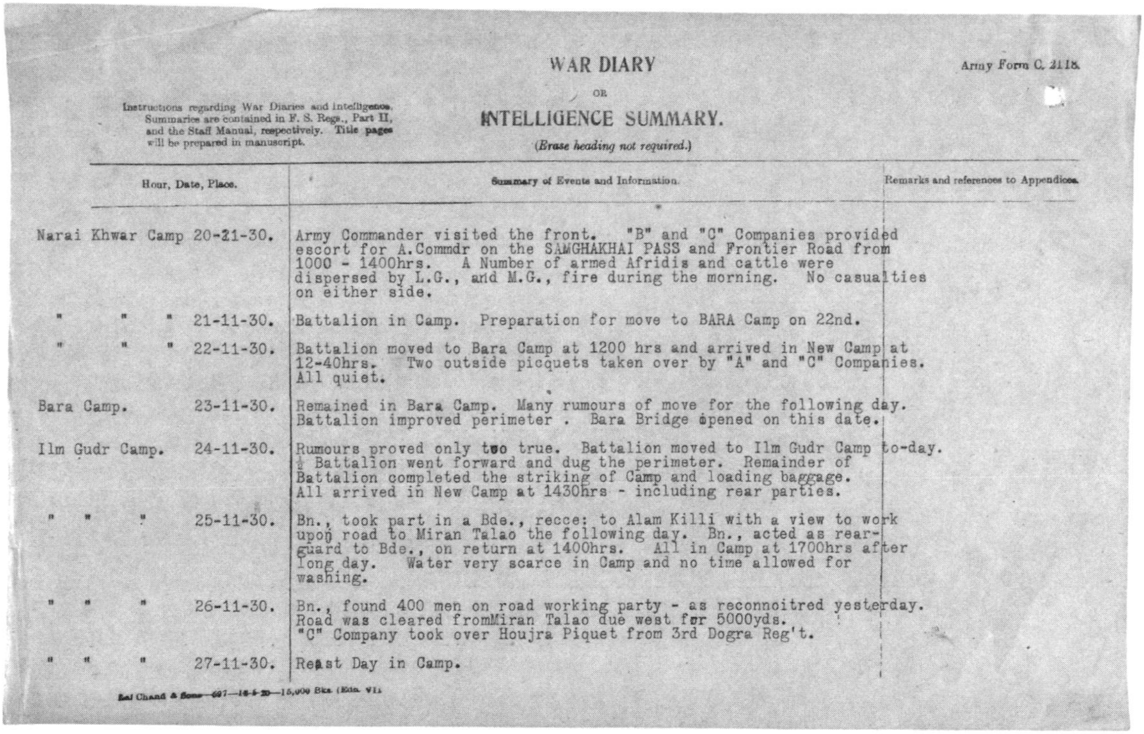

Instructions regarding War Diaries and Intelligence Summaries are contained in F. S. Regs., Part II, and the Staff Manual, respectively. Title pages will be prepared in manuscript.

WAR DIARY
OR
INTELLIGENCE SUMMARY.
(*Erase heading not required.*)

Army Form C. 2118.

Hour, Date, Place.	Summary of Events and Information.	Remarks and references to Appendices.
Narai Khwar Camp 20-21-30.	Army Commander visited the front. "B" and "C" Companies provided escort for A.Commdr on the SAMGHAKHAI PASS and Frontier Road from 1000 - 1400hrs. A Number of armed Afridis and cattle were dispersed by L.G., and M.G., fire during the morning. No casualties on either side.	
" " " 21-11-30.	Battalion in Camp. Preparation for move to BARA Camp on 22nd.	
" " " 22-11-30.	Battalion moved to Bara Camp at 1200 hrs and arrived in New Camp at 12-40hrs. Two outside picquets taken over by "A" and "C" Companies. All quiet.	
Bara Camp. 23-11-30.	Remained in Bara Camp. Many rumours of move for the following day. Battalion improved perimeter . Bara Bridge opened on this date.	
Ilm Gudr Camp. 24-11-30.	Rumours proved only two true. Battalion moved to Ilm Gudr Camp to-day. ½ Battalion went forward and dug the perimeter. Remainder of Battalion completed the striking of Camp and loading baggage. All arrived in New Camp at 1430hrs - including rear parties.	
" " " 25-11-30.	Bn., took part in a Bde., recce: to Alam Killi with a view to work upon road to Miran Talao the following day. Bn., acted as rear-guard to Bde., on return at 1400hrs. All in Camp at 1700hrs after long day. Water very scarce in Camp and no time allowed for washing.	
" " " 26-11-30.	Bn., found 400 men on road working party - as reconnoitred yesterday. Road was cleared fromMiran Talao due west for 5000yds. "C" Company took over Houjra Piquet from 3rd Dogra Reg't.	
" " " 27-11-30.	Reast Day in Camp.	

Lal Chand & Sons—697—18-5-30—15,000 Bks. (Edn. VI.)

18.4 Records at the British Library

Between 1919 and 1939, and even into 1940, a significant part of the British Army conducted a large number of operations in and around India, including the Third Afghan War in 1919, in Waziristan between 1919 and 1924, in Malabar in 1921/2 and in Burma between 1930 and 1932 and back on the North-West Frontier between 1930 and 1931 and again between 1935 and 1939. A consequence of all these operations and the places where they occurred is that there are a large number of records concerning them amongst the records of the India Office held by the British Library. The majority of records for these inter-war operations can be found in the series L/MIL/7.

18.5 The Peacetime Army

The British Army has expanded and contracted according to budgetary constraints and operational need and records concerning operations are most plentiful when it was at its biggest and busiest.

As already stated, the only year a soldier has not been killed on operations since before 1899, was in 1968. What this illustrates is the fact that the British Army, whether it be a wartime army, a regular-only army or an army made up of conscripts/national servicemen and regulars, the British Army and its personnel have been laying down their lives on behalf of the state for over 110 years without a break.

As the size of the Army has changed, so has its make-up, with regiments being created, amalgamated and disbanded as Treasury and the army's commitments have changed. Perhaps one of the best sources for looking at how the structure and make-up of the Army has changed is to consult the *Army List*.

The Ministry of Defence website *www.mod.uk* provides links to specific pages for all three armed services and they illustrate quite effectively how the armed forces have changed over the last 100 years.

18.6 Searching for Records

It possible to search the online catalogue for records in all of the above-mentioned records series but many of the units and organizations are abbreviated, so you may need to search very carefully.

19 GENERAL GENEALOGICAL RECORDS

There are many records held by other institution and organizations, where information about people who became soldiers, were soldiers and who died as soldiers may be found. There are also records, which, whilst not containing information about the active service of a soldier, record what are still important parts of a soldier's life.

19.1 Registers of Births, Marriages and Deaths

The record series WO 156 contains some 633 registers of baptisms, confirmations, marriages and deaths/burials for the period 1808–2004. The registers cover various parts of the world where the British Army has served and garrisoned. The registers include not only service personnel but also their wives and children. The most effective way to search these records is to know what event you seek and where it took place. The records in WO 156 are indexed by place and this is the easiest way to look for them when searching the catalogue.

A small number of regimental registers of births, baptisms, marriages and burials are held at the National Archives. Some of these were annotated with information on discharge; others have baptismal entries for children entered on the same page as the marriage certificate of the parents.

The vast majority of records of births, marriages and deaths after 1837, however, are held by the Office for National Statistics (ONS) and indexes may be consulted online. Civil registration records sometimes identify a soldier's regiment—for example, the registers of deaths in the Boer War and two world wars. A summary of the holdings is given in chapter 20.

Registers exist at the National Archives for:

3rd Battalion King's Own Yorkshire Light Infantry (formerly 1st West Yorkshire Militia): baptisms and marriages, 1865–1904 (WO 68/499/1).

6th Battalion, Rifle Brigade (formerly 114th Westmeath Militia): baptisms and marriages, 1834–1904 (WO 68/439).

Royal Artillery: marriages and baptisms, 1817–1827, 1860–1877 (WO 69/551–582).

Royal Horse Artillery: baptisms and marriages, 1859–1877 (WO 69/63–73).

3rd and 4th Battalions Somerset Light Infantry (formerly Somerset Militia): baptisms and marriages, 1836–1887, 1892–1903 (WO 68/441).

3rd Battalion West Norfolk Regiment: baptisms and marriages, 1863–1908 (WO 68/497).

3rd Battalion West Yorkshire Rifles (formerly 2nd West Yorkshire Militia): baptisms and marriages, 1832–1877 (WO 68/499).

In addition, there are registers of births at Dover Castle, 1865–1916 and 1929–1940; Shorncliffe and Hythe, 1878–1939; Buttervant, 1917–1922; and Fermoy, 1920–1921, in WO 156. WO 256 includes burial registers for the Canterbury garrison, 1808–1811, 1859–1884 and 1957–1958; and baptisms and banns of marriage for Army personnel in Palestine, 1939–1947.

Registers of baptisms, 1691–1812, marriages, 1691–1765, and burials, 1692–1856, for the Royal Hospital Chelsea are in RG 4/4330–4332, 4387.

During the eighteenth and early part of the nineteenth centuries applicants for government jobs, including the Army, had to supply a certificate showing their place and date of baptism in order to prove their adherence to the Church of England. A collection of these certificates for officers, extracted from other papers and dating between 1777 and 1892, is in WO 32/8903–8920 under code 21A. Each piece is indexed. Similar series of certificates, again for officers only, of births, baptisms, marriages, deaths and burials, 1755–1908, extracted from War Office papers and files, are in WO 42; a name index is at the beginning of the class list.

Notifications to the War Office of marriages by officers, 1799–1882, are in WO 25/3239–3245.

19.2   The Census

Apart from 1941, population censuses have been taken every ten years since 1801, but few returns relating to individuals survive before 1841. Census returns for England, Wales, the Isle of Man, and the Channel Islands for 1841 (HO 107), 1851 (HO 107), 1861 (RG 9), 1871 (RG 10), 1881 (RG 11), 1891 (RG 12) and 1901 (RG 13) are available via the computer terminals at the National Archives.

Census records for Scotland are held at the General Register Office for Scotland, New Register House, Edinburgh EH1 3YT. You can access Scottish census records via *www.scotlandspeople.gov.uk*.

The records include returns for all officers, soldiers, and their families living in barracks or other military establishments on census night, normally the first Sunday in April. The returns give details of where a person was born, marital state, age and occupation. As all of the surviving census records have been digitized, it is possible to search them by name.

Census records listing the birthplaces of a soldier's children may thereby tell you where he was stationed earlier in his career. By searching sources that give the location of units, such as the Monthly Returns described in section 1.4, you may be able to narrow down the number of regiments that your man may have belonged to. For example, if a child is recorded as having been born at Gibraltar in 1850, there may have only been four or five regiments stationed there in that year and so his or her father is likely to have served with one of those regiments.

19.3 Wills

Wills of many men are in the casualty returns in WO 25, with a few wills for officers in WO 42. Wills for soldiers who died abroad, before 1858, may be with the records of the Prerogative Court of Canterbury (PCC). Registered copies of PCC wills may be seen on DocumentsOnline. Further details are given in Research Guide, Legal Records Information 23, *Probate Records* and Miriam Scott's *Prerogative Court of Canterbury Wills and Other Probate Records* (PRO Readers' Guide No 15, 1997).

Copies of wills after 1858 are at the Principal Registry of the Family Division, First Avenue House, High Holborn, London WC1V 6NP.

20 RECORDS HELD BY OTHER INSTITUTIONS

Local record offices

Relatively few military records are held by local record offices. Those that are, however, are often of great interest to the family historian. Three different types of military records may be held by a local record office.

First, there are records created by local units, either volunteers or the regular Army. These may consist of service rolls, war diaries and internal records of the unit and can give an insight into the life of the service. Records of some territorial and auxiliary forces associations have been deposited at local record offices and may contain items of interest to family historians. Details of these records, for the First World War period, are in *The Location of British Army Records: a National Directory of World War I Sources* by Norman Holding.

Local record offices also hold records of local militia units. In particular, militia lists (of all men) and militia enrolment lists (of men chosen to serve) may survive for the period 1758 to 1831. These records, and others likely to be of use to the family historian, are described in *Militia Lists and Musters, 1757–1876*, by Jeremy Gibson and Mervyn Medlycott.

Records relating to military events, although not military records as such, include rolls of honour for men who served during the world wars, or lists of casualties taken from local newspapers. Photographs of parades and manoeuvres may also be held locally.

Brief details of the holdings of most record repositories in Britain are given in *British archives: a guide to archive resources in the United Kingdom* by Janet Foster and Julia Sheppard. The addresses of local record offices, together with times of opening, are given in *Record Repositories in Great Britain* (10th edition, PRO, 1997). Similar information is included in *Record offices: how to find them* by Jeremy Gibson, together with maps and other details.

National Register of Archives

The National Register of Archives (NRA) was set up by the Royal Commission on Historical Manuscripts in 1945 to collect and disseminate information about manuscript sources for British history outside public records. The NRA consists of more than 40,000 unpublished lists and catalogues of major collections. They describe the holdings of local record offices, national and university, and other specialist repositories. Many of these collections may contain records of use to the family or military historian.

The NRA and the Public Record Office are now a combined under one umbrella organization, The National Archives, therefore is it possible to access and contact the NRA resources at Kew.

Access to these lists and catalogues is available in the Open Reading Room at Kew and also via the National Archives website. The NRA also publish a useful free leaflet, *Sources for the History of the Armed Forces* (NRA Information Sheet no. 8), which lists many of the major sources for military records.

Imperial War Museum

The Imperial War Museum has a very large collection of private diaries, letters, papers and unpublished memoirs for all ranks in the Army from 1914 to the present and a large photographic library. These can be consulted by appointment. The Museum also maintains a comprehensive series of biographical files on persons decorated with the Victoria Cross or the George Cross since the inception of the awards. The address is:

Imperial War Museum, Lambeth Road, London SE1 6HZ
Tel: 020 7416 5000, *www.iwm.org.uk*

British Library, Oriental and India Office Collections, formerly India Office Library and Records (IOLR)

The IOLR hold very large collections of material relating to the British in India. They also hold 1,000 volumes of births, marriages and deaths returns between *c.*1683 and 1947. There are indexes to these records.

Further information about their holdings of use to the genealogist may be found in *Baxter's Guide: Biographical Sources In the India Office Records* by Ian Baxter. The address is:

British Library, Asia, Pacific and Africa Collections
96 Euston Road, London, NW1 2DB
Tel: 020 7412 7873, *www.bl.uk*

National Army Museum

The Museum has a large collection of private, regimental and related papers concerning the British Army, the Indian Army prior to 1947, and British colonial forces to relevant dates of independence.

The life of the ordinary soldier is well illustrated by letters, diaries, memoirs and poems written by men stationed in every corner of the globe. There is a fine representative collection of commissions of officers for both the British and Indian Armies.

The Museum holds regimental records for the 9th/12th Royal Lancers, Westminster Dragoons, Surrey Yeomanry and various Indian Army units. It also houses documents relating to the Irish regiments of the British Army disbanded upon the formation of the Irish Free State in 1922: the Royal Irish Regiment, Connaught Rangers (materials relating to the history of the Connaught Rangers, 1793–1916, are also held at the Public Record Office in WO 79), Leinster Regiment, Royal Munster Fusiliers and the Royal Dublin Fusiliers.

Of particular interest to the family historian is the card index of biographical information on officers of the East India Company, compiled by Major Vernon Hodson.

In addition, the Museum holds a comprehensive record of all military casualties from 1900 to the present day, giving next of kin, address and how personal possessions and money were dispersed.

The Museum also has a very large library of regimental histories, military biographies and *Army Lists*, together with collections of photographs and sound recordings of old soldiers. The address is:

National Army Museum, Royal Hospital Road, London, SW3 4HT
Tel: 020 7730 0717, *www.national-army-museum.ac.uk*

Regimental Museums

Many regiments have a museum, some of which have collections of records that could be of use to the family historian.

Military Museums in the UK gives the addresses of museums with a brief description of their collections. In addition, *The location of British Army records* by Norman Holding lists museums and gives some idea of the records that each one holds relating to the First World War, although these may have been deposited with organizations apart from specific regiments, such as local and county archives.

Office for National Statistics (General Register Office)

The history of Army registration of births, marriages and deaths is not quite clear. Most of the records held by the General Register Office cannot be inspected by the public, although some indexes may be seen at the National Archives at Kew. Once you have identified a relevant entry from the indexes you may order a copy of the entry as an official certificate for a fee. A few Army registers or records of births, marriages and deaths are in the National Archives (see 19.1); others may still be in the custody of the regiment.

The General Register Office has registers of Army births and marriages from 1761 to 1987, and of deaths from 1796 to 1987. There are several series, some of them overlapping, with an uncertain amount of duplication and omission. The regimental registers of births/baptisms and marriages run from 1761 to 1924, covering events in Britain (from 1761) and abroad (from c.1790). There is an index to the births (giving name, place, year and regiment), but not to the marriages. To find out details of a marriage, you have to know the husband's regiment and a rough date.

For enquiries about an overseas marriage, about birth and/or death registrations abroad and about changes to records of overseas *events*, write to:

Overseas Section, General Register Office, Trafalgar Road
Southport PR8 2HH
Tel: 0151 471 4801 (9.00 a.m. to 5.00 p.m., Monday to Friday)
Email: overseas.gro@ons.gsi.gov.uk
Fax: 01633 652988

Overlapping with the regimental registers are the Army chaplains' returns of births, baptisms, marriages, deaths and burials, 1796–1880. These all relate to events abroad, and they are indexed. Unfortunately, the indexes do not give the regiment by simply the name, place and date range. From 1881 they appear to be continued by the Army returns, 1881–1955, of births, marriages and deaths overseas. From 1920, entries relating to the Royal Air Force are included.

From 1956–1965, there are indexes to combined service department registers of births and marriages overseas: after 1965, separate service registers were abandoned, and entries were made in the general series of overseas registers.

Records for the Ionian Islands appear to have been kept separately. At Kew there are registers, 1818–1864, of births, marriages and deaths: the index is to a military register, a civil register and a chaplain's register. It gives names only. Other registers from the Ionian Islands are in the National Archives; the register for Zante gives baptisms, marriages, deaths and burials 1849–1859 (RG 33/82).

Fees, similar to those charged for copies of ordinary certificates, are payable. The address for postal enquiries is:

Certificate Services Section, General Register Office, PO Box 2
Southport PR8 2JD
Tel: 0845 603 7788, *www.gro.gov.uk*

Scotland

Census returns and certain registers relating to deaths of warrant officers, NCOs and men in the South African War (1899–1902) are held at the General Register Office for Scotland, New Register House, Edinburgh EH1 3YT. They also hold an incomplete set of birth, marriage and death registers for Scottish armed forces for the Second World War.

It may be possible to trace the present whereabouts of regimental collections through the Scottish United Services Museum, The Castle, Edinburgh EH1 2NG.

Ireland

Most nineteenth-century census records relating to Ireland have not survived, but census returns for 1901 and 1911 may be consulted at the National Archives of Ireland, Bishop Street, Dublin 8, Ireland.

Birth, marriage and death registers created under the Army Act 1879 for the period between 1880 and 1921 are held by the General Register Office, Joyce House, 8–11 Lombard Street, Dublin 2.

Society of Genealogists

The library of the Society has a number of useful books, including regimental histories and rolls of honour. In addition, the Society has produced leaflets on *Army muster and description books*, *Army research: selected bibliography* and *In search of a soldier ancestor*. The address is:

Society of Genealogists, 14 Charterhouse Buildings
Goswell Road, London EC1M 7BA
Tel: 020 7251 8799, *www.sog.org.uk*

21 RESEARCH TECHNIQUES

There are so many approaches to the records discussed in this book it may appear difficult to know where to begin. Here are some basic questions to consider:

Officer or other rank?

Date?

When did they serve?

What is your evidence—a certificate, medal, photograph, hearsay?

Do you know what regiment/corps they served in?

Where did they serve?

Answers!

If you can't find an officer in the *Army List*, especially after 1750, doubt must be cast upon their status. There is a possibility that the man in question may have been an officer in the Militia or Volunteers. There are separate *Militia Lists* in the library; try those or *Hart's Army List*. The person you are looking for may have been a Warrant Officer, if so, consider him as an other rank when looking at the records. Lists of Warrant Officers can be found in the *Army List,* as can lists of Warrant Officers in receipt of a pension. Using this last list can tell you when a man went to pension; from the date at which he disappears from it you get a rough, if not exact, date of death.

Dates are a historian's bread and butter, so it helps to be as accurate as possible. Dates of awards or commissions or on certificates can all help to narrow things down.

Knowing when a man or woman served can help, as it may limit the amount of information you are likely to find. Soldiers who only served a short-service engagement in the 1870s or 1880s, for example, are less likely to have a record of service in WO 97. Length of service can sometimes be estimated from the census or information on marriage or birth certificate.

If a man received a medal, have you identified it?

Medals are not only interesting to look at, they can also provide you with a snapshot of a particular incident. Most medals will be named, either around the edge or on the back. As long as the medal is legitimate, it will enable you to start your research from a particular time in a man's career. You will need to use the medal rolls in WO 100 as your starting point and then work backwards to find out when they joined the army and forwards to locate a date of discharge.

Photographs of soldiers are always useful ways of gathering information, but the interpretation of them requires a good knowledge of badges and uniforms. The fact that a man is wearing a peaked cap does not mean that he is an officer. A cane does not make him a sergeant major. Photographers used lots of devices to make their photographs more interesting. If you have a photograph of a person in uniform, have you looked at the back?

Knowing which regiment or corps an individual served in may dictate the direction of your research. While most of the British Army can be researched at the National Archives at Kew, the records of those who served in the Indian Army or the armies of the East India Company will require a visit to the British Library. There are plenty of websites concerning units of both the British and Indian Armies which may help you identify the unit and which archive you need to use first. Try *www.regiments.org*.

Knowing where an individual served may help narrow your research down. Some regiments were the only parts of the British Army who served in a particular place and consequently using the series WO 379 and WO 380 to see who served where and when may help.

'He came from so and so, so he must have joined the X regiment'

The fact that a man came from Somerset, for example, does not mean he joined the 13th Foot or Somerset Light Infantry. While certain areas had strong links with particular regiments, there was nothing to stop a recruiting party of one regiment from being in an area associated with another regiment and taking their potential recruits.

During the First World War a large number of 'Pals' units, not just infantry, were formed, where the majority of men within a given unit were united by an association such as place, type of employment or employer, and who then joined a newly created unit together. A very good series of books about many of the 'Pals' battalions of the First World War have been published by Pen and Sword.

'He was too old to serve in the First World War!'

Anyone could volunteer for service in the First World War but they had to be of the correct age and be physically fit. Not only did men under the age of 18 try to join up, but many old and bold soldiers who had seen service, in many cases pre-1900, tried to join up again. A large number of these soldiers saw service in the UK only, but many who had served in campaigns after 1890 also served overseas and earned more medals.

The oldest person who died as a result of active service was Henry Webber, who was 68 when he died in 1916. Henry Webber was older than Lord Kitchener!

When conscription was introduced in 1916, the age criteria was fixed at a given age range; before the war had ended, the range was extended to 18–56. With a maximum age of 56, it was possible for the army to conscript men who had been in the Army as early as 1878.

Of all the problems associated with the First World War records, one of the most frustrating is where an old soldier and, more importantly, his old papers were taken out of a dormant set and placed in the collection relating to First World War service, which was almost totally destroyed in 1940!

The Soldier

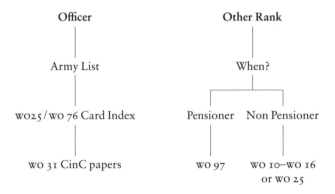

Casualties

It is a sad fact that, in the past, it was easier to research a man who died in service than one who survived.

If an individual died in a recognized campaign, battle or war, their name was recorded in a casualty roll, either official or something produced at a later date. Medal rolls are a useful way of checking when a man died, as they are frequently annotated with such information.

Until c.1895, widow's pensions were not an automatic right and consequently the papers of a man who died in service were usually destroyed. The only way of building a picture of a man's career would be to use the muster and pay lists in wo 10–wo 16.

Many of the casualty records in wo 25 contain information about men who left a unit rather than just those who died. In the nineteenth century, the term casualty related to those who were taken off the effective strength of a unit as well as those who died. The casualty records in wo 25 effectively list those who leave a given unit, alive or dead.

Commissioned from the Ranks

Researching a soldier who was commissioned from the ranks can cause problems, as the audit trail of records can be weaker than if they had remained an ordinary soldier. Once an ordinary soldiers was commissioned the key information, usually kept on his record of service, would have been noted on his new officer's record of service and then his soldier's papers would usually have been dispensed with. If all of the officer's records had survived, this would have caused no problems but very few records of commissioned officers from the late nineteenth century survive.

During the First World War the majority of officers were commissioned from the ranks and if their papers survive, their other ranks papers are usually with them.

No record of service

If a man died in service, was discharged by purchase or was discharged without a pension, you may have to create a picture of his career by using the musters. If you know a particular date when the individual was serving, use that as a starting point. By working backwards chronologically, you should find a date of attestation; by working forwards chronologically, you should eventually get a date of discharge.

Papers not in WO 97?

Due to the arrangement of WO 97, especially before 1872, it is very important to know which regiment/corps a man was discharged from. In many cases men changed regiments, either through operational need or in many cases because they wanted to stay in a particular place, in most cases India. In order to find the regiment/corps a man was discharged from, you have to look at the musters (WO 10–WO 16) for the unit and date where that information is known. By following the musters forwards chronologically, you should eventually discover to which unit the individual was transferred. Once you have the new unit, look at the appropriate WO 97.

Please note that it was not uncommon for a man to change unit more than once—so you may need to follow the process described above more than once.

APPENDIX 1

Organization Chart of the Army

This chart gives a very brief guide to the organization of the Army as it was between 1881 and 1945.

```
                Army Group
         (Second World War only)
                    |
                 Armies
                    |
                  Corps
                    |
                Divisions
                    |
                 Brigades
                    |
                Regiments
                    |
                Battalions
                    |
                Companies
                    |
                 Platoons
                    |
                 Sections
```

1. Army Group numbers should always be in Arabic numbers. The 21st Army Group (Second World War) consisted of the 2nd British Army and the 1st Canadian Army.
2. Army numbers should be in Arabic numbers, for example, 2nd Army.
3. Corps are always listed in Roman numerals, for example, III Corps.
4. Divisions are always listed with Arabic numbers, sometimes with a regional title, for example, 51st (Highland) Division.
5. Brigades are always listed with Arabic numbers, for example, 158th Brigade.

During the First World War, an Army could consist of two or three Corps; a Corps could consist of up to five Divisions; a Division usually consisted of three Brigades; a Brigade consisted of four Battalions of Infantry until early 1918 and only usually three Battalions by the end of the war.

APPENDIX 2

Ranks of the British Army

Commissioned Officers

Field Marshal
General
Lieutenant General
Major General
Brigadier
Colonel
Lieutenant Colonel
Major
Captain
Lieutenant
2nd Lieutenant

Non-commissioned officers and other ranks

Warrant Officer 1st Class
   = Regimental Sergeant Major
Warrant Officer 2nd Class
   = Company/Squadron Sergeant Major
Staff Sergeant
Sergeant
Corporal
Lance Corporal
Private

2nd Lieutenant replaced the ranks of Ensign (Infantry) and Cornet (Cavalry) in the mid-nineteenth century.

There were, and still are, a number of variations with regard to the rank of sergeant and these occur over time. To the actual term sergeant may be added one of the following prefixes—Colour, Battery, Quartermaster, Company. Many of the sergeant ranks in the Royal Engineers were preceded with their actual trade—for example, Foreman of Works Staff Sergeant or Engineering Clerk Sergeant. The Royal Engineers also used the rank 2nd Corporal.

Some ranks used by the Army can be deceptive. Corporal of Horse, for example, is a sergeant in the cavalry. If a soldier was a private, trooper, sapper or gunner, he was usually at the bottom of the promotion ladder; any other rank being further up it!

This is a very simplified table. Various branches and regiments have tended to give different names to different ranks. For example, in the Royal Artillery a Private is called a Gunner, in the Royal Engineers he is a Sapper, and in Cavalry regiments he may be called a Trooper.

APPENDIX 3

Useful Dates

Records of units and formations engaged in particular campaigns are listed in detail in M. Roper's *Records of the War Office and related departments 1660–1964* (PRO Handbook No. 29, 1998).

Campaigns and wars

1642–1649	English Civil War
1660, 25 May	Restoration of Charles I
1688	Glorious Revolution
1701–1713	War of Spanish Succession
1704, 13 August	Battle of Blenheim
1715	Jacobite Rebellion
1740–1748	War of Austrian Succession
1745	Jacobite Rebellion
1746, 16 April	Battle of Culloden
1756, 3 May– 1763, 10 February	Seven Years War
1775–1782	American War of Independence
1789	French Revolution
1793, 1 February– 1815, 22 June	Napoleonic Wars (or French Revolutionary Wars)
1808, 1 August– 1814, 30 March	Peninsular Campaign
1812, 19 June– 1815, 8 January	Second Anglo-American War (War of 1812)
1815, 18 June	Battle of Waterloo
1854, 14 September– 1856, 30 March	Crimean War
1854, 25 October– 1857, 6 December	Charge of the Light Brigade, Battle of Balaclava
1857, 10 May– 1860, 6 December	Indian Mutiny
1862–1864	Maori Wars in New Zealand
1878–1880	Second Afghan War
1878–1879	Zulu War
1879, 22 January	Massacre of British Troops at Isandhlwana, Zululand
1881	First South African (Boer) War
1881, 27 February	Defeat of British troops at Majuba Hill, South Africa
1882–1885	Egyptian and Sudan Campaigns
1885, 29 January	Relief of Khartoum
1898	Sudan campaign
1898, 2 September	Battle of Omdurman
1899, 12 October– 1902, 31 May	Second South African (Boer) War
1900, 28 February	Relief of Ladysmith, South Africa
1900, 17 May	Relief of Mafeking, South Africa
1914, 4 August– 1918, 11 November	First World War
1914, 22–23 August	Battle of Mons
1915, 25 April– 1916, 8 January	Gallipoli campaign, Turkey
1916, 24 April–1 May	Easter Rising, Dublin
1916, 1 July– 8 November	Battle of the Somme
1917, 31 July– 10 November	Battle of Passchendaele (Third Battle of Ypres)
1919, 6 May–8 Aug	Third Afghan War
1919, Oct 1– 1924 Mar 31	Operations in Waziristan
1922, 18 December	Last British troops leave Southern Ireland
1930, Dec 22– 1932 Mar 31	Operations in Burma
1936, Apr 19– 1939 Sept 3	Operations in Palestine
1939, 3 September– 1945, 2 September	Second World War
1940, 27 May–4 June	Evacuation from Dunkirk
1941, 22 April– 29 May	Greek and Crete campaigns
1942, 15 February	Surrender of Singapore
1942, 23 October	Start of Battle of El Alamein
1943, 10 July	Allies land in Sicily
1944, 6 June	Allies land in France (D-Day)
1945, 7 May	Germans surrender
1945, 14 August	Surrender of Japan (VJ-Day)
1947, 15 August	Last British troops leave India
1948, 14 May	Last British troops leave Palestine
1950, 26 June– 1953, 27 July	Korean War
1956, 31 October– 7 November	Suez Crisis

1969–31 July 2007	Operation Banner (operations in Northern Ireland)
1982, 2 April–14 June	Falklands War
1990, 2 August– 1991, 28 February	First Gulf War

Army history

1645	Formation of New Model Army
1661	Britain's oldest regiment, the Coldstream Guards, formed
1664	Royal Marines established
1684	Admission of first pensioners to the Royal Hospital Kilmainham, Ireland
1692	Admission of first pensioners to the Royal Hospital Chelsea
1708	Provision of pensions to widows of officers
1716	Royal Artillery founded
1717	Corps of Engineers founded
1740	First publication of the *Army List*
1757	Militia Act revives local militias
1760	Institution of soldiers' pension documents
1787	Corps of Engineers becomes Royal Engineers
1796	Establishment of Army Chaplains Department
1810	Army Medical Department established
1811	Royal Corps of Sappers and Miners set up
1833	Long Service and Good Conduct Medal instituted
1839–1915	*Hart's Army Lists*
1854	Institution of Distinguished Conduct Medal
1855	Ordnance Board abolished
1856	Victoria Cross instituted
1857	Army Hospital Corps formed
1859	Volunteer regiments formed
1867	Second Class Army Reserve established
1870	Army Enlistment Act introduces short service engagements of 12 years for other ranks
1870	Abolition of purchase of commission
1881	Abolition of numbered regiments of foot and their re-establishment as regiments with county affiliations

1881	Army Nursing Service formed
1886	Institution of Distinguished Service Order
1898	Royal Army Medical Corps formed by merger of Army Medical Department and Army Medical Staff Corps
1908	Creation of the Territorial Force
1916	Military Medal Instituted
1918, 1 April	Formation of Royal Air Force from Royal Flying Corps and Royal Naval Air Service
1922	Irish regiments disbanded on independence of Irish Free State
1940–1944	Home Guard (Local Defence Volunteers)

APPENDIX 4

Imperial Yeomanry Companies and Battalions

The majority of Imperial Yeomanry companies had their origins in the pre-1899 Yeomanry and others were given names when they were created between 1899 and 1902. Each company of the Imperial Yeomanry was placed into a battalion, in which it usually stayed for its service in South Africa. Unless otherwise stated, the first or only battalion number was the battalion in which the company served in both 1900 and 1901. If a company changed battalions, the first number is for 1900 and the second for 1901.

Company	Name or Title	Battalion
1 & 2	Wiltshire	1
3	Gloucestershire	1
4	Glamorganshire	1
5 & 103	Warwickshire	2
6 & 106	Staffordshire	4
7	Leicestershire	4
8 & 104	Derbyshire	4
9 & 11	Yorkshire	3
10	Sherwood Rangers	3
12	South Notts	3
13	Shropshire	5
14, 15, 100 & 101	Northumberland	5
16 & 102	Worcestershire	5
17	Ayrshire	6
18	Queen's Own Royal Glasgow	6
19	Lothian	6
20	Fife and Forfar Light Horse	6
21 & 22	Cheshire	2
23	Lancashire	8
24	Westmoreland and Cumberland	8
25	West Somerset	7
26	Dorsetshire	7
27	Devonshire	7
28	Bedfordshire	4
29	Denbighshire	9
30	Pembroke	9
31, 49 & 89	Montgomeryshire	9
32	Lancashire	2
33	Royal East Kent	11
34, 35 & 112	Middlesex	11
36	West Kent	9
37 & 38	Buckinghamshire	10
39	Berkshire	10
40	Oxfordshire	10
41	Hampshire	12 & 4
42	Hertfordshire	12
43 & 44	Suffolk	12
45	Dublin (1900 service only)	13
46	Belfast	13
47	Duke of Cambridge's Own (1900 service only)	13
48	North Somerset	7
51	Paget's Horse	8
52 & 68	Paget's Horse (1900 service only)	19
53	Royal East Kent	14 & 11
55	Northumberland	14 & 5
56 & 57	Buckinghamshire	15
58	Berkshire	15
59	Oxfordshire	15
60	North Irish Horse	17
61	South Irish Horse	17
62	Middlesex	14 & 11
63	Wiltshire	16 & 1
65	Leicestershire	17
66	Yorkshire	16 & 3
67, 70, 71 & 75	Sharpshooters	18
69	Sussex	14 & 7
72 & 79	Rough Riders (1900 service only)	20
73	Paget's Horse	19 & 12
74	Dublin	16 & 8
76 & 78	Rough Riders	20 & 22
77 & 105	Manchester	8
80–83	Sharpshooters	21
84 & 85	Rough Riders	22
86 & 87	Rough Riders	24
88	Welsh Yeomanry	9
90 & 93	Sharpshooters	23
94–97	Metropolitan Mounted Rifles	24
107	Lanarkshire	6
108	Royal Glasgow	6

Company	Name or Title	Battalion
109	Yorkshire Hussars	3
110	Northumberland	2
111	Yorkshire Dragoons	3
113 & 114	Served with Lovat's Scouts	
115, 117 & 118	Sharpshooters	25
116		25
119		26
120	Younghusband's Horse	26
121 & 122		26
123–126		27
127–130	Westminster Dragoons	28
131–134	Irish Horse	29
135–138		30
139–142	Fincastle's Horse	31
143–146		32
147–150		33
151–154		34
155–158		35
159–162		36
163–166		37
167–170		38
171–174		39
175 & 176	Irish Horse	29
177		31

APPENDIX 5

Regimental Order of Precedence

The following order of precedence is applicable to the First World War period, but it does represent information that may be needed to use many of the records for the period 1900–1920. The order is based on the date specific units were originally founded. The number at the end of each infantry regiment, starting with the Royal Scots, is the original numerical identity of the unit prior to 1881 and is the number used to identify the regiment in the index of officers' Long Numbers in WO 338.

1 Life Guards
2 Life Guards
Royal Horse Guards
Household Battalion
Royal Horse Artillery
1 King's Dragoon Guards
2 Dragoon Guards (Queen's Bays)
3 (Prince of Wales's) Dragoon Guards
4 (Royal Irish) Dragoon Guards
5 (Princess Charlotte of Wales's) Dragoon Guards
6 Dragoon Guards (Carabiniers)
7 (The Princess Royal's) Dragoon Guards
1 (Royal) Dragoons
2 Dragoons (Royal Scots Greys)
3 (King's Own) Hussars
4 (The Queen's Own) Hussars
5 (Royal Irish) Lancers
6 (Inniskilling) Dragoons
7 (Queen's Own) Hussars
8 (The King's Royal Irish) Hussars
9 (Queen's Royal) Lancers
10 (The Prince of Wales's Own) Hussars
11 Prince Albert's Own) Hussars
12 (The Prince of Wales's Royal) Lancers
13 Hussars
14 (King's) Hussars
15 (King's) Hussars
16 (The Queen's) Lancers
17 Lancers (Duke of Cambridge's Own)
18 Hussars
19 Hussars
20 Hussars
21 (Empress of India's) Lancers

The Yeomanry Regiments
Royal Artillery

Royal Field Artillery
Royal Engineers
Royal Flying Corps
Grenadier Guards
Coldstream Guards
Scots Guards
Irish Guards
Welsh Guards

Royal Scots (Lothian) 1
Queen's (Royal West Surrey) 2
Buffs (East Kent) 3
King's Own (Royal Lancaster) 4
Northumberland Fusiliers 5
Royal Warwickshire 6
Royal Fusiliers (City of London) 7
The King's (Liverpool) 8
Norfolk 9
Lincolnshire 10
Devonshire 11
Suffolk 12
Prince Albert's (Somerset Light Infantry) 13
Prince of Wales's Own (East Yorkshire) 14
East Yorkshire 15
Bedfordshire 16
Leicestershire 17
Royal Irish 18
Alexandra, Princess of Wales's (Yorkshire) 19
Lancashire Fusiliers 20
Royal Scots Fusiliers 21
Cheshire 22
Royal Welsh Fusiliers 23
South Wales Borderers 24
King's Own Scottish Borderers 25
Cameronians (Scottish Rifles) 26
Royal Inniskilling Fusiliers 27
Gloucestershire 28
Worcestershire 29
East Lancashire 30
East Surrey 31
Duke of Cornwall's Light Infantry 32
Duke of Wellington's (West Riding) 33
Border 34
Royal Sussex 35
Hampshire 37
South Staffordshire 38
Dorsetshire 39
Prince of Wales's Volunteers (South Lancashire) 40
Welsh 41

Black Watch (Royal Highlanders) 42
Oxfordshire and Buckinghamshire Light Infantry 43
Essex 44
Sherwood Foresters
    (Nottinghamshire and Derbyshire) 45
Loyal North Lancashire 47
Northamptonshire 48
Princess Charlotte of Wales's (Royal Berkshire) 49
Queen's Own (Royal West Kent) 50
King's Own (Yorkshire Light Infantry) 51
King's (Shropshire Light Infantry) 53
Duke of Cambridge's Own (Middlesex) 57
King's Royal Rifle Corps 60
Duke of Edinburgh's (Wiltshire) 62
Manchester 63
Prince of Wales's (North Staffordshire) 64
York and Lancaster 65
Durham Light Infantry 68
Highland Light Infantry 71
Seaforth Highlanders (Ross-shire Buffs,
    The Duke of Albany's) 72
Gordon Highlanders 75
Queen's Own Cameron Highlanders 79
Royal Irish Rifles 83
Princess Victoria's (Royal Irish Fusiliers) 87
Connaught Rangers 88
Princess Louise's
    (Argyll and Sutherland Highlanders) 91
Prince of Wales's Leinster (Royal Canadians) 100
Royal Munster Fusiliers 101
Royal Dublin Fusiliers 102
Rifle Brigade
Royal Army Chaplains Department
Army Service Corps
Royal Army Medical Corps
Army Ordnance Corps
Army Veterinary Corps
Machine Gun Corps
Royal Tank Corps
Labour Corps
Honourable Artillery Company
Monmouthshire Regiment
Cambridgeshire Regiment
London Regiment
Hertfordshire Regiment
Northern Cyclist Battalion
Highland Cyclist Battalion
Kent Cyclist Battalion
Huntingdon Cyclist Battalion.

This order of precedence is based on the *Army List* of August 1914, to which have been added a number of units created between 1914 and 1918.

A number of Irish regiments were disbanded in 1922 and other units, such as the Parachute Regiment and the Special Air Service, were created in the Second World War. In order to see more recent orders of precedence, use the *Army List*.

APPENDIX 6

Key War Office Records and how they are made available

Series Format	Original	Film/Fiche	Digitized
WO 10–17	X		
WO 22	X		
WO 23	X		
WO 25	X	X	
WO 68	X		
WO 69	X		
WO 76		X	
WO 95	X		X
WO 100		X	
WO 145	X		
WO 146	X		
WO 338		X	
WO 339	X		
WO 344	X		
WO 345	X		
WO 363		X	X
WO 364		X	X
WO 373	X	X	X
WO 374	X		
WO 398		X	X
WO 399	X		
WO 400	X		

FURTHER READING AND WEBSITES

The best general introduction to family history in the Public Record Office is Amanda Bevan's revised edition of *Tracing Your Ancestors in the Public Record Office* (7th edition, TNA, 2006). Section 18 in the book covers many of the classes of military records of genealogical interest at the National Archives.

The Office also produces a number of Research Guides, formerly Records Information Leaflets, on many subjects of interest to the family historian. The guides are intended to be used at Kew in conjunction with the records. The guides are continually evolving and new leaflets are always being produced. Please ask in the Open Reading Room.

The Research Guides can be downloaded via *www.nationalarchives.gov.uk/gettingstarted/guides.htm?source=ddmenu_research1*.

In addition, there are a number of source sheets which aim to provide searchers with lists of references on popular topics.

Stella Colwell, *Family Roots* (London, 1991) gives many examples of military records to be found at the National Archives and includes a brief account of finding ancestors who served in the Army.

An idiosyncratic account of how to trace individuals in Army records is Gerald Hamilton-Edwards' *In Search of Army Ancestry* (Chichester, 1977). A.R.H. Montague, *How to trace your military ancestors in Australia and New Zealand* (Sydney, 1989) is a useful illustrated guide to military records of value to genealogists in Australia and New Zealand. Many queries about military records are answered in Pauline Saul, *The family historian's enquire within* (3rd edition, FFHS, 1995).

There are several general histories of the British Army which can provide background information for the family historian, such as David Ascoli, *A Companion to the British Army, 1660–1983* (London, 1983). A useful introduction to the organization of the Army before 1914 is given in John M. Kitzmiller II, *In Search of the 'Forlorn Hope': a Comprehensive Guide to Locating British Regiments and their Records, 1640 to World War One* (2 vols, Salt Lake City, 1988). A good general history of the British Army is Corelli Barnett, *Britain and her army* (London, 1970).

An interesting account of the life of the soldier is Victor Neuburg, *Gone for a soldier* (London, 1989). Byron Farwell, *For queen and country: a social history of the Victorian and Edwardian army* (London, 1981) is a well-written introduction to the life many ancestors must have experienced. A pictorial introduction to the life of the Scottish soldier is Jenni Calder, *The story of the Scottish soldier, 1600–1914* (HMSO, 1987).

General Works

P. E. Abbott, *Recipients of the Distinguished Conduct Medal 1855–1909* (London, 1992)

D. Ascoli, *A Companion to the British Army, 1660–1983* (London, 1983)

K. Asplin, *The Roll of The Imperial Yeomanry, Scottish Horse and Lovats Scouts, Second Boer War Africa 1899–1902*, (privately published, 2000)

P. A. Bailey *Researching Ancestors in the East India Company Armies* (FIBIS, 2006)

D. J. Barnes, 'Identification and Dating: Military Uniforms', in *Family History Focus*, ed. D. J. Steel and L. Taylor (Guildford, 1984)

I. Baxter, *Baxter's Guide: Biographical Sources In the India Office Records* (FIBIS, 2004)

C. C. Bayley, *Mercenaries for the Crimea* (London, 1977)

J. D. Beckett, *An index to the regimental registers of the Royal Hospital Chelsea 1806–1838* (Manchester and Lancashire FHS, 1993)

J. Bradley *et al., Roll call! A guide to genealogical sources in the Australian War Memorial* (Canberra, 1986)

J. M. Brereton, *Guide to regiments and corps of the British Army and the regular establishment* (Bodley Head, 1985)

A. P. Bruce, *An Annotated Bibliography of the British Army, 1660–1714* (London, 1975)

A. Bruce, *The Purchase System in the British Army, 1660–1871* (London, 1980)

E. Bull, *Aided immigration from Britain to South Africa, 1857–1867* (Pretoria, 1990)

S. Colwell, *Family Roots* (London, 1991)

F. and A. Cook, *The Casualty Roll for the Crimea* (London, 1976)

R. Coombs, *Before Endeavours Fade* (After The Battle, 2006)

C. Dalton, *English Army Lists and Commission Registers, 1661–1714* (6 vols, London, 1892–1904, reprinted by Francis Edwards, 1960)

C. Dalton, *George I's Army, 1714–1727* (2 vols, London, 1910–1912)

P. Dennis, *The Territorial Army 1907–1940* (Royal Historical Society, 1987)

M. G. Dooner, *The Last Post being a roll of all Officers (Naval, Military and Colonial) who gave their names for Queen, King and Country in the South Africa War, 1899–1902* (Hayward, reprinted 1980)

R. Drew, *List of Commissioned Medical Officers of the Army, 1660–1960* (2 vols, 1925, 1968)

A. Farrington, *Guide to the records of the India Office military department* (India Office Library and Records, 1982)

B. Farwell, *Armies of the Raj* (London, 1990)

C. Firth and G. Davis, *The Regimental History of Cromwell's Army* (Oxford, 1940)

Y. Fitzmaurice, *Army Deserters from HM Service* (Forest Hill, Victoria, 1988)

J. Foster, *British archives: a guide to archive resources in the United Kingdom* (Palgrave, 4th edition, 2002).

I. Gentles, *The New Model Army* (Blackwell, 1992)

J. Gibson and A. Dell, *Tudor and Stuart Muster Rolls* (FFHS, 1991)

J. Gibson, and A. Dell, *Tudor and Stuart Muster Rolls — A Directory of Holdings in the British Isles* (FFHS, 1991 edition)

J. Gibson and M. Medlycott, *Militia Lists and Musters, 1757–1876* (FFHS, 1994)

G. Hamilton-Edwards, *In Search of Army Ancestry* (London, 1977)

I. Hallows, *Regiments and corps of the British Army* (Arms and Armour, 1991)

B. Harris: *A Dorset Rifleman: the Recollections of Benjamin Harris*, edited by Eileen Hathaway (Shinglepicker, 1996)

J. Hayward, D. Birch and R. Bishop, *British Battles and Medals* (Spink, 2006)

V. C. P. Hodgson, *Lists of Officers of the Bengal Army* (London, 1927–1928, revised 1968)

N. Holding, *The Location of British Army Records: a National Directory of World War One Sources* (FFHS, 3rd edn, 1991)

N. Holding, *More Sources of World War One Army Ancestry* (FFHS, 1991)

N. Holding, *World War One Army Ancestry* (FFHS, 1997)

N. Holding and I. Swinnerton, *World War I Army Ancestry* (FFHS, 2004)

N. Holme, *The Noble 24th* (Savannah, 1999)

S. and B. Jarvis, *Cross of Sacrifice* series (Roberts Medals, 1993 onwards)

J. M. Kitzmiller II, *In Search of the 'Forlorn Hope': a Comprehensive Guide to Locating British Regiments and their Records 1640 to World War One* (Salt Lake City, 1988)

M. E. S. Laws, *Battery Records of the Royal Artillery, 1716–1877* (Woolwich, 1952–1970)

A. Lawrence, *Parliamentary Army Chaplains 1642–1651* (Royal Historical Society, 1990)

R. T. J. Lombard, *Handbook for Genealogical Research in South Africa* (Pretoria, 1990)

F. C. Markwell and P. Saul, *The family historians enquire within* (3rd edition, FFHS, 1991)

M. Mann, 'The Corps of Invalids', *Journal of the Society for Army Historical Research* vol. 66, no. 1 (1988)

P. McDermott, *For Distinguished Conduct in the Field: Register of The DCM 1920–1992* (Hayward, 1994)

M. Medlycott, 'Some Georgian 'Censuses': the Militia Lists and 'Defence' Lists', *Genealogists' Magazine*, vol. XXIII, pp 55–59

Sir O'Moore Creagh and Miss E. Humphries, *Register of the DSO* (London, 1923)

E. Peacock, *Army Lists of the Roundheads and Cavaliers* (London, 1863)

R. Perkins, *Regiments and Corps of the British Empire and Commonwealth, a critical bibliography* (privately published, 1994)

Public Record Office, *Alphabetical Guide to certain War Office and other Military Records preserved in the Public Record Office* (PRO Lists and Indexes, vol. LXIII)

A. Rawson, *British Army Handbook 1914–1818* (Sutton, 2006)

E. E. Rich, 'The Population of Elizabethan England', *Economic History Review,* 2nd ser., vol. II, pp 247–265 (Discusses the Elizabethan muster rolls)

M. Roper, *The Records of the War Office and related departments 1660–1964* (PRO, 1998)

W. Spencer, *Records of the Militia and Volunteer Forces 1757–1945* (London, 1997)

W. Spencer, *Air Force Records: A Guide for Family Historians* (TNA, 2008)

W. Spencer, *First World War Army Service Records* (TNA, 4th ed., 2008)

W. Spencer, *Medals: The Researcher's Guide* (TNA, 2006)

H. Strachan, *Wellington's Legacy: Reform of the British Army, 1830–1854* (Manchester University Press, 1984).

A. Swinson ed., *A Register of the Regiments and Corps of the British Army: the Ancestry of the Regiments and Corps of the Regular Establishments of the Army* (London, 1975)

R. R. Temple, 'The Original Officer List of the New Model Army', *Bulletin of the Institute of Historical Research,* LIX (1986)

R. W. Walker, *To what end did they die? Officers who died at Gallipoli* (R. W. Walker Publications, 1985)

R. W. Walker, *Recipients of the DCM 1914–1920* (Midland, 1981)

C. T. Watts and M. J. Watts, 'In Search of a Soldier Ancestor', *Genealogists' Magazine,* vol. XIX, pp 125–128

A. S. White, *A Bibliography of the Regiments and Corps of the British Army* (London, 1965, reprint 1988)

L. B. Whittaker, *United Kingdom, November 1944* (Newport, Gwent, 1990)

T. Wise and S. Wise, *A Guide to Military Museums and Other Places of Military Interest* (Doncaster, 2001)

W. Woolmore, *Steinaecker's Horse* (South African Country Life, 2006)

J. Young, *'They Fell like Stones': casualties of the Zulu War, 1879* (Greenhill, 1991)

TNA publications, and those of the Federation of Family History Societies (FFHS), are on sale at the TNA shop at Kew and online at *www.national archives.gov.uk/bookshop.*

Useful Websites

Advice about websites can be detailed or simple, but I prefer to just flag them up as they can change and people use them in different ways. The following websites all provide information about service personnel, alive or dead, and the records relating to them.

www.cwgc.org

www.gazettes-online.co.uk

www.ancestry.co.uk

www.1914-1918.net

www.awm.gov.au

www.archives.ca

www.nationalarchives.gov.uk/documentsonline

www.bl.uk

INDEX

E

E 101 19
E 121 22
E 182 49–50, 72
East India Company 91–3,
    148, 152
*East India Register and
    Directory* 92
Efficiency Medal
    (Territorial) 86
emigrants 58, 104
English Civil War 23, 21–3
Enrolled Pensioners 107
Exchequer accounts 19,
    20–1
expeditionary force 13

F

Fencible Infantry and
    Cavalry 69
field officers 24
First World War 13, 16,
    85, 98–9, 120–30,
    152–3, 154
    prisoners of war 114–16
FO 383 114
foreign medals 86
Foreign Office 86, 114
foreign troops in British
    pay 101–4
Foreign Veterans Battalion
    103

G

gallantry, awards for 81–3
genealogical records 42,
    143–5, 149
general courts martial 87
general officers 24
General Register Office
    149–50
General Staff 13
Gradation Lists 26
gunners *see* Royal
    Artillery

H

Haldane reforms 13
half pay 33
Hanoverian army 102

Harding, Colour Sergeant
    John 61–2
Harris, Private Benjamin
    Randell 44, 59
Hessian troops 101–2
higher command 16–17
Hodson's Index 94, 148
Holberton, Lieutenant
    Colonel 127, 128
Home Guard 71, 132–6
Home Office Military
    Papers 71
Household Battalion 122
Household Cavalry 47–8
HS 9 138

I

Imperial War Museum
    147
Imperial Yeomanry 97, 47,
    62–3, 72, 157–8
in-pensions 51, 57
indentures 18, 18–19
India 91–4, 141, 142
    British Army in 91, 93–4
India Office Library and
    Records (IOLR) 147
Indian Army 91–3, 94, 152
Indian Army Lists 92
infantry regiments 13–14
inspection returns 32
intelligence summaries
    126
    see also war diaries
International Committee
    of the Red Cross 118
invalids 107–8
Ionian Islands 149
Ireland 12, 150
Isandhlwana, Battle of 61

J

J 135 89, 90
J 152 90
Judge Advocate General's
    Office 88

K

Kilmainham, Royal
    Hospital 45, 51, 52, 57
King's African Rifles 98

King's German Legion
    102–3
King's South Africa
    Medal 47, 98, 109
knight service 18–19
Korean War 99, 118
KV series 113

L

L/MIL/9–14 92–3, 94
*List of Officers taken
    prisoner in the various
    Theatres of War
    between August 1914
    and November 1918*
    114–16
Local Defence Volunteers
    71, 132
    see also Home Guard
Local Militia 69
local record offices 16, 72,
    73, 136, 146
localization 12
London Gazette 28, 81,
    126
Long Service and Good
    Conduct Medal 85
long-service medals 85–6

M

marriage certificates 35
marriage registers 143–4,
    149
Medal Index Cards 125–6
medal rolls 84, 84–5, 98,
    125–6, 152, 153
medals 81, 83–6, 151–2
    campaign medals 83–5,
    125–6, 136
medical records 124–5
medical services 108–9
medieval sources 18–19
Mentions in Despatches
    (MiD) 126
meritorious service
    awards 81–3
Meritorious Service
    Medal (MSM) 85–6,
    126
MH 106 124
Military Cross 81
Military General Service

Medal (MGS) 59, 81,
    84
military intelligence 113
Military Medal (MM) 81,
    126
Military Register, The 27
Military Secretary 31–2
Military Service Tribunals
    129
Military Train 107
militia 11, 12, 13, 69–77,
    146; muster for War-
    wickshire 70; monthly
    return for West Kent
    73
Militia Act 1757 69
Militia Lists 151
miners 67, 68
Ministry of Defence 104,
    122, 131, 136, 142
Moffatt, Private John
    59–60
Most Excellent Order of
    the British Empire 81
Most Honourable Order
    of the Bath 82
muster rolls 41–2, 48–9,
    60, 72, 153, 154
    Tudor and Stuart 19, 70,
    19–21

N

Napoleonic Wars 102
National Archives, The
    7–8, 147
National Army Museum
    42–3, 94, 148
National Register of
    Archives (NRA) 147
New Zealand 58, 99–100
Niger and West Africa
    Force 98
Nightingale, Florence
    109
non-commissioned
    officers (NCOs) 17,
    41, 155
    Indian Army 93
Notley, Lydia 109, 110
North America 96
notification books 28
nurses 110, 50, 109–10,
    129–30, 138